Remembering Herbie

Celebrating the Life and Times
of Hockey Legend Herb Brooks

by
Ross Bernstein

"Remembering Herbie"

"Celebrating the Life and Times of Hockey Legend Herb Brooks"
by Ross Bernstein

Self Published

(WWW.BERNSTEINBOOKS.COM)

ISBN#: 0-9634871-6-7

Distributed by Adventure Publications (800) 678-7006

Printed by Printing Enterprises: New Brighton, Minn.

Photos courtesy of the Brooks Family,
the U.S. Hockey Hall of Fame and the University of Minnesota

*A portion of the proceeds from the sale of this book
will go to the newly created Herb Brooks Foundation.
Thank you for your support!*

**DONATIONS TO THE NEWLY CREATED
"HERB BROOK FOUNDATION" CAN BE SENT TO:**

**RBC Dain Rauscher
Attn: Dan Brooks
60 South Sixth Street
Minneapolis, MN 55402
(612) 371-2396**

(Contributions are 501C3 Tax Deductible)

In Memory of Herbie Brooks

*"You were born to be a player. You were
meant to be here. This moment is yours."*

August 5, 1937 — August 11, 2003

Thanks to all of the people who were kind enough to share their personal memories of Herbie for the book:

Badalich, Steve	McClanahan, Rob
Baker, Bill	Messin, Frank
Bessone, Amo	Micheletti, Joe
Blais, Dean	Nanne, Lou
Blatherwick, Jack	Ostby, Paul
Bloom, Butch	Paradise, Bob
Boo, Jim	Paradise, Kelly
Brooks, Dan	Parise, J.P.
Brooks, Dave	Patrick, Craig
Brooks, Patti	Pavelich, Mark
Broten, Neal	Peters, Bob
Buetow, Brad	Phippen, Pat
Bush, Walter	Pleau, Larry
Butters, Bill	Polich, Mike
Christoff, Steve	Rahn, Noel
Coppo, Paul	Ramsey, Mike
Cotroneo, Lou	Reid, Tom
Dahl, Craig	Rink, Bob
Eruzione, Mike	Rosen, Mark
Ferris, Wayne	Saatzer, Don
Findley, Jim	Sarner, Craig
Fotiu, Nick	Sauer, Jeff
Gambucci, Gary	Schmit, Joe
Gilbert, John	Schneider, Buzz
Grillo, Chuck	Sertich, Mike
Harrington, John	Sheehy, Neil
Hedican, Bret	Smith, Gary
Hendrickson, Larry	Sonmor, Glen
Holmgren, Paul	Strelow, Warren
Holtz, Lou	Strobel, Eric
Houle, LeRoy	Telander, Bruce
Housley, Phil	Ulseth, Steve
Ikola, Willard	Utecht, Bob
Johnson, Paul	Vairo, Lou
Knoblauch, Dave	Vannelli, Tom
Larson, Reed	Verchota, Phil
Lawton, Brian	Walters, Charley
Lucia, Don	Wigen, Roger
Malone, Greg	Williamson, Murray
Mayasich, John	Wong, Gregg
Mazzocco, Frank	Woog, Doug

"BROOKSISMS"

Original sayings, as told by Herb Brooks... and retold by 1980 Olympians John Harrington, Dave Silk and Mike Eruzione:

"You're playing worse every day, and right now you're playing like it is next month..."

"You look like you have a five pound fart on your head..."

"We'll do everything together but chase the same girl..."

"Gentlemen, you don't have enough talent to win on talent alone..."

"Hey Ref, you should take a two week vacation and then retire..."

"I am going to be your coach but I am not going to be your friend..."

"Gentlemen, if you don't have your teammates respect, you don't have anything..."

"Don't dump the puck in, that went out with short pants..."

"It's confusion by design, but there's a method to our madness..."

"Gentlemen, let's not be a whore out there..."

"You look like a monkey screwing a football out there..."

"If you make a mistake out there, make it by co-mission instead of by o-mission..."

"We're going to climb into their jockstraps out there..."

"In front of the net, it's bloody nose alley..."

"Catch a pass like that and you're going to get your bleepin' unit knocked off..."

"You've already made the first mistake, so don't make the second one..."

"Boys, I'm asking you to go to the well again..."

"There's a fine line between class and no class..."

"There's a fine line between guts and brains..."

"Respect the game of hockey and it will reward you in many ways..."

"I'd love to pay $10 to watch any one of you play in the NHL..."

"You're halfway between the sh-- and the sweat..."

"Throw the puck back and weave, weave, weave... but don't just weave for the sake of weaving..."

"Let's be idealistic, but let's be practical..."

"Screw that, I am not that type of guy..."

"Whose got one?... Whose got two?..."

"I don't care what your agent says..."

"Speed, deception and puck control..."

"Let's cut their throats gentlemen..."

"We'll be pissin' in the wind..."

"You can't be common, the common man goes nowhere; you have to be uncommon..."

"If you want to bring a hard hat and lunch pail to work, that is fine with me..."

"If you don't respect your opponent, you're going to get raped out there..."

"Hey, you're a defenseman first and a forward second..."

"You'll take it to the grave..."

"You see the tiger, you walk up to him, spit in his eye, and then shoot em'..."

"I wouldn't ask my family to do what this team has done..."

"Boys, the well's getting deeper and the water's getting colder..."

"Play well here, and it's money in your back pocket..."

"You're just plain stupid..."

"Or we'll all be belly-up in the tank..."

"Blah, Blah, Blah..."

It is amazing to think that it was actually because of Herb Brooks that I even got into hockey. You see, I grew up in Fairmont and didn't really start to even play the game until I was about 10 years old. Hockey wasn't very big in Southern Minnesota and not only did we not have an indoor arena in town, we barely had an outdoor rink that was playable. But, after the Miracle on Ice in 1980, all of my buddies got into hockey in a big way. My family moved to a new house on a lake that same year and we used to make a rink behind my house. It was awesome, we would be out there all night. Hockey was suddenly the thing to do, and I became hooked.

Now, because we didn't really have any coaches, other than the guys who were nice enough to volunteer their time and flood the rink at night, most of my buddies and I had to go to hockey camps to learn the game. So, the first Summer camp I ever went to, Minnesota Hockey Schools, was at Shattuck Military Academy in nearby Faribault. It was run by Herb Brooks, the very same guy whose Olympic team had just inspired me to go out and buy my first pair of skates — a used pair of Bauer Huggers from Coast to Coast Hardware, I can still remember them.

I remember seeing Herbie for the first time. I was immediately impressed by him, his presence was just larger than life. I remember when he would skate around and tell you how to do certain drills and critique your style. He commanded such respect and the kids were just in awe of him. Well, for me, that first impression never really changed.

Our paths didn't cross again for many years later, until 1992, when I wrote my very first book entitled *"Gopher Hockey by the Hockey Gopher."* You see, I had a silly notion of trying out for the mighty Gopher Hockey team as a freshman at the University of Minnesota. I loved hockey. I loved watching it, I loved playing it and I loved everything about it. The only problem was, I just wasn't very good at it. So, after a brief "cup of coffee" as they say, as a pylon with the junior varsity team, I was cut. Sad? Sure, but I still wanted to do my part. So, I later became the team mascot, "Goldy the Gopher." I remember, at the time Goldy had always been a member of the band — but the administration was tired of having Bucky the Badger coming over here and kicking the snot out of our beloved rodent. So they sought out to find a new, tougher Goldy, who would not get pushed around. From what I understand, the criteria was simple: you had to know how to play hockey and you had to be a complete idiot. I apparently fit on both accounts. The rest, they say, was history.

After a two-year stint as Goldy, I decided to write a book about my experiences at old Mariucci Arena and about all the trouble I had gotten into while trying to fire up the Gophers and amuse the fans. From there, the book took on a life of its own. Really, it sort of turned into a history of the program as told through the eyes of hundreds of former players, coaches and media personalities. I just started interviewing and recording, and some 200 people later, the book came to life. One of those people who I interviewed was Herb Brooks. Herb was coaching with the New Jersey Devils at the time, but was more than gracious to let me interview him. In fact, he thought the idea of it all was downright hilarious. He loved the fact that even though I wasn't good enough to make the team, that I hung in there and did my part to help the program in an entirely different capacity. Herb appreciated the fact that I was doing my part, albeit infinitesimal, and he respected the fact that I was preserving history and paying homage to a lot of people who he respected, like John Mariucci. From that moment on, I was all right with Herb Brooks. I was in the fraternity — not the inner circle mind you, no way, that was reserved for hockey's elite, but, incredibly, it would be the beginning of a very different type of relationship which would grow and manifest into something very special over the ensuing decade.

Through the years I would call Herb to interview him for various book projects or magazine articles I was writing. Conversations with Herb were neither short in length, nor short in passion. Herb had issues with people and with causes, and if you were willing to listen, you would pretty much get to hear it all. Disseminating the information when it was all said and done, however, was an entirely different animal. Typically, he would want to see whatever it was that I was writing about him before it went to press. That was OK, but trying to transcribe a Herb Brooks interview was like negotiating your way through the gauntlet. It was a venerable minefield of stories, facts and opinions that were "on the record" one minute and then "off the record" the next, to the point where you really didn't know what the heck he wanted you to print. Now, for those of you who knew Herb, you knew that he was a pretty intense guy. He just had that special way of, let's see… how would I say this? Ah, yes, scaring the sh-- out of you! I mean, I was downright scared to death of the guy. So, after I would send him something to see, I would get that dreaded phone call. Answering the phone was like going to the principal's office, you just had that same sick feeling like you were going to get it — and get it good. Herb was a details guy and you simply did not want to get something wrong or disappoint him. You know, I later learned that Herb was a master at reverse psychology and used to drive his players insane. The same was true for writers. His heart was usually in the right place, but having Herb redo and critique your work was an editorial adventure much along the same lines as his legendary practices — by the time you were done with them you were so mentally and physically exhausted that you simply didn't have the strength to say no.

We got through it though, and even became friends. In fact, when Herb called me last year to ask me to write his book, I was completely blown away. He told me that he wanted to really get into public speaking and that like the other speakers on the circuit, he too needed to have a book. So, I did a bunch of research for him and got the ball rolling. It was a new "project" for Herbie, and for those of you who are in the know, projects with Herbie tended to take on a life of their own. The phone calls increased, and so did the level of excitement on my end. It was fun and it was significant. I remember asking him why he chose me to be his guy on this. He said he trusted me. He said that he had been approached by several big name journalists, guys from ESPN and guys from the East Coast, but he wanted to keep it local, with someone he knew he could trust. He said I had earned that. Wow. That was Herbie, always rooting for the little guy, the underdog, willing to go out on a limb to give a guy a break. Like so many of his players, I too didn't want to let him down.

So, I began contacting publishers and literary agents to start shopping the concept. I will never forget one of our first conversations with International Management Group, or IMG. They are the "Jerry McGuire's" of the sports world, and no one is bigger and better with regards to representing the world's top talent. Anyway, I worked like a dog and pulled every string I could to set up a conference call with one of their literary agents. They have a literary arm as well and publish a ton of big time sports books that come out every year. So, I sent them a big proposal and then set up the call. We are all set. Finally, I have the agent on one line and Herbie on the other. We start to talk and a little while into the conference call the agent starts to ask some pretty obvious questions about who Herb is and what sport he is involved with. Click. That was it. Herb had been insulted by the agent's lack of knowledge and had had enough. We were back to square one. That was Herbie.

From there, we talked to some other publishers and finally just decided to do it ourselves. Under this scenario, I was going to act as Herb's agent, publicist, writer and personal assistant. Now, I write five books a year and am a work-at-home-dad who takes care of a 15-month-old daughter, so I have a pretty full plate as it is. Really, I had no idea what the hell I was getting myself into to tell you the truth. But, I wanted to be there for Herbie and I wanted to see this project come to life. By now we were talking about doing a series of motivational, self-help books, tied into hockey as a metaphor for life and business. Herbie spoke at a lot of big Fortune 500 functions to a lot of heavy hitters and used to hate it when other speakers spouted off about their "pop psychology bull-sh--!" Herbie wanted to do something totally different, totally outside the box and these books were going to really set him apart. His same no nonsense, tell-it-like-it-is attitude was going to come screaming through the pages, and that excited me. I felt like he was preparing me to take on the Russians, I couldn't wait to get going.

So, we started talking and talking and talking. We spent the last year and a half going over details of the books and how we were going to write them, distribute them and market them. We even talked about tying in a radio or TV show with them, to build a "Herbie franchise," so to speak, around his name and his pedigree. Herbie could never pull the trigger though. There was always something that would come up to delay the project or that would make him change his mind a thousand times on how he wanted the books to be laid out. Then, with the new movie about him coming out, he wanted to tie the book into that as well. (Disney is doing a movie about the 1980 Olympic Team called *"Miracle,"* in which Kurt Russell plays Herb. I used to tease him about how he got a lot younger this time around, versus the first movie about the Miracle on Ice back in the '80s in which Herb was portrayed by an aging Karl Malden! "Patti wanted Robert Redford to play me for the new one and she wanted to play herself — I think that says it all," Herbie would joke.)

Anyway, I could see how hard it was for him to make big decisions. Case in point: he accepted and turned down the New York Rangers job this last year about three hundred times too. I even remember telling Herbie right before he left for the 2002 Olympics that he needed to be sure to get me the contact information for the Today Show, because NBC was doing several big features on him during that time. I told him that his Q-score, an advertising measuring tool, would never be higher after the Olympics and that the book should come out right away after that, so we needed to strike while the irons were still hot. I told him that I would coordinate his publicity and make sure that he was booked on all of the talk shows and that the book would be a big hit. He agreed.

Time would pass, Herbie would get busy on other projects, and then I would get his calls. Our conversations were sort of like "Tuesdays with Morrie." (*"Tuesdays with Morrie"* was a best-selling book written by Mitch Albom, which chronicled the intimate friendship between Mitch and his old college professor and mentor, Morrie, on every Tuesday, while Morrie was dying from ALS.) Only for me, it was "Monday, Wednesday, Thursday, Friday and Sunday Nights with Herbie..." He was relentless, and our talks would go on for hours. It was great though, talking about everything from what was wrong with hockey today, to how the Wild were doing. We would talk about life, it was wonderful. I was fascinated, and I felt blessed to be on the other end of the phone, talking to a man who I respected and admired so much. I think that Herbie looked at me as the "new guard." I was a young guy with a passion for hockey. Herbie knew that and knew that I could get his message across, whether that was through my books or through articles I would write about him in American Hockey Magazine or Minnesota Hockey Journal. I still wasn't in the inner circle, but I was close, and that was awesome.

When Herbie finally turned down the Rangers job this Summer, he told me that he was committed to getting the book done. He wanted it to tie in with the movie and he wanted to get going. In fact, we talked about changing the outline up at

Giant's Ridge in Biwabik, the night before he died at the U.S. Hockey Hall of Fame golf tournament. Herb was in his element that night. All of his pals were there and he was having a ball. I remember, Bobby and Brett Hull were being honored and while they were speaking, they acknowledged Herbie, who was sitting way in the back enjoying the time out of the spotlight with some of his old buddies. Herb graciously acknowledged them back, but didn't want to distract from their moment in the sun. After the dinner I had a beer with Herb and we talked, it was great. I remember sitting with a couple of guys I knew back in college at dinner and afterward they asked me to introduce them to Herbie. I did, and Herb was as gracious as could be. People would come up and ask for his autograph and he talked to all of them. He asked them sincere questions about how they were doing, and made them feel important.

Well, I hit the sack around midnight, and I saw Herb that next morning out on the course as we were about to start the golf tournament. We were delayed for whatever reason, so I went over and hung out with him, John Mayasich and Paulie Coppo, his old pals, as they were warming up. It was early, and we were all tired. I will never forget as we stood there in the grass, talking and laughing. Herbie was giving me tips on how to hold my club and telling me that I needed to keep my arm straight when I swung. That was Herbie, coaching right up until the end. I told him I would work on it and that I hoped he had a fun round of golf with his pals. I said that I hoped he had a good trip to Chicago that night and that I would call him later that week to get together for the book. Those were the last words that I ever got to say to my old friend. Herb died later that day in a terrible car accident on his way home from the tournament.

What a great final weekend it was for Herb though. He was surrounded by his best friends, eating great food, laughing, relaxing and playing golf — all of his favorite things. And, he was in his element, surrounded by hockey fans who adored him. It is only fitting that Herb would spend his final days on this earth in such a wonderful environment. Add to that the fact that he was there to help the Hall of Fame raise money and it was a fitting ending to an incredible life. Herb was a giver, and did whatever he could to give back to the sport which he so dearly loved.

As I got into my car that afternoon with my wife and daughter to drive home from our cabin, which was nearby on Lake Nichols, I turned on the radio. To my shock and horror, I heard what had happened. Like everybody else, I simply couldn't believe it. I pulled over and hugged my wife. Then, ironically, I hugged my four year old Jack Russell Terrier, who I had named *"Herbie Brooks Bernstein,"* in honor of my idol. I then peered into the back seat and looked at my daughter, Campbell. I thought about life and how precious it was and how quickly it could be taken from you. I cried. Herbie used to always ask about my daughter. He loved being a grandpa and that was the softer side of Herb that really made you melt. He used to always tease me about naming her Campbell and asking if I was going to name my next kids Norris or Smyth, in reference to the old NHL conferences of the same name. That was Herbie, always putting a hockey spin on everything.

As we drove home we listened to the radio. Of course, it was non-stop talk about Herbie. For two and a half hours, we listened to people talk, cry, tell stories and share what an impact he had had on their lives. When I turned on my cell phone it was full of messages from friends of mine who wanted to see if I was all right. I was devastated. But, as we listened further and got past the initial shock of it all, it was sort of like therapy. Hearing what everyone was saying really moved me. You see, like Herbie, I too wanted to do my part. So, I decided right then that I would turn our book project that we had been working on into a memorial, a tribute to someone I worshiped. Then, I decided to donate some of the proceeds to his cause. That would be the right thing to do and that would be how I could do my part. Herbie felt so passionately about building the base of the pyramid, getting more and more people involved in the sport at the bottom, where it was widest. He knew that if the sport was to grow that we needed more people getting involved in it from the grass roots level, from kids to coaches to volunteers. He just felt so strongly that everyone needed to do their part, for the good of the game. That is what Herbie had been doing that weekend, doing his part for the good of hockey. He had been carrying the torch for his mentor, John Mariucci, the Godfather of Minnesota hockey. It would now be up to everyone else to carry the torch for Herbie, and I wanted to do my part.

As we got closer and closer to the Twin Cities, we knew that we would have to confront our worst nightmare head on. We were heading south, on I-35, and on a direct course to pass by the crash site in Forest Lake. It was so tough, I wanted to turn around and find a different way home. As we approached and saw the news vans, helicopters and onlookers, I tried to stay strong. I just couldn't believe that my friend, who I was with just hours earlier that morning, was gone, and I was about to pass, literally, by where he had so suddenly died. Then, as we slowed down, I saw a makeshift memorial on the side of the road which someone had erected of a cross made from two hockey sticks covered by a Gopher Hockey jersey. I lost it.

The next few days were tough, and the funeral was even tougher. It was beautiful though, and so fitting. Appropriately, it was held at the Cathedral in St. Paul, where Herbie's roots ran deep. Everybody from the world of hockey was there, along with so many others. People from all walks of life just wanted to come out and pay their respects to a man who truly made a difference to them in this world. From the rich and famous to the poor and homeless, they were all there. It was a spectacle I will certainly never forget. When I got home I called my dad, Don. He and Herb are exactly the same age, 66, and I told him that I loved him. I told him that I wanted him to make sure that he ate right and kept on exercising, because I wanted him around for a long, long time to be with me and his granddaughter. Then, I called my mom, and told her that I loved her too. I also told her that she had better start wearing her seat belt, and reluctantly, she agreed. She would never do it before that, but after seeing the affect that Herbie's accident had on me, she changed her mind.

Well, a few weeks later, I forced myself to get going on the new book. It was so tough. I didn't know where to begin, so I just jumped in and started interviewing people who were close to him. Nearly 100 people later, I had a book. I didn't want to do a biography, that will be a book for someone else. For me, I wanted to touch on Herbie's achievements and contributions, and then tell his story through the eyes of those who knew him best. I would call it "Remembering Herbie," and that is exactly what it is. As I began interviewing people, I could see what an amazing impact he had had on so many lives. Dozens and dozens and dozens of grown men openly wept on the phone with me. They laughed, they cried and they remembered Herbie. It was wonderful. While some people opened up about what he meant to them as a person, others shared hilarious stories. I know it is cliché, but I really did want to celebrate his life, and I think I was able to do that.

I tried to interview a broad sampling of those who knew him best, so I talked to former teammates of his from St. Paul Johnson High School, the Gophers and from U.S. Olympic & National Teams. I spoke to former players of his from the Gophers, the Olympics, the New York Rangers, the Minnesota North Stars, the New Jersey Devils and the Pittsburgh Penguins. Then, I talked to friends, neighbors, acquaintances and colleagues. I was even able to interview his wife, Patti, and kids, Danny and Kelly. They are such strong, amazing people and I can't begin to thank them enough for their help and willingness to share their memories of someone they so deeply loved.

I found that as I wrote the book and talked to more and more people, a picture was emerging of who Herb Brooks really was. The common denominators throughout the book are simply fascinating. The way he motivated people, the *"Brooksisms"* he was so famous for saying, the way he never forgot where he came from, the way he championed the underdog, the way he was always looking to make hockey better, the way he could never make up his mind and the way he loved his family. All of those things and so much more came out in the book in a way that I know Herbie would be proud of.

For me, it was therapeutic. I was able to talk about Herbie every day for several months and that was wonderful. For others, however, I think I was more like the grim reaper, calling them and asking them to deal with something that they were not yet ready to deal with. Some people avoided me like the plague, not returning my calls or asking instead if they could just e-mail me their responses to my questions. Others just said no, and that they weren't ready to talk about it. I totally respected that. I just wanted them to have the opportunity to be a part of it if they wanted to. Others opened up and poured out their emotions to me like I was their shrink. It was incredible. I just wanted to get as many people in the book as possible, to honor a man who I thought so much of. I really felt a great sense of responsibility in doing this. I wanted to get it right. I wanted to honor his legacy the right way. I wanted to make sure that I spoke to the right people and asked the right questions.

You know, I even talked to a few people who were notorious for bucking heads with Herbie. Do you know why? Because not even Herb Brooks would want a book written about him which was 100% gushy. He would just as soon take a slap shot to the groin than to have to read all of that, so I mixed it up and got some other opinions too. I know that he would be glad with my decision.

Well, I hope I nailed it. I have never put more effort or passion into anything in my entire life. And do you know what? That is exactly what Herbie would have expected of me. Just when you thought you didn't have anything left in the tank, and were running on fumes, that is when Herbie put the hammer down and demanded more. That is why Herbie was a winner.

You know, I found it fascinating that one man could have so many "best friends." I swear, at least three dozen people that I talked to were convinced that Herbie was their best friend. That is incredible to me. People just wanted to be around him, they wanted his attention, his guidance, his approval, his love and his friendship. Herbie was infectious that way. Everybody wanted a piece of him, and it is remarkable to think that he gave as much of himself as he did to so many people and to so many causes. He grew on you. After a while, you would even sort of start to sound like him. I remember talking to my wife one time after a marathon Herbie phone call and I said some profound cliché, like I really knew what I was talking about. She just kind of looked at me and asked if I had just talked to Herbie. Busted! He just made you want to be like him, and that was something that started for me way back at his hockey camp in Faribault when I was a peewee.

I have to tell you, the way people talked about Herbie in the book was simply incredible. I have never heard so many wonderful things about one person in my entire life. I really think he could have been anything in this world, even the President of the United States. I am not kidding. And hey, politics intrigued him. He had it in his blood. After all, his father was a good friend of fellow East Sider, Wendell Anderson, and even served as his campaign chairman when he ran for governor. Herbie could motivate people and just get their attention, that's why both Democrats and Republicans alike each tried to get him to run for office on numerous occasions. He wanted no part of it though. Herbie was tough, controversial and said whatever was on his mind, whenever he wanted. That was the charm as well as the dark side of Herbie, and that is what made him such an interesting public figure. Through it all though, he always wanted to do what was right. He was so principled, so determined and so passionate about things that he believed in, that once he got something in his head, it was going to get done — no matter what. That was Herbie. I think about the now infamous saying which will forever be linked to his legacy, *"Do you believe in miracles?"* Yes!? Well… Herb didn't. Sure, he was a dreamer, but Herbie believed in hard work, commitment and integrity. There were no short-cuts or divine interventions for this guy. It was all about hard work, commitment and passion.

Described as the ultimate motivator, a brilliant tactician, a superb innovator and a driven perfectionist, Herbie was smart, innovative and intense. He was also stubborn, aggravating, pig-headed and extremely complex. Ask him what time it was and he would tell you how to build a watch. That was Herbie. You truly never knew what you were going to get when you talked to him. He was part philosopher, part politician, part psychologist, part teacher, part public speaker and even part stand-up comedian. Most importantly, however, Herbie was part dreamer. And luckily for us his obsession was hockey, and through that he changed the face of American history. Through his hard work, dedication and determination, Herbie affected generations of American hockey players. He spent countless hours building the game from the grass roots level and did whatever he could to get more rinks built and more kids playing hockey. It was always about the kids with Herbie, and his heart was always, always in the right place. For that, we all owe Herb Brooks a tremendous debt of gratitude. He was truly a one of a kind.

Ironically, one of the questions that I recently asked Herbie was about how he would want his coaching epitaph to read, or how he would want to be remembered when it was all said and done. This was what he had to say: *"He sacrificed for the unknown and had truly piece of mind. You know, I have always felt strongly about the name on the front of the sweater being much more important than the name on the back. They'll forget about individuals in this world, but they'll always remember the teams. That is how I want to be remembered."*

This project was the adventure of a lifetime for me and something I will never forget. Herbie touched so many lives in his 66 years on this earth and I feel so genuinely touched and honored that mine was one of them. I am so happy to be able to have done this for my friend and hope that in the end what it does is to preserve his legacy and keep it going for many, many years to come. I learned so much from him and will never forget him. Now that he is gone I will only have memories. But, every time I see my dog, I will think of my old friend and smile.

"Herbie Bernstein"

So, thanks to all of the people who were gracious enough to let me interview them for this book. I appreciate it and I know that Herbie would too. To be honest, I could only hope to die so beloved and so well thought of. Sure, he left us far too soon, but the guy really ly went out on top of his game.

Simply put, Herb Brooks was a giant among legends and the best of the very best. Period. He will be dearly missed and it is now up to all of us to keep his torch burning brightly. That is what Herbie would have wanted. He wouldn't want us sitting around mourning over him, he would want us out there, each doing his or her part, for hockey.

Thanks Herbie, we will miss you.

HERBERT PAUL BROOKS

August 5, 1937 — August, 11, 2003

This is the story of Herbie Brooks, which is simply as amazing as he was...

Born in St. Paul on August 5, 1937, Herb Brooks grew up in a modest duplex at the corner of Payne and Ivy, the son of a plumber who found himself selling insurance after the Great Depression. Herb's family loved hockey. His father was a well known amateur hockey player in the 1920s, while his kid brother, David, would go on to play for the Gophers in the early 1960s and also on the 1964 U.S. Olympic team as well. As a boy growing up on St. Paul's tough East Side, a training ground for many future Minnesota hockey stars, Herb was a typical hockey playing rink-rat. He would go on to star at St. Paul Johnson High School from 1952-55. As a senior, the speedy forward led Johnson to a 26-1-2 record en route to winning the state championship. Here is how it all went down:

The 1955 Minnesota State High School Hockey Tournament started out innocently enough, until the third quarterfinal game rolled around. That game, between Minneapolis South and Thief River Falls, would prove to be, arguably, the most famous of all-time. That's because it lasted an incredible 11 overtimes, the longest game ever to be played in tourney history. The game roared back and forth all night. Well, after nine overtimes, and no end in sight, the officials decided to start the evening game between St. Paul Johnson and Roseau at 11:30 pm. The two games then rotated back and forth in between periods. Finally at 1:50 of the 11th extra session, South's Jim Westby scored the game winner to end the unbelievable marathon. Incidentally, and completely overshadowed, Ken Fanger's first period goal was all that Johnson needed to hang on for a 1-0 win over Roseau in their quarterfinal game. Then, in the semifinals, a kid by the name of Herb Brooks put his Johnson squad up 1-0 midway through the first, while Stu Anderson and Roger Wigen each tallied in the third to give the Governors a 3-1 win, and a ticket to the

The 1955 State Champs from St. Paul Johnson

Front Row: Karl Dahlberg, Herb Brooks, Roger Wigens, Tom Wahman, Jack Holstrom, John Patton.
Second Row: R. Gustafson (Coach), Rodney Anderson, Chuck Rodgers, Ken Fanger, Bill McKechnie, Ryan Ostebo, Stu Anderson, Tony Hudalla (Student Manager).

Finals. There, Johnson and their Mill City rivals from Southwest faced off for all the marbles in front of a packed St. Paul Auditorium crowd. The hero of the game would prove to be none other than Herbie, who got the Governors on the board at 2:32 of the first period. His teammate, Stu Anderson, then tallied less than seven minutes later, only to see Brooks score his second of the game just a minute and a half after that. It would prove to be the final nail in the coffin as Coach Rube Gustafson's Governors cruised to a 3-1 victory.

"Winning the state championship was great, but my most memorable moment is not from the title game but the game we had to follow!" said Herbie of the 11-over-time quarterfinal thriller. "We had to wait and wait in the dressing room; we'd take our skates off, put them on, shuffle our feet, this and that. It was hard to wait, and it was after one in the morning when our game was finally over, but we won and went on to win the championship. Winning the state championship, that represented your neighborhood. I would have to say that it was my biggest thrill ever. It was just the guys in the neighborhood and that was special."

An outstanding athlete, Herb also earned three varsity letters as a first baseman on the Johnson baseball team as well. Before long, the colleges were calling.

"I had an interview with the Air Force Academy, because I really wanted to be a fighter pilot," said Brooks. "Unfortunately, because I was slightly color blind, I washed out of the Academy. I also had a scholarship at the University of Michigan, but my dad encouraged me to walk on at the University of Minnesota and try to play for John Mariucci, so that was the route I took."

At Minnesota, Brooks became known for his blinding speed. "He was one of the fastest, if not the fastest, player in college hockey in that era," Mariucci would later recall. Brooks would learn a lot from "Maroosh," saying that he had more to do with shaping his ideas in hockey than any other individual.

"In all social causes to better an institution, there's always got to be a rallying force, a catalyst, a glue, and a magnet, and that's what John was, for American hockey," Herbie once said in a Star Tribune article. "The rest of us just filled in after him."

"At first I was scared to death of him," said Herbie. "I was fresh out of high school. I remember in practices my first year he used to call me Pete. For the longest time he never knew my name, and I was terrified of him.

"He was like a father to me, we were very close. He wasn't long on words, and didn't want to be everybody's buddy like some coaches try to be. John was an entirely different guy as a coach. You took care of yourself under John. He never called you to take care of you, or told you to go to class. His psychology of coaching was to take care of yourself, or get the hell out. You grew up pretty fast under John. He was a throwback, and was an entirely different coach than you'd see today. He was such a great guy. I remember the day they renamed the arena in his name. It was his happiest day, and such a memorable moment for him.

"I patterned several aspects of my coaching after John. He was a pioneer and faced immense competition as a coach. When the '80 Olympic team won the gold, John said it was one more piece to the puzzle for American hockey. I shared these hopes, dreams and aspirations with him, and was proud of the fact that there were 12 of us from Minnesota on that team."

Brooks wore a Golden Gopher sweater from 1957-59, scoring 45 points over his three-year career. He graduated from the U of M in 1961 with a B.A. in Psychology — a degree he would put to use in more ways than one over the ensuing years to come.

Dreams Can Come True
The next phase of Brooks' life involved his lifelong dream, the Olympics. After graduating, he began to build a successful career in the insurance business, but never fully got away from the game that continued to dominate his life. He would play off and on with some local semipro teams, including the St. Paul Steers and Rochester Mustangs over the next several years, while also selling insurance as well. Then, he tried out for the U.S. Olympic team which was set to play in Squaw Valley, Calif, for the 1960 Winter Games. He played well, eluding every cut except the final one, when he was literally the last player to be released from the team's final roster. He was devastated.

Herb then sat at home with his father and watched his buddies from the neighborhood, some of the same kids who he used to play hockey with out on the frozen ponds, bring home the gold. Herb was torn. On one hand he was genuinely happy for his old pals. On the other he was jealous as hell, because they were living out his dream. At that very moment Herb's father, Herb Sr., looked at him and said: "Looks like Coach cut the right guy…" It was right then and there, on

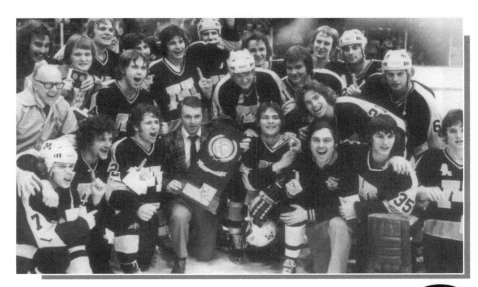

February 27, 1960, that Herbie knew his destiny. He was going to make the 1964 team, and one day, he was going to coach an Olympic team. Period.

Brooks worked like a dog, and for his efforts spent nearly a decade playing for either U.S. Olympic or National teams. In fact, from 1961-70, he played on two Olympic teams and five National teams — more than any player in the history of United States hockey — even captaining several teams along the way.

"To me the Olympics are not about 'Dream Teams,' they're more about dreamers," said Herb. "They're not about medals, but the pursuit of medals. The Olympics are not about being No. 1, they're about sacrificing and trying to be No. 1. That's why the Olympics will always be special to me."

Finding His True Calling
Herbie went into coaching after that, becoming an assistant under Coach Glen Sonmor at the U of M. At the same time, he pioneered Junior Hockey in the state as the first coach of the Minnesota Junior Stars in the Minnesota/Ontario Junior-A League. In 1970, Herb was considered for the head coaching job at the University of Wisconsin, a job which ultimately went to fellow Minnesotan Bob Johnson. How scary to think that if that had happened it might have been "Badger-Herbie" instead of "Badger Bob!" Luckily for us, that next year Sonmor left to become the coach of the WHA's Fighting Saints. The following season Brooks was named as the Gophers' new head coach. The youngest college hockey coach in the country, Brooks would inherit a program that had just finished in last place. The challenge of turning it all around was just what Herb was looking for.

The chant "Her-bee!, Her-bee!" would become an all too familiar sound at the "Old Barn" throughout the tenure of the man who would become Minnesota's

greatest hockey coach. Brooks instilled a new brand of pride and tradition that next season, starting with his newly designed jerseys which proudly featured the Minnesota "M" on the front. Brooks promised he would bring, "exciting, dynamic people into the program," and he kept his word. In only seven years, he would build a dynasty at Minnesota. More importantly, he did it all with Minnesota kids.

With his extensive knowledge and experience in European hockey, Herb became an advocate of the Russian style of play and in particular, the coaching style of Anatoli Tarasov. He would instill this philosophy in motivating his own players. From 1972-79, Brooks was simply dominant. With his no-nonsense attitude, he went on to win the first three national championships in

Gopher Hockey history: 1973, 1976 and 1979. While at the University of Minnesota, Brooks won 175 games, lost 100, and tied 20 for a .636 winning percentage. Brooks also guided five All-Americans: Les Auge, Mike Polich, Tim Harrer, Neal Broten and Steve Ulseth, while 23 of his protégés went on to play in the NHL as well.

"We went to the finals four of my seven years there, and we made a great run of it," said Brooks. "I think I put a lot of pressure on the players, and I had a lot of expectations of them. I didn't give them an 'out,' and I think I was always able to find the kids who were really competitive. The common denominator of all the guys who played throughout my seven years was that they were really competitive, very hungry, very focused, and mentally tough — to go along with whatever talent they had. I think that really carried us."

Do You Believe in Miracles?...Yes!

The next chapter of Brooks' life was the one that would make him a household name, the legendary "Miracle on Ice." Sure, he had built the University of Minnesota hockey program into a dynasty, but for Herbie, coaching the Gophers was just another rung on the ladder. You see, for Herbie, coaching the Olympics had always been what it was all about. That was his dream, to coach the U.S. squad at the Olympics. Now, his dream was about to become a reality. He was about to make history.

"The Olympians, the amazing athletes like Jesse Owens, they are the ones who have always captivated me," said Brooks. "The Olympics are a world sporting spectacle on an international stage. It is national pride with so much wonderful history. I grew up with that history, so to me the Olympics transcend the game itself."

After coaching the 1979 U.S. National team at the World Games in Moscow, Herbie was then named as the coach of the fabled 1980 U.S. Olympic team.

"Having played international hockey for so many years, it gives me an awfully warm feeling to be selected as head coach for the 1980 Olympics," said Brooks of his new job. "I'm extremely honored and humbled. To be picked when there are so many outstanding amateur hockey coaches in the nation, well, let's just say it's something I never really expected to happen."

The Americans, who, since the inception of the Winter Games, had won one gold medal (1960), four silver medals (1924, 1952, 1956 & 1972), and one bronze (1936), were eager to bring home some hardware on their native soil. Having finished fourth during the previous Olympics, in 1976, at Innsbruck, Austria, under coach Bob Johnson, the U.S. knew it would never have a better opportunity than the one they had in front of them right then in Lake Placid, N.Y.

Brooks now had the responsibility of selecting the 20 players to fill out his roster. He didn't want to take any chances, so he went with who he knew and who he could trust — local boys. He researched countless candidates, made thousands of phone calls, and tried to find out which players he could count on when it really mattered. That was what it was all about for Herbie.

"When he had to pick the 1980 Olympic team, I remember Herbie calling the high schools of the potential Olympians to find out their records on grades, if they got into trouble, did drugs, and what kind of people they were," recalled Herb's brother Dave. "When I asked him why the hell he was doing that, he said that he wanted to know what kind of player he was going to have when it came down to the last two minutes of a game. He said he wanted to know which kids he should have on the ice come clutch time."

When it was all said and done, fully 12 Minnesotans had made the final cut. In addition, nine were players that Brooks had coached as Gophers: Roseau's Neal Broten, Grand Rapids' Bill Baker, White Bear Lake's Steve Janaszak, Rochester's Eric Strobel, Duluth's Phil Verchota, Minneapolis' Mike Ramsey, Babbitt's Buzz Schneider, St. Paul's Robb McClanahan and Richfield's Steve Christoff. The three other Minnesotans were: Warroad's Dave Christian, who played at North Dakota, and Virginia's John Harrington and Eveleth's Mark Pavelich — both of whom played at Minnesota-Duluth.

From there, Herbie worked them relentlessly, taking them on a world-wide tour to test them both mentally and physically. In early September, the team began

as challenging an exhibition schedule as had ever been organized for an American Olympic squad. Beginning with an initial European tour, the team played a 61-game pre-Olympic schedule against foreign, college and professional teams, ultimately finishing with a 42-16-3 record. It was during this time together that the players were introduced to Brooks' new offensive game-plan called, the "weave." Brooks felt that if his club was going to compete against Europeans, they had better learn how to play like Europeans.

Brooks' free-flowing, crisscrossing offensive style allowed his players to be creative. It was a loose style which allowed for a lot of improvisation, or "sophisticated pond hockey," as Herbie would call it. It was an amalgam of the North American style with the

European game, and it worked. Brooks pushed the kids relentlessly. He watched their diet, had them do dry-land training in soccer fields to work on their footwork and flexibility, and trained them like they had never been trained. He challenged them, prodded them, screamed at them and drove them beyond what they thought they could achieve. They were in shape too, as he worked them to death in his legendary practices. He wanted to make sure that they were ready to go in the third period of a big game. He was their motivator, their teacher, their psychologist and their father — all wrapped up into one. And, he was their worst nightmare too. He was tough as hell on them, never cutting them any slack.

Entering the XIIIth Winter Olympic Games, the team was a decided underdog, an evaluation that seemed to be confirmed by a 10-3 defeat at the hands of the mighty Soviets in the final exhibition game in New York City's Madison Square Garden. Though seeded seventh in the 12-nation pool, the Americans felt that they had something to prove. The Yanks took on Sweden in the opening game, as Bill Baker scored with 27 seconds remaining in the third period to give the U.S. a 2-2 tie. The goal acted as a catalyst for the young Americans, who then upset Czechoslovakia, and the amazing Stastny brothers, 7-3, thanks to goals from Pavelich, Schneider, Verchota and McClanahan. After beating both Norway and Romania, now only West Germany (the team that knocked them out of the bronze medal in 1976), stood in the way of getting into the medal round.

Down 2-0 in the first, the Minnesota boys came through big as McClanahan and Broten each tallied to tie it up. McClanahan then scored again on another breakaway in the third, and Phil Verchota lit the lamp late to give the U.S. a 4-2 win over the West Germans. This gave the Americans a round robin record of 4-0-1, and a date with the Soviets — who were led by Vladislav Tretiak, the world's premier goaltender. The Soviets, who had outscored their opponents 51-11 through their first five games, were just another of a long line of dynasty teams which had won the last four Olympic golds, and five of the last six. In fact, the only team to beat them since 1956 was the U.S. squad, 20 years earlier in 1960.

Going for Gold
Herbie now had his boys right where he wanted them. He knew that the Soviets were ripe for defeat. Sure, they were technically superior to any team in the world.

1980
UNITED STATES OLYMPIC HOCKEY TEAM
XIII WINTER OLYMPICS
GOLD MEDALIST

Front Row (L-R) Steve Janaszak, Bill Baker, Mark Johnson, Craig Patrick (Ass't Coach/Ass't GM), Mike Eruzione (Captain), Herb Brooks (Head Coach), Buzz Schneider, Jack O'Callahan, Jim Craig

Middle Row (L-R) Bob Suter, Rob McClanahan, Mark Wells, Bud Kessel (Equipment Manager), V. George Nagobads (Physician), Gary Smith (Trainer), Robert Fleming (Chairman), Ralph Jasinski (General Manager), Warren Strelow (Goalkeeping Coach), Bruce Horsch, Neal Broten, Mark Pavelich

Back Row (L-R) Phil Verchota, Steve Christoff, Les Auge, Dave Delich, Jack Hughes, Ken Morrow, Mike Ramsey, Dave Christian, Ralph Cox, Dave Silk, John Harrington, Eric Strobel

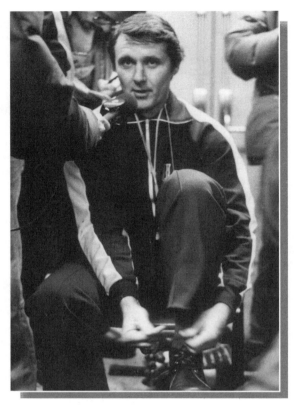

They were fast, strong and better in nearly every way. Every way but one, they lacked heart — something Brooks was banking on. He knew that they were overconfident and knew that the time was right to go for it. And that is just what he did. The game had all the hype imaginable, with political and social implications written all over it. Amidst the backdrop of the Iranian hostage crisis, the Soviet invasion of Afghanistan, the realization that the U.S. economy was in disarray with interest rates and inflation soaring — not to mention the fact that President Carter had already announced an American boycott of the Summer Olympics in Moscow, the team hit the ice. Talk about pressure.

With that, the "Iron Range" line of Pavelich, Harrington and Schneider got the Americans on the board, when, down 1-0, Pavelich fed Schneider for a nice slap shot which found the top corner. The Russians answered back three minutes later, only to see Mark Johnson tie it up with just seconds to go in the period on a nice open ice steal and break-away. When they returned to the ice following the intermission, the U.S. team was shocked to see that Soviet coach Victor Tikhanov had replaced Tretiak in goal with backup goaltender Vladimir Myshkin. While it would appear that the great bear was wounded, the Soviets came back to take the lead, having now out-shot the Yanks 30-10 through two periods. Johnson then got his second of the game at 8:39 of the third to tie it at 3-3, setting up the heroics for the Iron Rangers.

Midway through the third, Schneider dumped the puck into the Russian zone and Harrington dug it out to his old UMD wingmate Mark Pavelich. Pavelich then floated a perfect pass to the top of the circle where team captain Mike Eruzione fired home "the shot heard 'round the world." The final 10 minutes of the game were probably the longest in U.S. hockey history, but the Americans somehow held on behind goalie Jim Craig's brilliant netminding down the stretch. Then, as the crowd counted down the final seconds, famed television announcer Al Michaels shouted *"Do you believe in miracles,...Yes!"* Our boys had done it. And with that, the Americans had made it into the gold medal game.

After the players were through celebrating on the ice, Herbie, ever the psychologist, quickly put them back in their place in the locker room. He screamed at them not to get too cocky, and that they were just lucky, and hadn't won anything yet. The next day at practice, Brooks put the team through a grueling workout, constantly reinforcing to his men that he was not their friend, and they had proved nothing up to that point. This was all part of his ingenious master plan, to get the players to despise him, and force them to rally amongst themselves to become stronger.

In the gold medal game the U.S. would face Finland, a team which had beaten the Czechs in the other semifinal. It was during this game which Herbie would utter the famous words: *"You were born to be a player. You were meant to be here. This moment is yours."* His team would respond, big time.

Despite being down early in the second period, Steve Christoff got the Americans on the board at 4:39 with a nice wrister down low. The Finns hung tough, however, and went into the third up 2-1. After an emotional speech between the intermission from Brooks, reminding his players ever so eloquently that they would regret this moment for the rest of their collective lives if they let it slip away, the U.S. came out inspired and tried to make history. The constant reminder of Herbie saying *"Play your game... Play your game,"* was comforting to the players, who knew that they were on the verge of making history.

The hero this time would prove to be Phil Verchota, who took a Dave Christian pass in the left circle and found the back of the net at 2:25. With that, the Americans started to smell blood and immediately went for the jugular. Just three minutes later, Robbie McClanahan went five-hole with a Mark Johnson pass to give the U.S. a 3-2 lead. Johnson then saved the day by adding a shorthanded backhand goal of his own just minutes later to give the U.S. a two-goal safety net. From there, Jim Craig just hung on for the final few minutes of the game as Al Michaels this time screamed: *"This impossible dream, comes true!"* It was suddenly pandemonium in Lake Placid, as the players threw their sticks into the crowd and formed a human hog pile at center ice to the chants of *"USA! USA!"* Herbie, meanwhile, thrust his arm into the air in a brief moment of uncharacteristic jubilation and sat-

isfaction, only to then sneak out the back door, leaving the players to celebrate their achievement amongst themselves.

Afterward, many of the players were visibly moved by what they had done, as evidenced during the singing of the National Anthem, where the entire team gathered on the top podium to sing the Star-Spangled Banner.

While Mark Johnson, son of ex-Gopher, "Badger Bob" Johnson, led the team in scoring, the Iron Range Line of Schneider-Pavelich-Harrington led the team's four lines in scoring with 17 goals and 20 assists. Brilliant goaltending by Jim Craig, who played all seven contests, was a big factor in the victory, as was the stellar play of defensemen Dave Christian, Ken Morrow, Mike Ramsey, Neal Broten and Bill

Baker.

The event will forever remain etched in our memories as one of the greatest sporting events of all-time. Looking back, the icy miracle was achieved by enormous ambition, coupled with great passing, checking, speed, and sound puck-control. Shrewdly, Brooks refused to play the typical dump-and-chase style of hockey that was so prevalent in American hockey.

"I didn't want the team throwing the puck away with no reason," he said. "That's stupid. It's the same as punting on first down. The style I wanted combined the determined checking of the North American game and the best features of the European game."

A Lasting Legacy

A grateful nation, saddened by what was happening in the world, hailed the team as heroes. A visit to the White House followed, as well as appearances in cities across the land. Covers of Wheaties boxes, magazines, awards, honors, speaking engagements and a whole lot of hoopla would follow for all the players. In the heart of the Cold War, beating the mighty Soviets was something bigger than they could've ever imagined. The country went crazy with a newly found sense of national pride, all thanks to Herbie's incredible achievement. Sports Illustrated went on to name the team, collectively, as *"Sportsmen of the Year;"* Life Magazine declared it as the *"Sports Achievement of the Decade;"* and ABC Sports announcer, Jim McCay, went on to call the spectacle, *"The greatest upset in the history of sports."*

"They were really mentally tough and goal-oriented," said Brooks. "They came from all different walks of life, many having competed against one another, but they came together and grew to be a real close team. I pushed this team really hard, I mean I really pushed them! But they had the ability to answer the bell. Our style of play was probably different than anything in North America. We adopted more of a hybrid style of play — a bit of the Canadian school and a little bit of the European school. The players took to it like ducks to water, and they really had a lot of fun playing it. We were a fast, creative team that played extremely disciplined without the puck. Throughout the Olympics, they had a great resiliency about them. I mean they came from behind six or seven times to win. They just kept on moving and working and digging. I think we were as good a conditioned team as there was in the world, outside maybe the Soviet Union. We got hot and

lucky at the right times, and it was just an incredible experience for all of us."

After the Olympics, all of the players went their separate ways. Many went on to play professional hockey, while others went into business and began their careers elsewhere. They would not all be reunited again, however, until 2002, when the team was brought together in an emotional gala to collectively light the Olympic caldron at the Winter Games at Salt Lake City.

Looking back, the event was extremely significant for the growth of American hockey. The historic win brought hockey to the front-page of newspapers everywhere, and forever opened the door to the NHL for American-born players from below the 49th parallel. The impact of the event was far reaching, and is still being felt today. Since that milestone game back in 1980, hockey in the United States has grown significantly at both the professional and amateur levels. The fact that we now have hockey in Arizona, North Carolina, Florida, California and Texas can all be traced back, in part, to the Miracle on Ice. Herb Brooks had a great deal to do with that. The event would later be named as the "Sporting Event of the 20th Century," not bad for a kid from Payne Avenue in St. Paul.

From the Big Apple to St. Cloud to the Met to Jersey to Pittsburgh, the Adventure Continued...

After coaching in Davos, Switzerland, that next year, where he rested and reevaluated his future, Herb's coaching success continued in the National Hockey League with the New York Rangers. Herbie took the Big Apple by storm, even being named as the NHL Coach of the Year in 1982, his rookie season. Brooks would guide the Rangers for four seasons, leading his team to the playoffs each year and earning 100 victories faster than any other Ranger coach before him. In all, Brooks coached the Rangers to a .532 winning percentage and twice he led the team into the second round of the playoffs, losing both times to rival New York Islanders teams which went on to win Stanley Cups.

In the pros, Herbie did things which were truly revolutionary at the time. He had off-season training back when off season training consisted of golf and fishing. He brought in his old buddy from Minnesota, Jack Blatherwick, to teach his players about exercise physiology, and it worked. He even monitored his players' body fat and insisted that they eat right, and even chew sugar free gum. Then, he instilled a European style of hockey into the rough and tumble, clutch and grab, dump and chase North American game which had been commonplace for decades. People thought he was crazy, but when his "Smurfs" beat the mighty Broad Street Bullies by skating around them, no one was laughing. Herb truly changed the game. (Many of his players were small and quick, earning the nickname "Smurfs," in reference to the little blue cartoon characters.)

Herb's Broadway stint with the Rangers lasted until 1985. He had just gotten tired of dealing with tem-

peramental and arrogant millionaire players who didn't show him the same respect that he had been accustomed to, and wanted out. It was drastically different from coaching amateur kids in college and in the Olympics. He was also frustrated with the team's lack of personnel moves. In college, if he needed a quick centerman, he would recruit one. Here, it was more difficult to get the management to make a deal for what he wanted. Couple that with the fact that his dad had died during training camp that year, and the fact that he was tired of living in hotel rooms away from his family, and the writing was on the wall.

When Herb came home, he took some time off to recharge his batteries. He accepted a sales position with local Jostens, selling "national prestige awards" to big-time clients including the NFL and NBA. A year later, however, Herb got the coaching itch. So, in an amazing move, Brooks accepted the head coaching position at St. Cloud State University in 1986. He would be revered as the school's savior, leading the Huskies to a third place finish in the national small-college tournament, and more importantly, getting the program elevated to NCAA Division I status. He stayed for only a year, but with his clout, got the school a beautiful new arena and really got the Huskies' program turned around. He did it as a personal favor to John Mariucci, and once again, it was classic Herbie, helping out the underdog.

"St. Cloud was a very positive experience for me, and John was very influential in that endeavor as well," said Herb. "We felt that there were more kids in Minnesota than opportunities for them. He encouraged me to go up there for a year, get the program from Division III to Division I, raise money for the new rinks, and get them going in the right direction. Then I left. John was very much a visionary, and had a lot to do with my decision in going up there."

The next stop in Brooks' hockey resume was Bloomington, to coach the NHL's Minnesota North Stars. It was another homecoming of sorts, as Herb took over the reigns from Lorne Henning and became the first Minnesota native to coach the team. The season, however, didn't go well for Brooks. Lou Nanne had just resigned as the teams' general manager and newcomer Jack Ferreira had just come in. Unable to overcome an enormous number of injuries, the Stars finished in the Norris Division cellar that year. So, citing philosophical differences with management, Brooks resigned after the season. It was a bad deal all the way around.

Brooks then took some well deserved time away from coaching for a few years after that to embark on a successful business career which included motivational speaking, TV analysis, NHL scouting and occasional coaching. Then, in 1991, he got back into the action when he took over the New Jersey Devils minor league team in Utica, NY, and was later promoted to be the head coach of the NHL team in 1992. There, he guided the Devils for one season, compiling a record of 40-37-7 along the way.

It is interesting to note that Herb lobbied to coach the 1992 U.S. Olympic team at that time. He proposed the development of a full-time U.S. National team, made up of non-NHL players which would stay together through the 1994 Olympics in Lillehammer as well. But USA Hockey officials were only willing to hire him for the 1992 Winter Games, so Herb, very principled, walked away.

After scouting and working in the private sector, Brooks got the coaching bug yet again a few years later, when he agreed to guide the French Olympic team at the 1998 Winter Games in Nagano, Japan, — even upsetting Team USA, 3-1, in the World Championships just prior to the tournament. Herbie just loved to coach and loved new challenges.

Following that, Brooks became a full-time scout with the NHL's Pittsburgh Penguins, ultimately taking over as the teams' head coach in 1999. Herb really didn't want to take over as the Penguins' head coach, but did it out of loyalty. Yet, he seized the moment, demanding speed, hard work, excitement and fun from his players. He was determined to make things happen and happen they did, as his club rallied back from a lousy start to end up with a respectable 29-23-5 finish and a first-round playoff series win.

Herbie then came full circle again in 2002 when he guided the U.S. Olympic team to a dramatic silver medal at the Winter Games in Salt Lake City. There, Herbie was a kid in a candy store, guiding Americas best professional players in a venue so near and dear to his heart. Once again, Herbie had made America proud. A 6-0 opening round win over Finland sparked America's interest and set an early tone for Team USA. Later, after beating Russia, 3-2, in the semifinals, it all came down to the wire in the gold medal game against Canada. There, the U.S. hung tough through two periods, but came up short in the third, losing 5-2 in a thriller. It wouldn't have been a miracle this time around, but Herb certainly brought some magic back to the game and fans of American hockey loved every minute of it. Just his mere presence behind the bench brought back so many wonderful memories of that special time in Lake Placid some 22 years earlier.

The New York Rangers came calling again in 2003, but Herbie had had

Herbie with John Mariucci

enough, even turning down a multimillion-dollar multi-year offer. He was serving as the director of player development for the Penguins at the time and did not want to get back into the rat race. He was enjoying life and enjoying the fruits of his labor. He had five grandchildren now and was having a ball. Sure, it was tempting for him, as he went back and forth over many sleepless nights debating whether or not he wanted to get back into the New York City sports scene or not. But in the end, he chose to stay put. When it was all said and done, Brooks' career NHL coaching record with the Penguins, North Stars, Devils and Rangers added up to a respectable 219-221-66.

A True Legend with a Truly Amazing Legacy
Tragically, on the afternoon of August 11, 2003, Herb was killed in a one car accident just north of Minneapolis on Interstate 35 near Forest Lake. Ironically, he was returning home from the U.S. Hockey Hall of Fame Golf Tournament in Biwabik Minn., where he was once again doing his part to promote the growth of American hockey. He was just 66 years old. Herb's funeral was a venerable who's who of the hockey world, with several thousand dignitaries, politicians, family members, friends, coaches and fans alike, all coming out to pay their respect to one of the true patriarchs of the game. Honorary pall bearers carrying hockey sticks saluted Herbie as he left the St. Paul Cathedral while a formation of World War II planes flew overhead in his honor. The funeral mass began with a lone bagpiper playing "Amazing Grace," and ended with the singing "The Battle Hymn of the Republic." In typical Herbie fashion, the Mass was a wonderful mix of the rich and famous alongside the blue-collar and poor. Former Gopher Billy Butters and former Olympian Mike Eruzione each spoke beautifully in his honor as well. Then, in a lighter moment, fell St. Paulite Reverend Malone spoke of Herbie's East Side roots.

"I have a message for the East Siders here," he said, "and this is coming from someone who grew up three doors down from the old Harding High School. Consider just some of the accomplishments of Herb Brooks, as hockey player at the University of Minnesota and for two Olympic teams, coach of three Gopher national champion teams, coach of U.S. Olympic hockey teams that won the 1980 gold medal and 2002 silver and as a professional coach. Incredible. But for a moment, imagine if he had lived on the right side of the East Side and gone to Harding, not Johnson. It boggles the imagination!" The church erupted with laughter and smiles. Even Herbie would've cracked a smile at that one.

Throughout his career Herb earned great recognition both individually and for his country. He has also been inducted into the U.S. Hockey Hall of Fame, the International Ice Hockey Hall of Fame, the University of Minnesota and the State of Minnesota Halls of Fames, while also receiving the coveted Lester Patrick Award for his contributions to American hockey as well.

As a public speaker, Herb was one of the very best, frequently being asked to speak to the executives of such companies as Bristol-Myers, General Mills, IBM, 3M, Levi Strauss, General Electric, Sports Illustrated, Jostens, U.S. Postal Service, All State Insurance, General Foods, Nations Bank, GTE and XEROX. There, he would speak about team building, leadership, perseverance and commitment. He would also talk about dreams, because Herbie was a dreamer. He encouraged those in attendance to believe in their dreams and follow their passions. When he was done, oftentimes those in attendance would rise up in unison and applaud, pausing only long enough to wipe away their tears. After listening to him speak, nearly everybody in the room thought that they too could beat the mighty Soviets. That was Herbie.

One of our nation's most charismatic and innovative coaches, Herb Brooks was a true American hero and a real Minnesota treasure. Whether he was competing in the business world, on the ice, or even on the diamond of a world championship fast-pitch softball team, he took the same no-nonsense attitude and intensity to whatever he did, and that's why he was so successful. His legacy will live on forever in the youth of America as they continue to enjoy the fruits of his hard work. In the world of coaching, no one, was larger than Herb Brooks. He was simply the best of the absolute best, and will dearly be missed.

As it has been said so many times, Herb never forgot where he came from. Whether he was enjoying a burger and talking hockey at Serlin's Cafe on upper Payne Avenue, or having a cold one with his high school pals at Yarusso's, Brooks stayed true to his colorful working-class neighborhood roots. On St. Paul's East Side, Herbie was royalty, but if you asked Herbie, he would just say that he was a "Joe Six Pack" from Payne Avenue.

There will be a statue of Herbie erected in St. Paul's Rice Park across from the one of F. Scott Fitzgerald. Ironically, it was Fitzgerald who wrote the now infamous line: *"Show me a hero and I will show you a tragedy."* Gone from this earth, Herbie has earned his place in sports immortality.

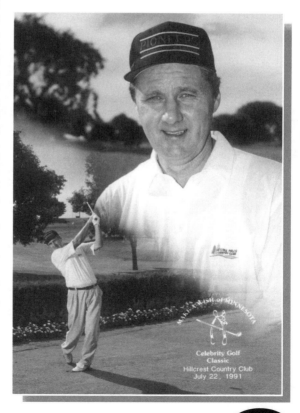

Celebrity Golf
Classic
Hillcrest Country Club
July 22, 1991

"Growing up in St. Paul I was a typical youth hockey player that hung around the rink and just fell in love with the game," said Herb. "I think I was just like any other kid in that when I had a chance to finally make my high school team, it was a big thrill. Then, to win the state championship was very gratifying because it represented the guys I grew up with in the neighborhood. It was a grass-roots type of thrill, and those things stay you for the rest of your life."

"I think that sports really affects the quality of our lives in a positive way here in the state of Minnesota, and I think that what has happened here over the years, has given us a lot to feel good about. We have such a rich sports legacy with so many outstanding athletes, great teams, great fans, great moments, and great people, and that has all gone into making our proud heritage."

"Like so many people, I too am a real Minnesota sports fan. I love to read the sports page and see what is going on. I follow it all, from the amateurs to the college kids to the pros. I am extremely interested in all of our athletes, at all levels, and follow all of our teams very closely. I enjoy reading about our teams and our players and try to keep up with it as much as possible. Of all the athletes I admire I feel that gymnasts are the most unique. They just might be the greatest athletes in the world. Who can do what they can do? I just marvel at them."

"With regards to my own coaching style, I believe in setting high standards for my players. I never wanted to let them slide or have any sort of comfort zone. It is a combination of pushing or pulling them to those standards. I don't think good coaches put greatness into their athletes. You try to create an environment for athletes to pull this greatness out."

"I would also say that I am definitely not a book coach. In fact, I think there are too many book coaches today. You know it's like 'Time-out, I gotta run to the library...' Instead, I would encourage those coaches to study and do research on the academic side of coaching. Then they could try to incorporate that research along with their personality to see how they can best sell those X's and O's to their players. Because really, when you are a coach you are just selling. You are selling team building, you are selling your systems of play, you are selling everything associated with making an individual better, and collectively your team better. I also think they

The Brooks Brothers: Herbie and Dave

have to be instinctive and be able to react on the turn of a dime, particularly under pressure. Coaching is really a battle for the hearts and minds of your athletes. It is as simple as that."

"I am also a big believer in the philosophy of 'it's not what you say, but how you say it.' I think having the ability to communicate and, once again, having the ability to sell your beliefs is the key to being a successful coach. You have to give your players something to believe in, then they will have something to belong to. Once they have something belong to, then they have something to follow."

"Has coaching has changed over the years? There is no question. I think that every sport has changed, particularly in terms of the knowledge of physiology. Coaches today are also more knowledgeable than ever before as they look at and understand the game. Are they more dynamic? Are they more believable? Are they more personable? Do they have more leadership? I really don't know. But I do think the way they present and prepare for their competition has definitely changed."

"Overall, I think there is a real bright future for hockey in Minnesota. We have the infrastructure in place, we have a lot of wonderful volunteers and we have some very dedicated coaches out there. But I think we have to always remember, at least on the amateur side, what this is for. It is for our young people so that they have a real meaningful environment to play and learn the game. There are a lot of positive things, but we also have to watch out for the 'doing too much too soon for too few' syndrome. Basically, we need to stop narrowing the base of our pyramid. We have to understand that when you have competition without preparation, then there is no real development. Sure, we've got to take care of our elite players by challenging them and bringing them along, but at the same time we can't let other kids, with latent development, fall through the cracks. And these triple A pro-

grams, showcase teams, and select programs do little for the real developmental of our players. That is a big concern."

"I also believe that we have more athletes than we have opportunities for them. Sure, we have five division one hockey schools in Minnesota right now, and that is great, but we could easily support another two or three in the area. I think that North Dakota State and Iowa State could make the jump right away for starters. We also have some great division two and three schools here, but overall we have a lot of kids who have the ability to compete at a higher level if given the opportunity."

"Lastly, I feel that we need some changes in high school hockey, particularly at the Minnesota State High School League, which, in my opinion, is really forced mediocrity. There is a lot of room for improvement

there. I think that the MSHSL should be asking our coaches one simple question: 'How can we make our student athletes better?'. Nobody knows more what should be done better than our high school coaches and we must listen to them. We should always be looking for new ways to make progress for our athletes. That is the bottom line."

"You know, someone recently asked me at a seminar why I would coach the 2002 Olympic Hockey team after winning the gold medal in 1980, and risk losing credibility. I told him that I was a psychology major in college and asked if he was familiar with Sigmund Freud. Some of Freud's writings dealt with people who avoid stress, competition and anxiety, oftentimes tranquilizing themselves. They wind up sort of sleep-walking through life, never really understanding their true capabilities. So, I guess I never wanted to step away from a challenge, and I am very glad I did it. We came up just short in that gold medal game against Canada, but it was a marvelous experience. I am much better off for having taken on that challenge. That is what life is all about."

HERE ARE SOME MORE QUOTES FROM HERBIE:

HOW WOULD YOU DESCRIBE YOUR COACHING STYLE? "As far as Xs and Os are concerned, I tried to blend the European style of hockey with the North American style —a hybrid system that was unique and different. I basically wanted to create an environment to give this game back to the players as much as possible. At the same time, bringing out their creativity and ability to react at the highest possible tempo. As far as my psychological/motivational style, I believe in setting high standards for players, being open and honest with the players, and respecting an honest effort. I am always looking at an athlete and a team and addressing the psycho/physiological being."

HOW DID YOU MOTIVATE YOUR PLAYERS? "Motivation is really a combination of things. Obviously communication is very important. It is the ability to sell a concept. Sometimes it's the all important four words: 'ask questions and listen.' Coaching is selling. You're just selling Xs and O's and you're selling team building. So, to be a good coach you have to be a good salesman. You have to get your players to somehow buy into your system and your philosophies. That is the key. Players must know that you care about them. I am not a touchy-feely type of a person but I try to show my respect and caring for them in other ways."

WHO WERE YOUR COACHING MENTORS? "Certainly John Mariucci was first and foremost. I will always remember when I first started coaching with the Gophers and he told me that this job is not just being the coach at the University of Minnesota. He said it was much bigger than that and told me it was about doing whatever you possibly could to help make hockey better in the state of Minnesota. That is why I went to St. Cloud State to coach, because it was that important to John Mariucci. He said it was not about what you accomplish, but what you really contribute towards. John gave countless hours of his time to youth hockey associations through whatever means he could to promote the game. I have tried to follow his lead. I learned a great deal from Glen Sonmor as well. He always talked about the importance of not only looking at the qualifications of players but also at the qualities of players. He reinforced to me that while skills are important, you need people with character. I also learned a lot from Murray Williamson while playing for him in the Olympics. He was very organized all the time and had a good time-line for the season. He was always trying to think outside the box. Most recently I have learned a lot about physiology as it applies to hockey from Jack Blatherwick — a brilliant man."

IF YOU COULD MAGICALLY GO BACK IN TIME TO THE FIRST YEAR YOU WERE A HEAD COACH AND GIVE YOURSELF SOME ADVICE FOR THE FUTURE, KNOWING WHAT YOU KNOW NOW, BACK THEN, WHAT WOULD YOU SAY TO YOURSELF? "When I started coaching at the University of Minnesota it was a stressful time. After Glen Sonmor left the program to coach professionally in the World Hockey Association, the team slid into last place in the WCHA, and the crowds at Williams Arena were only around 2,500 per game. We had to do a lot of things fast. Even though Glen left a core of good players, I didn't have the luxury of being as patient and understanding as I probably would have liked to have been. I was just in overdrive trying to get so much done with very little resources. I wish I had a little more patience and was a little more understanding."

WHAT ARE THE CHARACTERISTICS OF WINNERS? "I don't know if there is any one real definition of a winner. Winners in my opinion are those who are willing to make sacrifices for the unknown, both for themselves and for the team. Once you have that, then the results take care of themselves."

Maroosh makes peace between Herbie and Badger Bob

WHAT ARE THE CHARACTERISTICS OF LEADERS? "Again, I don't know if there is any one real definition of a leader. Leadership is not a function of titles but of relationships. You have to wear a lot of different hats as a leader. There is a time to talk and a time to listen, and a good leader knows this. Leadership is a much debated topic. Leaders are visionaries. Leaders are not managers. Leaders give people something to believe in, then they've got something to belong to and then they have something to follow. That is a real key component of a good leader. Most importantly, leadership is the battle for the hearts and minds of others. It is not a spectator sport. It is not necessarily a popularity contest. Leaders have to show good habits. They have to display a sincere purpose and have passion for what they are doing."

WHAT WAS THE KEY TO RECRUITING? "Playing, hard work and communication — a never ending battle in your scouting trying to find quality people. You win with people, not with talent. So the quality of the people is very important in building your team. I always looked for people with a solid value system. I recruited kids from a cross-section of different personalities, talents and styles of play. Recruiting is basically work, more work and it is never ending."

HOW DID YOU BUILD TEAM UNITY & CHEMISTRY? "It's up to the coach to create an environment which has a high level of comradeship, at all times reinforcing team concepts stressing strength of association and the power that can be attained when working together. The team reflects your value system, your instincts, your philosophies, and it is just matter of how well you can articulate it and sell it to your players."

WHAT MOTIVATES YOU? "As a player it was the goals that I set for myself. If you don't have goals you are going to be used by people who do have them. When I started coaching at the University of Minnesota I wanted to coach an NCAA championship team. And, I wanted to coach an Olympic team. While at the University, I also wanted to create a positive environment for our players so that they could grow as people, grow as athletes, and receive a good education. But the overriding motivation for me while at the University of Minnesota was to coach an Olympic team. To do that, I knew that we had to be very successful in order to be considered. The entire time I was there though, I was thinking about coaching the Olympic team. I am very proud of winning three NCAA national titles, but to go on to become the coach of Team USA was what it was all about for me. After the Olympics I had to re-evaluate what I wanted, and decided the next challenge would be in the National Hockey League. My motivation there was to win a Stanley Cup. That is a very elusive thing though that requires a lot of variables to fall into place."

ON PRACTICING: "I believe my practices were demanding and hopefully challenging. I tried to make our practices almost atypical situations so that games were easier — easier to adjust to the play, easier to read plays, easier to function on the ice. I was always striving to bring them out of their psycho-physiological comfort zones so that they were always improving their quickness, their execution of plays and the sharpness of their minds. I just always felt that the pace and the ability to execute at a high tempo was crucial. That way we were prepared for any set of circumstances that might have been thrown at us. I was always trying to lift the floor of their comfort zones during practice all the time."

WHAT'S THE BIGGEST THING YOU'VE LEARNED FROM COACHING THAT YOU'VE BEEN ABLE TO APPLY TO YOUR EVERYDAY LIFE? "Making sacrifices."

WHAT ARE THE KEY INGREDIENTS TO CREATING A CHAMPIONSHIP TEAM? "You've got to have talent. Period. Then, you have to have people who, in some way shape or form, understand that the name on the front of the jersey is more important than the one on the back."

WHAT WOULD YOU WANT TO SAY TO YOUR FANS, BOOSTERS, AND ALUMNI WHO HAVE SUPPORTED YOU ALL THESE YEARS? "Thank you for your support. (long pause and a chuckle…) I hope you got your money's worth!"

WHAT DID IT MEAN FOR YOU TO BE A GOPHER? "An awful lot. At the time there were very few alternatives for us coming out of high school because of the heavy influence on Canadian athletes in college hockey. It was really tough. Luckily, John Mariucci kept the door open for us. We had a few other alternatives, but not many — certainly not all the options that kids have today. So, for me to be able to play at the University of Minnesota was a real honor and it meant a lot. Then, to come back as a coach was also very special."

ON BEING THE COACH OF THE "TEAM OF THE CENTURY," THE 1980 "MIRACLE ON ICE": "It was a great thrill to represent your country on the Olympic stage with some great athletes. Without a doubt it was a dream come true for me."

ON ST. CLOUD STATE: "It was a wonderful experience. The President of St. Cloud State, Dr. McDonald, along with Bill Radovich, a St. Cloud State Vice President, Morris Kurtz, the Athletic Director, various members of the administration, and many

people in the St. Cloud community, wanted to have a Division One hockey program. We sold the concept to the state legislature, the governor, and the people of Central Minnesota, raised $10 million dollars, built the arena and somehow got it done. Look at them now, it's a great, great story."

ON THE TRANSITION TO THE PROS FROM COLLEGE: "You really have to be able to function on the fly at that level due to the fact that there is not a lot of preparation and practice time. With players on individual contracts, building team goals can be a challenge and at times difficult. It is a lot more challenging than being a college coach."

ON MAKING YOUTH AND HIGH SCHOOL HOCKEY BETTER: "We have to broaden the base of the pyramid, recognize the late talent of individuals, and value and understand the need for preparation of skill development. Competition without preparation is anti-development and we are on a slippery slope in youth hockey today with the 'Triple A' and 'Showcase' concepts. I think in high school they must play at least 30 games in a season and with 20 minute periods. We have the coaches, players and the infrastructure to do this and hopefully that can get done."

ON THE NHL GIVING A LITTLE MORE TO THE USA: "Again, I feel that to grow the game of hockey we need to broaden the base of our pyramid with regards to development and participation. If we broaden the base, geometrically speaking, then the peak, or the National Hockey League, will grow higher and higher. Having said that, I think it is important for the NHL to look more closely at the grass-roots movements of USA Hockey and reward them a little bit more. To better understand this you have to look at the Canadian Junior system where the NHL rewards those teams with literally millions and millions of dollars in the form of compensation for their players being drafted. 'That's why those teams want as many players drafted as possible — it's pay-day!' I think that more of those 'draft money' dollars should come to USA Hockey instead to further support our college and university programs as well as our American junior leagues along with various amateur programs. I think that their financial formula should be revisited and that USA Hockey deserves a little bit more. Our American-trained college players are among the very best in the world and I for one think that it is about time that we were on level playing field with Canada. Now, as far as where those dollars should go, I think they should go to both the people who are getting the job done as well as those who are starting and developing new programs and want to get the job done in the future. We need to open a dialogue and then see what can happen."

ON OUTDOOR RINKS: "I think we are doing well to improve our infrastructure to increase the number of rinks in America, but we can do more. Let's be real, arenas cost a lot of money, and I think there might be some more efficient uses of our hard-earned money to build them. Whenever a new arena is built there are hundreds of thousands of dollars that are appropriated to things that do not affect change or help the athletes or coaches. We need ice sheets, locker rooms and ice resurfacers. We don't always need, however, weight rooms, restaurants, beautiful lobbies and architectural niceties. Sure, they are nice, but they cost a lot of money. We have to ask ourselves, who are we building these for: the fans or for the kids? Perhaps instead of building such elaborate indoor facilities, we should go back to constructing more outdoor rinks with artificial ice. This is what baseball, soccer and basketball have over hockey — kids can hone their games virtually anywhere. Hockey is unique, we need ice. Sure, there are thousands of lakes and ponds, but the weather doesn't always cooperate. So we need more good quality outdoor ice sheets in order for our kids to get in more practice time. With girls hockey growing in popularity, ice-time has never been more scarce. This is another way to help out. So maybe the next time they want to build a community rink for $5 million, they should look instead to build 5 to 10 outdoor lighted artificial rinks, with warming houses, where kids could play consistently for six months out of the year. And, while youth associations could have structured practices here, it would also be a great place for kids to learn the game. Oftentimes that is where kids learn their creativity, playing pick-up games against other kids in an unstructured, informal environment with no coaches screaming at them."

ON CLUB HOCKEY: "A problem we are seeing right now is that a lot of our kids have no where to go after high school. I mean we are turning out kids, bringing them up and increasing participation, but then all of a sudden they get to a certain level and there are no more opportunities for them. As a result, too many good kids are being forced out of the game way too early. That is where club hockey comes in. Right now there are roughly 200 schools playing club hockey. Now, I think that it would be incredible if we could start to get some more of these programs to make that jump to D-I varsity status. That is really what the game needs right now. It would not only get more kids playing hockey, it would build the game's fan base, and the game would expand to more of a nation-wide game. Who knows? Maybe one day Georgia Tech will be playing Southern Cal for the national championship? Wouldn't that be something? I mean there are so many programs that are very close: Iowa State, North Dakota

State, Colorado State, Arizona State, and maybe even St. Thomas University right here in Minneapolis. Why not? So, overall we need to reach down and help to create more opportunities for our players. And by helping them, we are helping ourselves by growing the game and ultimately growing the pyramid's base even wider. This is another key area where the NHL could step in and help financially to grow the game at this level."

ON EUROPEANS, PROFESSIONAL COACHES AND "20-MINUTE PLAYERS": "Why are the Europeans producing so much talent these days? Well, in Europe they have a better ratio of games to practices, and in the United States we are turning out a bunch of 20-minute hockey players — that is a serious problem. It takes an hour for kids to get to the rink and get ready. They play one-third of the one hour game for a total of 20 minutes, and then it takes another hour to get undressed and go home. That means a kid is only playing 20-minutes of hockey out of a three-hour afternoon.

"The bottom line is that we need more emphasis on development, pure and simple, and one way to achieve that is by hiring professional coaches who can coach other coaches. Sure, we have coaching clinics and certification programs, but is it enough? Now, this is in no way intended to be a back-handed slap at our youth coaches and volunteers who are giving up their time and energy to help teach our kids. Rather, it is something to consider to help our kids get better. If a program were to hire a young professional coach to help teach and train the volunteer coaches at a grass-roots level, wouldn't that make everyone better? Now, does it cost money? Sure, but that is one area where the Europeans are advancing much quicker than we are and as a result they are producing more talent on to the next levels. I think we should open a dialogue and discuss it, that's all."

ON THE NHL BEING JUST 15% AMERICAN: "This may or may not be cyclical. Sure, I am concerned, but you have to ask who we are losing market-share to. The answer to that is Europe, not Canada. Once again, we need to look at what Europe is doing to get better and try to get better ourselves. We need to make some changes and that can only be good for the game. Tolstoy once said 'Everybody wants to change the world, but they don't want to change themselves.' So, we all have to change our thinking and focus on getting our kids better. I have always been a student of the Europeans' philosophies and styles of hockey. Having said that I don't think that they are necessarily better athletes. They are just trained differently, with much more emphasis put on skill development, pace of execution and repetition. Are Europeans better athletes? No. Are they more competitive people? Certainly not. And, are their more opportunities for them? Not even close. I mean we have more rinks in Minnesota alone than in most of Europe. They work with what they've got though, and are not afraid to do exhaustive dry-land training to hone their skills. I remember watching a bunch of kids practicing on a basketball court in Czechoslovakia one time, working on their back cross-overs, their break-outs and on their power-play in just tennis shoes. They were mastering the spatial relationships and working with what they had. There are only a few rinks in all of Prague, so how do they produce so much top-level talent? It is strictly a matter of development and the way that they are introduced to the development sequence of skills that they learn."

ON CHANGING THE GAME: "I have written to Mr. Bettman on several occasions to express my opinions on several matters of change within the NHL such as eliminating the red line and moving the goal line out. The players are bigger, faster and stronger and the game is not keeping up. Hey, we are in the entertainment business. Is it right to ask fans to pay a hundred bucks to be put to sleep?"

ON RECENTLY WINNING THE LESTER PATRICK AWARD: "It is my understanding the Lester Patrick Award honors service to USA Hockey. Now, while I am very grateful and humbled to win the honor, I have to say that with all due respect a lot of the past winners of the award have really done nothing for American hockey. The award, from what I thought, was about service, and not about one's personal accomplishments that he may have had as a player, coach, executive, general manager or what have you. So this thing has been passed around through the NHL's good ol' boys network for years and I think it is a shame. I do feel very honored, however, because I have done a lot to contribute to the growth of American hockey. I have always tried to affect change and help the growth of the game, so in that regard it is very gratifying."

ON THE OLYMPIC EXPERIENCE: "The Olympic experience is just unbelievable. To be able to represent your country is a tremendous honor. I have seen it all. I was the last guy cut on the gold medal winning 1960 team, but I went on to play on both the 1964 and 1968 teams. Then, to coach the 1980 team was a dream-come-true, and later to be able to come back and coach again in 2002 was very meaningful. Now, as far as the parallels between 1980 and 2002, it was not even close. The young people we had in 1980, it was a bunch of college kids. We were trying to take them out of their comfort zone of being college athletes, college All-Americans, and play at a certain tempo of world class competition in the Olympic Games. But this (the NHLers) is a different thing. I'm not going to be introducing a lot of things to these athletes. I'm not going to be telling them things they don't already know. They all come from good programs and have had excellent coaches. It's more of a reminder. It's really their show. The strategy comes down to how well we adapt to the different styles. The Europeans, who play on larger ice sheets, have more finesse players, while the North Americans play a much more physical game. In addition, the 1980 team trained and practiced together for a very long time, while the 2002 club got just a few days together before we hit the ice. We did spend a week together this Summer at a training camp and that was a lot of fun. The players were very up-tempo and excited to be there and that was a lot of fun. Chris Chelios was the captain and it was his team. I could feel their enthusiasm and it was very motivating for me to get back into it."

ON AMATEURS VS. PROS PLAYING IN THE OLYMPICS: "As far as the argument over whether it should be amateurs or pros playing, I will say that while I do understand the business side with regards to visibility, marketing and dollars, I also have to say that it is unfortunate that if a kid wants to one day play on an Olympic team, he has to first become an NHL All-Star. But it is all part of change and while it is debatable, this is where we are at and we will make the best of it.

The 1979 National Champion Gophers

Row 1 (L-R) – Steve Janaszak, Rob McClanahan, Joe Baker, Phil Verchota, Head Coach Herb Brooks, Captain Bill Baker, Athletic Director Paul Giel, Steve Christoff, Eric Strobel, Don Micheletti, Jim Jetland.
Row 2 (L-R) – Dave Terwilliger, Mike Greeder, Jeff Teal, Student Trainer Jim Mulcahy, Trainer Mike Bell, Asst. Coach Brad Buetow, Asst. Coach John Perpich, Asst. Coach Mike Foley, Student Manager Steve Tollund, Student Manager Fred Field, Mike Ramsey, Brad Doshan, Tim Harrer.
Row 3 (L-R) – Steve Ulseth, Neal Broten, Kevin Hartzell, Brian Zins, Jay Larson, Bob Bergloff, Steve Pepper, Peter Hayek, John Meredith, Wayne Larson, Bart Larson.

ON HIGH SCHOOL HOCKEY IN MINNESOTA: "I think there is a lack of progressive thinking on the part of the Minnesota State High School League. Their mentality is more of a forced mediocrity and I think that there are some things that could be done differently. Most importantly, I think that the kids should be able to play an additional six to eight games throughout the course of the season and those games should be increased to 20-minute periods. That alone would add the equivalent of about six games a year in just ice-time alone. And, while the tournament is going on in March, the vast majority of kids are standing around in snow banks by the end of February. So, the season could be extended to mid-March with no problem. I think that all the sports should be adjusted to the particular dynamics of that individual sport to make this all work out — so it's very doable. Even though there are more than 250 Minnesotans playing D-I hockey in our country right now, I think that can still be improved. We have the No. 1 high school program in the country here in Minnesota and I never want it to become complacent. Overall, I would like to see more public representation on the

The 1974 National Champion Gophers

Row 1 (L-R) – Equipment Manager Dick Brown, John Matschke, John Perpich, Eric Lookwood, Team Captain Brad Shelstad, Bill Moen, Cal Cossalter, John Harris, Manager Dennis Cossalter.
Row 2 (L-R) – Dr. V. George Nagobads (team doctor), Brad Marrow, John Sheridan, Bruce Carlson, Doug Falls, Dick Spannbauer, Mike Phippen, Robby Harris, Les Auge, Tim Carlson, Athletics Director Paul Giel, Head Coach Herb Brooks.
Row 3 (L-R) – Tom Vannelli, Warren Miller, Tom Dahlheim, Joe Micheletti, Bill "Buzz" Schneider, Mike Polich, Pat Phippen, Manager David Gurovitsch.

The 1976 National Champion Gophers

Row 1 (L-R) – Jeff Tscherne, Joe Micheletti, Brad Morrow, Warren Miller, Captain Pat Phippen, Tom Vannelli, Tom Younghans, Bryan Fredrickson, Tom Mohr.
Row 2 (L-R) – Ken Yackel, Don Madson, Jim Boo, Russ Anderson, Head Coach Herb Brooks, Asst. Coach Brad Buetow, Trainer Gary Smith, Reed Larson, Mark Lambert, Tim Rainey, Steve Janaszak.
Row 3 (L-R) – Bob Fish, Tom Gorence, Rob Larson, Phil Verchota, Tony Dorn, Joe Baker, Bill Baker, Dan Bonk, Bruce Lind, Mark Conway.

MSHSL though. They make a lot of unilateral, authoritarian decisions without the real debate and discussions that I think are needed."

ON THE STATE OF THE STATE: "Overall, there has been great progress in American hockey over the past 25 years or so. For us to keep on moving forward though, we really need to encourage the debate, the dialogue and the discussion for change. We should be respectful of one another, understand differing philosophies and work together to make American hockey better. We have so many great athletes in our country and I think that our future is unbelievable. We just have to work on our developmental programs and keep it going. Locally, I think there are too many AAA, showcase and elite camps, etc., for young kids today and as a result we are creating a bunch of robots. We need to make it fun for our kids and let them learn to love this game the way we did. Kids love to play and we need to give this game back to them. Our coaches need to make practices more fun by making drills that are both fun and competitive that will challenge the kids to find the games within the game. We are doing a great job though. Our girls programs are continually getting better, we're getting more and more kids onto the next level and the rest will eventually take care of itself."

ON GIVING BACK: "I look back and think about my father who started one of the very first youth hockey associations in the state of Minnesota. From that I saw the spirit of volunteerism on a first hand basis and think it is a very powerful and tremendous thing. Now, moving on, I saw that same spirit when I was coaching at the University of Minnesota. One of my mentors was John Mariucci, who told me that I was more than just a coach and that I needed to reach out and help the growth of the game throughout the state. I have always remembered that and as a result have always tried to do as much as I could to help the coaches, administrators and volunteers to grow the game. Maybe the biggest thing I have done was to take St. Cloud State from a D-III school to D-I. And hey, look at them now, they've got a new arena and are one of college hockey's best teams. Once again, it was John Mariucci who convinced me to take that job and it is really one of the best things I have ever done in hockey. I made only $15,000 that season, but would do it all over again in a heart beat. It was a real labor of love and that's what it's all about — giving back to the game."

FOREWORD
BY LOU NANNE

Herbie and I go way back. He was just finishing up at the University when I came there in 1959 and then we played together on several teams after that. During that time we played together in Rochester, on the U.S. National Team and the U.S. Olympic Team. Then, when I decided to turn pro, I asked him if he wanted to take over my job as the freshmen coach at the University of Minnesota. So, I went to Glen Sonmor and Marsh Ryman and asked them to hire him. Later on I was part of the Olympic Committee that hired him to coach the 1980 U.S. Olympic Team and I even hired him myself to coach the North Stars in 1987. We have just had a lifetime of hockey together.

Herbie was a lot of things to me. He was a friend, a teammate, an employee and just a tremendous person. I valued his friendship and his loyalty immensely. We had a lot of very good times together and I am going to really miss him as you would do with any close friend. We played together, we traveled together and we even roomed together. I got to know him before he was married and then watched him grow as a person once he was married. Then, to watch him become a husband and father, and later a coach, that was so great to see. I just thought the world of the guy. His death really increased my awareness of my own mortality. You just realize how short life is and that things can happen so unexpectedly. I still can't believe he is gone. It just doesn't seem real.

You know, as far as hockey was concerned, Herbie just loved the game and was tireless in his pursuit to see it improved. He continually strived for the betterment of the sport and was determined to do whatever he could to make it grow and get stronger. He was also constantly trying to find ways to teach kids at a young age to play the game better. He was always looking for ways to improve how we were teaching them the fundamentals and was just passionate about his beliefs in that. He was genuinely concerned about players at all levels and wanted to make sure that they were advancing and getting better as they moved up the ranks.

Herbie was a rare individual who could talk about the game of hockey all day long. He just loved it. He was intrigued with it; he was enamored with it; he was enchanted by it; and was genuinely interested in seeing kids get better at it. He was just absorbed with hockey, and that is what made Herbie, Herbie. He would eventually get burned out and try to get away from the game every now and then, but he would always come back. Even this last year, with the New York Rangers job, he just couldn't make up his mind as to whether or not he wanted to get back into the game or not. You just never knew with Herbie. That might have been his best quality and it might have been his worst, I don't know. The most consistent thing about Herb Brooks, was his inconsistency to do the things you thought he was going to do. If you thought he was going to coach team ABC, he would instead coach team XYZ. That was just his style, he always kept you guessing. It wasn't necessarily always about money either, it was just about whatever he felt was the right fit for him at that particular moment in his life.

As far as Herbie's style went, he was obviously much tougher on the college and Olympic kids than he was on the guys at the professional level. He knew that you had to handle people differently and he adjusted accordingly. I will say this about his coaching style though, I don't think that there was anybody better at getting his team ready and appropriately conditioned to play than Herb Brooks. He worked his guys tirelessly and really got them into shape. That was one thing that you could bet on no matter where he was coaching, that his team was going to be well conditioned. Period. I think he got some of that from John Mariucci, because he used to work the hell out of all of us too! Herbie, however, took that to a different level, because he just felt so strongly about it. And, it paid off for him, because his teams were always ready to go in the third period when other teams were tired. In addition to being in shape, his teams were always capable of handling the puck and they always had speed, so that was also a big part of it as well.

He endlessly studied the game. He was fascinated by what the Europeans and Russians were doing and always wanted to learn from what they were doing and then make it better. He was truly a student of the game in every sense. He was fascinated by speed, movement and how things worked. That was his style, and his players played hard for him. He demanded excellence and he got it. Herbie was always in a tireless pursuit of finding ways to get our kids to be able to play better. His biggest obsession as of late was to get our younger kids to have better fundamentals and to learn the game better. He didn't like all of the structure that was in the game at that level right now. He didn't want them over-coached, but he wanted them taught properly, and that was something he worked very hard at. He had so many ideas and thoughts of how we could do that better, and that is what drove him.

He cared so much about the game, and since he had become a grandparent, I believe that made him see things differently on how the game should be played for future generations.

You know, after reflecting, I would have to say that Herbie's best quality might have been his love for his family. He never showed people his true affections, but I know that his kids and grandkids were the absolute joys of his life. I can't imagine how much they are going to miss him. We are all going to miss him. He was a great friend, and a great friend to hockey. I am very proud that I got to share as much of my life with him as I did. I will never forget him. He was a one of a kind, that was for sure.

FOREWORD
BY GLEN SONMOR

I first met Herbie in the Fall of 1955 when I was the freshmen coach at the University of Minnesota. You know, I had just lost my eye the year before while playing for Cleveland during a game in Pittsburgh. Shortly thereafter, John Mariucci, who I had gotten to know while playing with the Minneapolis Millers, called me in the hospital and told me not to worry about a thing and said that I could come back to Minnesota to be his freshmen coach with the Gophers. Herbie was a freshman on that team and I could see then that he had a lot of talent. He was such a gifted player and was a real leader. The players respected him and he worked very hard at whatever he was doing. Well, I left that next year, but when I came back to Minnesota in the late 1960s to take over as the head coach of the Gophers, Herbie wound up serving as one of my assistants. Herbie, of course, later took over the program a few years later when I left to coach the Fighting Saints, and that was when he got his first big break. And boy oh boy, did he ever make the most of it. Three national championships in eight seasons, that was just incredible what he did there, and he was just getting started too. Then, to see what he did in 1980, with the Olympic team, and then in the NHL — he was just a great coach at so many different levels. And I truly understood that because I also coached at those same levels, both with the Gophers and the North Stars, so we had a lot in common and would share a lot with each other over the years.

I knew he would make a great coach, even back then. He just had that special quality about him which made him a winner. He was so intelligent too. He had an ability to see everything that was going on around him and then was able pick out what was really important. Combine that with his unbelievable work ethic, and you knew he was going to be successful in whatever he did in life. That was Herbie. As a coach, he was such a great tactician. His players maybe didn't love him, but they respected him and went to war for him. He was a no nonsense kind of a guy behind the bench and that was all part of what made him a success. He didn't let anything slide either. I mean if something or somebody had to be confronted, then he would confront that situation right away and get it behind him. And what a great motivator he was. He could get his players to do things that they never imagined they were capable of doing and that was just a marvelous quality. His honesty and forthrightness might have been his best qualities though. There was never any question as to where you stood with Herbie.

Herbie set such an example for all of us with his absolute concern for the game of hockey. He truly championed American hockey, and even more specifically, Minnesota hockey. His commitment to making sure that Minnesota kids had every advantage was incredible, and we should all be grateful to him for that. He really carried that forward from John Mariucci's vision and that will probably be his legacy I think. So, all of us need to work a little harder to keep that going now that Herbie is gone. His commitment to make sure that Minnesota kids had every chance to succeed is what drove him. He would go to war over his beliefs and that is what made him so unique. In fact, I have not met anybody in my life who was more committed to what he believed in and was willing to risk anything and everything to champion that, than Herb Brooks. He just didn't care. He took up unpopular causes and wasn't afraid to stand up and say that something wasn't right.

He had such a great dedication to the game of hockey and just totally loved it in every aspect. He was so resolute in standing by everything he believed in. His passion was unparalleled and there wasn't anything that he wouldn't help you with if you needed him. Where there was something he really believed in, he would see it through to the end no matter what the consequences were. And he proved that time and again, even recently, when he gave up several lucrative jobs because there were things behind the scenes which he didn't believe in. He was just a man of uncompromising standards and was willing to walk away from millions of dollars for what he believed in. That is amazing to me.

Herbie also had a great sense of humor, and not a lot of people knew that because you had to really get to know him to see it. I also think that a lot of people didn't see the lively and playful side of him. Herbie liked to present to the world a sometimes very stern persona, but there was a completely different side to him in that he truly loved life and had so much fun. He was very close with his family and really had a passion for what he was doing, both in hockey and in life. To me, Herbie was the result of giving of yourself completely to whatever cause you believed in and seeing it through to the end. Dedication and hard work just exemplified everything he believed in and I admired that in him so much for that. What a remarkable person.

Herbie also always took time for people, wrote them notes, and really made a difference in a lot of people's lives. He had such a wide circle of friends, and that made him unique too. I remember once he went into a biker bar in St. Cloud and sat with a bunch of rowdy bikers, just drinking beer and hanging out all night. He even got them all to come to a game. That was Herbie, he just touched an awful lot of people, including a lot of people outside of the world of hockey.

You know, Herbie was just a really good friend. He was also a wonderful hockey resource, and I had so many great conversations with him over the years about hockey. I am going to miss that. He was such an interesting person. And we didn't always agree with each other either, but that was OK. We agreed to disagree quite a bit, but he had such a passion for what he believed in and I really respected that. He was always a delight to see wherever I would run into him and he was always so genuinely concerned about me and about how I was doing. I just really felt that he was a brilliant coach, a great friend, a great person, and I admired him a great deal. What else can I say? Herbie was my friend, and I am going to miss him dearly. Hockey is going to miss him too, because he was a great, great man. So, goodbye dear friend, you left us far too soon.

WHAT DID HERBIE MEAN TO YOU? "Herbie was my protector. I just felt so safe with him. And I don't know, maybe that is a wife thing — like you don't feel that you have to lock the doors when he is home, or the fact that you just don't get scared of things when he is around. He was just always there for me and I will miss that so much. It was just different when he was around. It was so special, no matter what we were doing. I just loved him so much. You know, Herbie was gone a lot, traveling, so I became really independent. Someone recently asked me if I was going to sell my house and I said 'Why would I do that?' And they said, 'Well what will you do if your oven goes out or something?' I said, 'I will call the repair man to come and fix it.' I have always been very independent and I have always kind of been my own person. Now, however, I am feeling the hole, the emptiness, because he always made me feel so safe, and that will be hard to get past."

WHAT WAS THE SECRET TO HERBIE'S SUCCESS? "Herbie was a psychologist. He really understood people and knew how to motivate them to get the most out of them. He was just such a good motivator. You know, not only was he a psychology major at the University of Minnesota, he also had an economics degree. So, he was very smart too, and really just a brilliant person. I think that combination was what really made him so unique. I know that I have never met anybody like him, and I know there will never be anybody like him again."

WHAT WAS HERBIE'S BEST QUALITY? "Probably honesty. He was just a brilliant mind and that was a big part of who he was too. He just understood people so well. He also had integrity and that made him a special person."

ON BEING MRS. HERBIE BROOKS: "We were a lot a like, but we were polar

opposites as well. Our relationship had always been kind of good cop — bad cop with the kids. He was the disciplinarian and I was the softie. It was funny, people would meet me after they knew him and could not believe that we were married because we were just so opposite. I think another thing that helped our marriage was that I honestly do not know the difference between a hockey puck and a grapefruit. So, when he came home from traveling, or just from coaching, there was never any hockey talk with us. I think that was healthy for him and for me too. Our house was kind of like an oasis for him to just get away from it all. And that was important to him. I think that was why he enjoyed yard work and gardening so much too, because it was just him turning off hockey to focus on something else entirely different."

ON HERBIE'S IMPACT ON OTHERS: "I remember shortly after the funeral, I had a UPS man on my doorstep sobbing. I don't think Herbie even knew the guy's name, but he told me that Herbie would always come out and talk to him and always made time for him when he came over. And it was never about hockey, it was about the trees, the dog or whatever. I have gotten some amazing letters from people all over country over the past couple of months and it has just been incredible. One letter came from a guy who was an investment banker from New York City. Well, he was in a hotel in Houston on business, and just felt the need to write me a letter. In it, he said that he had attended one of Herbie's hockey camps at Shattuck back in 1976. He said he was the worst hockey player there and that he struggled just to get through the week. But afterward, Herbie had told his mother that he was a hard worker. He said that meant so much to him and that he has carried that through his entire life. Things like that just blow me away. I knew that he was a pretty special person and that he made a difference in a lot of people's lives, but now that he is gone I can really see it in a much different light. I think I was even a little bit naive about the way so many people felt about him. I wanted to have the funeral at the little convent in Shoreview, I just had no idea that he had had such an impact on so many people. To me he was just a husband, dad and grandpa who trimmed the trees and took out the garbage. I could really not fathom the outpouring of emotion that came after the accident. It still amazes me. It is still so shocking to me to even think about it. I still can't believe he is gone."

ON HERBIE'S DIVERSE CIRCLE OF FRIENDS: "My best friend, Gretchen Badalich, and I used to always tease Herbie about his multiple personalities. I mean we used to kiddingly say, 'would the real Herb Brooks please stand up...' because he had such a diverse cross-section of friends. He was wanted by kings in one moment and then ran around with the tree trimmer in the next. That was Herbie. Look at his pall bearers. Other than Lou Nanne, who was a friend for 100 years, they were all old blue collar, salt of the earth friends of his. I can even remember when we lived in New York and he was coaching the Rangers, I would drive down to pick him up at Madison Square Garden and he would come walking out with his arm around the janitor. He loved people and just truly never forget where he came from.

"The St. Paul Hotel has this wall of fame of famous Minnesotans who are now deceased. On it are pictures of people like Judy Garland, Hubert Humphrey and F. Scott Fitzgerald. Each picture has their name, what they did, their birth and death dates, and then one line about them. Well, Danny and I had to go down there and figure out what in the world to put in this one line about Herbie. I mean talk about concise, one line to sum up your life. So, underneath *'hockey legend,'* we put *'I am just a guy from the East Side...'* Because that really kind of said it all with him, he just truly never forgot his roots and he was very proud of where he came from."

WHAT WILL HERBIE'S LEGACY BE IN YOUR OPINION? "Sure, the 1980 Olympics were a wonderful thing and they will probably follow him forever, but I would hope that his legacy would be his children and his grandchildren to tell you the truth. You know, look at Kelly's two little twin boys. Both of their grandfathers as well as their great grandfather are in the U.S. Hockey Hall of Fame, with Herbie and Bob Paradise, and then Bobby Dill — who is on their father's side. Not to mention Mike Gibbons, the champion boxer, who was Dill's uncle as well. So, that is an amazing athletic genetic link that those little boys have. All that feisty toughness from both sides of the family, but hey, who knows? Maybe they will wind up playing the violin instead!'"

ON THE SOFTER SIDE OF HERB: "There was a whole other side to Herbie beyond that rough hockey exterior. He loved musicals, he loved gymnastics, he loved gardening and oh, he loved his grandchildren. He just couldn't get enough of those kids. I think a lot of that stemmed from the fact that he was gone a lot on the road for his own kids when they were growing up, and wanted to make up for lost time. He was actually a very sensitive person. He was very caring and loving and would do anything for anyone who he loved. That was Herbie. He was always concerned about others and always wanted to take care of his friends. Hockey was just one part of his life, to me there was so much more."

ON HERBIE'S PALS: "You know, when I wrote thank you letters to all the pall bearers, because all of those guys are my friends, I told them to not quit calling me to say hi. I really got to know all of those guys over the years. They would call for Herbie, and he would be gone, so we would wind up talking for an hour. It was wonderful. I even told them all in my final parting line that 'Herbie loved you and so do I.' But really, they have been so supportive of me and the family and that has meant so much to us. Herbie had some wonderful friends and they will always be like family to us. Those were his friends who he stuck with for a thousand years and he loved them. They meant the world to him."

WHAT IMPACT HAS HERBIE HAD ON YOUR LIFE? "Herbie was my whole life. He got into my psyche and became a part of me. I was always on my toes around him, that was for sure. I mean that is 38 years of your life that you are talking about. I just feel like I have a big hole in my heart now. I miss him so much. Our whole life together was an adventure and I would do it all over again in a heartbeat."

ON SAYING GOOD BYE: "You know, I think about Herbie's mother, who is 93 years old. She had to go through all of this twice, first with her husband and now again with Herbie. I just think, 'how unfair is that for her.' She is so strong, and I just feel so badly for her. It has been tough on us all, but we are getting through it. As for me, I have no regrets. Herbie and I just had a wonderful life together. I actually talked to him the night before the accident, and I know that he knew the way I felt about him. I loved him dearly, and that will never change. It was just so sad that it had to end the way that it did. That was the worst day of my life. But, I know that he was up at the Hockey Hall of Fame golf tournament with his very best friends and doing what he loved to do. So, that was nice too, that he was able to spend his last days with people who loved him."

WHAT DID YOUR DAD MEAN TO YOU? "My father was sort of a two-tiered person. He was obviously a father who tried to raise me the best that he could by teaching me lessons in life. Then, he was also another person where he was my idol, and I was a fan of his. I mean I grew up loving the sport of hockey just loving the Gophers, the Olympic team and the New York Rangers. So, I was a fan of his and a fan of his teams. It was kind of a weird relationship sometimes. I mean it would be like if you grew up loving baseball in Minnesota and idolizing Kirby Puckett and Rod Carew, only they told you what time you had to be home at night. So, being a sports fan I really looked up to my dad, which made it tough sometimes. But, it was a really unique experience and I wouldn't have traded it for the world. I mean I got to live every win and loss, just like my dad. So, when the Gophers won, I was on top of the world, but if they lost, I couldn't get out of bed the next day — just like my dad. I just experienced every emotion there was as a kid, through my dad's teams. You know, if your father was an accountant, or a lawyer or a teacher, you just didn't have those type of emotions, so that was unique, but special at the same time."

ON GROWING UP AS THE SON OF THE LEGENDARY HERB BROOKS: "I was lucky, I got to see the world through hockey. While my dad was coaching the Rangers, our family lived just outside of New York City in Greenwich, Conn., from 1981-85. I have so many great memories of living in New York. I was just a kid, so I was able to just sort of soak it all in. I remember going to Madison Square Garden to watch the team and hanging out in the locker room was amazing. Then, when we would drive out to Long Island to play the Islanders, dad would pick up Craig Patrick and Walt Tkachuk, his assistants, and I would just sit in the back seat and be in awe of those guys as they talked hockey. I got to travel all over with the team, it was great. By 1985, I was 16 years old, and I can remember when like John Vanbiesbrouck was an 18-year-old rookie goaltender with the Rangers. We became friends and it was crazy because he had more in com-

mon with me than he did with half of the players on the team. Another guy was Chris Contos, and I can remember just hanging out with him and playing Pac Man at team hotels together. It was great though, and I have some wonderful memories of those days. I also got to see what kind of a guy my dad was from the players perspectives, and that was special too."

ON YOUR DAD NEVER FORGETTING HIS PAYNE AVENUE ROOTS: "I personally think my dad would have been a great politician, but he might have been too principled. My dad also loved the little guy. He just loved the blue collar guy, the underdog — that was huge with him. He wanted to be the little guy, the down-and-out guy, and that was just part of his soul I think. I remember back about 10 years ago, I was back from college and working. Well, I joined Midland Hills Country Club and somehow talked my father into joining as well. He loved to golf with a passion, but being a member of a country club wasn't big with him. He just wasn't a part of that whole social/economic thing that went along with being a member of a snooty club. So, I met him one Saturday morning out there for a round of golf. I showed up and it was real early in the morning, so I parked right out in front, like in the first stall. I am then looking around for my dad, and I don't see him. Then, I look way down, like a couple hundred yards away, where the maintenance guys and groundskeepers parked, and I see his old beat up pick-up truck. So, I asked him why he parked all the way down there and he said that he was just too embarrassed to have all of the big-shot members see his old truck and that they might laugh. He said he just liked to be with the grounds crew guys, where he felt more at home. That was my dad.

"It was funny, my mom and I even had a nickname for him, the 'down-and-out-guy,' because he just wanted to be the union guy who was out of work and just down and out. I remember one time I saw him and told him that I had just been out hitting some balls at the range and he said, 'hey, me too, where did you go?' So, I said I was up at White Bear Yacht Club, and Mr. down-and-out-guy says, 'oh yeah, I just went up to see the little farmer at Shadow Ridge to hit my little bucket of balls...' Like I was supposed to feel sorry for him or something! I mean come on, financially he could afford to join any club in town without batting an eye, but he just liked to do his own thing and not make a big scene. That was just not him.

"My dad just really liked to associate himself with the blue collar people that he identified most with. I think that was evident at his funeral when so many down and out people showed up to pay their respects to him. That part of him is real important to me now. One image that I will always remember from the funeral, was as we were leaving the cathedral and walking with the pall-bearers down the steps and over to the limousines. When we got down the hill I saw this guy, a truly poor soul, with his shoes untied and his Twins hat on crooked. He had like five programs from the funeral in his hand and he was just standing there at full attention, saluting my dad and crying as we walked by. It was sort of like that image of J.F.K. Jr. at his dad's funeral, and that image of this down-and out-guy to me was just so poignant. It totally captured the moment of what my dad was all about."

"You know my dad's best friend was LeRoy Houle, a tree trimmer and landscaper who he met after the 1980 Olympics, and I think that LeRoy personified the guy my dad wanted to be. He is just a very simple, blue collar guy, and my dad just loved him. We all love him, he is just the greatest guy. I mean for my dad, all the stuff that came along with being who he was, like the hob-knobbing with the big-wigs and the public speaking, that was just something that he did out of obligation. He was very loyal and that was all stuff that came along with being a celebrity. He did it because it went along with the territory, but deep down, my dad would much rather have been out working in the yard with LeRoy and then having a beer and relaxing. Sure, he could hob-knob at the country clubs with the best of them, but that was not who he was. Really, even to this day, if Mario Lemieux or Wayne Gretzky walked into our house to pay their respects to my dad, I would be very impressed and in awe of them, but if LeRoy walked in I would cry like a baby. He is just that type of person and our family loves him."

WHAT'S THE BIGGEST THING YOU LEARNED FROM YOUR DAD? "My dad had one very simple saying that he told me before I started college at the University of Denver. I was going to try to make the hockey team there and was nervous. They had just won the WCHA the year before and were really good. So, my dad just said to me 'be the first one on the ice, the last one to leave and keep your mouth shut.' That was it, very simple and to the point, just like my dad. Well, I did, and I made the team. So, I applied that same theory to my life in whatever I did, and it has been great. It is so simple. If you show up, keep your mouth shut and work hard, you will get ahead in life. Now, I am a stock broker and I have been able to be very successful by following that motto. He instilled a lot of lessons upon me over the years and they have all centered around working hard and being prepared – really the same principles that he preached to his players all through the years.

"You know, my dad loved to battle. Unfortunately, the years that he was out of hockey, he sometimes created his own battles to sort of satisfy that inner urge that he had for battling. I think that coaching was a great outlet for him because it was the ultimate battle. Later on in life, when he was semi-retired from coaching, he used to create battles with me just for fun I think! He was a lot of fun though and I enjoyed arguing with him — even though he would usually win. He was so smart. My dad was also a hell-raiser and a rebel. I always thought that he would have been a great trial lawyer, a '60s radical, war-time general, or, a great hockey coach, and thank God for all of us that he chose the latter."

WHAT WILL YOUR DAD'S LEGACY BE IN YOUR OPINION? "My dad will have a lot of legacies to a lot of different people, whether that was the 1980 Olympic team — the biggest upset victory in the history of sports, or the Gophers, or what have you. But for me, his hockey legacy was being the coach of the New York Rangers. Sure, the 1980 Olympics were an amazing part of our history, but I get a little frustrated with that because I think he should be remembered for so much more than just that one event. I mean when you look at some of the things that he did after the Olympics, like during his time in New York, that was phenomenal. Unfortunately, however, his teams had to go through the New York Islanders at that time, who were arguably one of the greatest dynasties in the history of the National Hockey League. So, who knows, maybe he would've been able to have had more success if that had not been the case. Then, he did a great job in Pittsburgh and had a fine year in New Jersey as well. He did some great things at St. Cloud State, and of course with the Gophers too. His year with the North Stars was tough because of all their injuries, but it was a special time for him nonetheless. So, if his legacy will wind up being the Olympics then that is OK, because he was always in such awe of the Olympics as a kid and really all throughout his entire career.

"My dad could just get guys to believe that they could do anything and the 1980 team was a prime example of that. He studied and studied and knew that the Russians were overconfident and just ripe to be beaten. He worked so hard for that and it literally consumed his life. I remember having dinner with he and my mom and sister in this little bistro in Lake Placid during the Olympics. It was like the first time we had actually gotten to spend any time with him in a while because he had been so busy. I can still remember he sat there the entire time, face down, scribbling line combinations on a napkin during the entire meal. That was my dad, he was just so into it. He was an emotional wreck, but so focused on the task at hand. It was amazing to see. And who can argue with the results?

"You know, I would sort of correlate my dad's career with that of Francis Ford Coppola. I mean when his name comes up, people immediately think of the Godfather. He was an innovative young director at the time who took an unknown group of actors and created a thing of beauty that will go down as one of the greatest movies ever made. Since then, he has made some great movies and has done a lot of good things, but people will always remember him for the Godfather. I think the same is true for my dad. Sure, he orchestrated the greatest upset in the history of sports, but I think it is important to remember that he went on to do some wonderful things in the world of coaching too. Really, he brought a game to the NHL that they had never before seen in the early 1980s. I can still remember when my dad was with the Rangers, they used to call them the 'Smurfs,' because they had a bunch of little, quick skaters who could skate circles around everyone, including the legendary 'Broad Street Bullies' of Philadelphia. Philly was so tough at that time, but dad's teams just owned them, it was awesome. It was a revolutionary system he ran and it was years ahead of its time. Now, it is the standard. So, my dad was a real innovator and took a lot of chances which literally changed the game. I think that is all a part of his legacy too.

"He was just a gamer. He loved pressure and thrived under pressure. While most people got nervous over a test at school or over a big game, or what have you, my dad always used to say that tests and games were the fun parts, because you could just go out there and react. The hard part was in the preparation and the practicing that all went into it prior to that. My dad couldn't understand people who panicked under pressure and didn't act up to their true abilities. My dad was just always prepared, no matter what he did. I remember what Steve Ulseth, a former player of his with the Gophers, once told me. He said that guys couldn't stand him (Herbie) during the week of practice because he was so tough on them. But then, when they were in the national championship game, and it was 3-2 late in the third period, and they looked back behind the bench and saw my dad, calm and collected, leading them, they thanked their lucky stars that it was him back there and not somebody else. Preparation was just the utmost thing to him and I think his players totally respected that."

WHAT IMPACT DID YOUR DAD HAVE ON YOUR LIFE? "My dad was such a down to earth kind of guy. He was just a great guy. You know, I especially loved being around him these past three or four years, when he got to spend time with his grandkids. That had such a profound impact on me and I will always remember seeing how he was with my two daughters and my nieces and nephews. He would do anything, just anything for those kids. He wanted them over all the time, he would call me and say, 'come on, bring Grace over and let her spend the night...', and that was so much fun. Memories like that just make me love my kids even that much more. He loved them so much and unfortunately he will not be able to watch them grow up. That will be tough."

WHAT IS THE ONE THING THAT YOU WOULD WANT YOUR DAD TO KNOW ABOUT THE WAY YOU FELT ABOUT HIM? "My dad and I did not have a conventional father-son relationship. You know, let me give you an example.

I am a huge golf fan and while I was watching the U.S. Open (golf) this year, I was taken back by watching Jim Furyk, who won the tournament. I watched his dad, who is his coach, as he followed him around the course on that last day. Then, when he won, they were hugging and kissing and talking about how they had breakfast together that day and that it was even more special because it was Father's Day. I remember afterwards when Jim said 'I love you dad,' and his father replied, "I love you too, son.' It was really touching. Now, if that were me at the U.S. Open, that never would have happened. Our relationship was not like that at all. My dad was just not a lovey, touchy-feely, kind of a guy. But, I would want my dad to know that I still felt the same way that Jim Furyk did . So, if I ever got into a situation like that, whether it was in business or in my family life, or whatever, even though I was not going to be able to hug and kiss and tell my dad that I loved him, I was OK with that because I had already told him that many, many times in my heart and in my soul.

"I have one story that was very poignant in my life and I have never really told it to anybody before. You know, my dad treated his father that same way too. But he loved him deeply and respected him a great deal. My grandpa was a lot like my Uncle Dave, the life of the party and very outgoing and gregarious. But my dad was more shy and quiet. So, their relationship wasn't real touchy-feely either. Now, my grandfather died when my dad was in New York, coaching the Rangers. He died on the golf course in October of 1984 and my dad had just left for training camp. Two weeks prior to him leaving, we all played a round of golf together over at Goodridge Golf Course over by Aldrich Arena. My dad was begging my grandfather to let him buy him a cart to drive. My grandfather, meanwhile, was very stubborn and insisted on walking. So, fast-forward to a few weeks later when my dad was off at training camp, and my grandfather was out golfing. He is on the 17th hole, hits his tee shot, walks 50 yards towards his ball, and then falls over and dies of a massive heart attack right there on the fairway. So, my dad flew home for the funeral. Now, I remember during that week that when he was home, he was a wreck. I can still remember trying to fall asleep up in my bed and hearing him just crying downstairs because he was so upset and distraught over the fact that he hadn't been able to tell his father that he loved him. It was very, very hard on him. Even though my grandfather knew, my dad just never told him that. So, from that point on, my dad really wasn't ever the same. I mean six months later he and Craig Patrick had a falling out and he was released from the Rangers. I think that his father's death had a lot to do with that.

Anyway, a few years later, it was like my junior year at college, and I was home. So, I am packing up and am about to leave to drive back out to school. I will never forget, it was like five in the morning and I wanted to get an early start to get on the road. Meanwhile, it is just pouring rain outside, and I am getting my car and U-Haul all packed up to leave. Well, my dad is up and like a mad-man, he is just following me around the house. I mean he is literally, like right on my heals as I am running around the house and trying to get packed up to leave. Finally, I am all ready to go and I make a mad-dash out to my car so I won't get soaking wet. So, I go, and sure enough, my dad is still right on my heals. As I run to my car, my dad grabs my shoulder, turns me around and looks at me. I mean there is like a five second pause as we are standing there in the rain, and it seemed like 15 minutes. He looked me right in the eye, took a deep breath, and said ' I love you.' Then, he ran back into the house. That was it. Wow! Not a day goes by in my life where I don't see that image of the rain pouring down and hearing those words from my father. I think I cried the whole way to Colorado. I knew what was going through his mind and knew that he did not want to make the same mistake of not telling me that he loved me like he had done to his father. That haunted him. So, I will remember that for the rest of my life."

ON GENETICS: "Sure, I think I have some of his feistiness. I still catch myself saying 'OK, you are starting to act like your dad…'. For instance, one time at work I had to go through a bunch of licensing requirement bull-sh-- for some project and I simply didn't want to do it. I was all mad and felt like screaming, 'We should be producing revenue and if you don't like it, then you can have the bleeping CEO call me!' Well, I caught myself and said 'Oh my God, you sound just like my old man!' There I was, trying to raise hell and create a battle for the sake of creating one, I suppose. So, I think I have a lot of my dad in me, both good and bad. And do you know what? That is great."

WHAT WAS YOUR DAD'S BEST QUALITY? "He had so many good qualities both as a person and as a coach. His best quality as a coach, in my opinion, was probably his ability to motivate. That is what made him such a great leader. Obviously, he was great with the X's and O's part of it, and he knew the game very well, but he put his psychology degree to work every day. I mean let me tell you, he did this as a father every day as well. He was the ultimate reverse psychologist. He knew just where to stick that knife to make it count. He knew your hot-buttons and had an unbelievable, uncanny ability to know how to motivate you in a reverse way. Whether it was me, or his players, we performed not to satisfy ourselves, but rather it was a 'f--- you, I'll show you, I am going to prove to you that I can do it' response. I used to watch my dad from a far get under the skin of his players. He studied their personalities and knew just how to treat each of them so that they would perform their best. Again, he would take that knife and stick it in and then twist it just the right way. But you know what? They all overachieved because they all wanted to prove him wrong.

"Then, I think my dad's best quality as a person was his humbleness. He was just so down to earth in everything he did. He was not a materialistic person at all. I mean, my mom and I used to laugh about that all the time. Some of the shoes he wore and the cars he drove were great examples of that. He was also very, very principled. I never knew him to screw anybody, or to lie to anybody and he was not manipulative for self gain. He was very honest too. Case in point, one of the reasons why me dad was not re-hired as the North Stars coach when Jack Ferreira took over at the GM was over a letter that Jack wrote to the team's scouting department. In it, he wrote 'Henry Howell' instead of 'Harry Howell,' who was one of the team's scouts. Harry Howell, meanwhile, is an NHL Hall of Famer and my dad had a great deal of respect for the guy. Now, with all due respect to Jack, I am sure it was probably just a typo, my dad went ballistic. My dad always stuck up for the little guy and was so insulted that Jack would show such disrespect for this guy who, despite being a Hall of Famer, was not a real big-wig within the organization. Well, dad took it personally and went after Jack. He pissed him off then to the point where Jack basically said, 'screw you, we will hire someone else to be our coach.' I mean my dad probably had an ulterior motive for getting fired, but he loved the battles and was just so principled in what he felt was right."

WHAT WAS THE SECRET TO YOUR DAD'S SUCCESS? "My dad could just get people to believe in whatever it was he was passionate about at that moment and then sell them on completing that mission at hand. As a coach, he treated everybody so differently, versus a lot of coaches who treat everyone the same way. I mean, my dad could treat the prima-donna in a way where he would stroke his ego, and not battle with him. That was unique. As a result, he got the best out of them. Then, he knew when to be tough on some guys and to just leave them alone at other times as well. Again, there was a method to his madness, but he was a brilliant motivator and could really get people to believe in his causes, whatever they were. Guys would just go to battle for him and follow him anywhere. He was really able to get the best out of people. You know, I never played for him, but I felt like I did because I was in every locker room of every team he ever coached. I literally snuck into his locker rooms as a kid and hid behind poles or trash cans and he did not know even that I was in there most of the time. So, I got to see him work his magic first hand. I also learned a lot of great four letter words as a kid too!"

LIKE YOUR DAD CARRIED JOHN MARIUCCI'S TORCH, HOW ARE YOU NOW GOING TO DO YOUR PART TO CARRY YOUR DAD'S TORCH? "That will be hard, because I am not in the hockey industry per say. Obviously, I can carry the torch personally, like how I conduct myself on a day-to-day basis. I think the big thing now will be making sure that his mission for the game of hockey in the United States for coaches and players is carried out. He really wanted to see kids, players and coaches overachieve both on and off the ice and that was his vision. Presently, I am working with a lot of great people who were very close to him on creating a foundation in his honor. So, hopefully the 'Herb Brooks Foundation' will be able to keep his dreams alive well into the future."

ON SAYING GOOD BYE: "I just look back and, especially now, I really appreciate my dad. I mean how many kids can say that their dad was their hero? I don't know, but I certainly did. It was such an honor to be his son and the memories that I have of him mean more to me than almost anything in the world. My dad gave me so much and I just hope that I can be as good a father to my own kids as he was to me. I was lucky. I got to see the world through hockey and I got to be with my dad for every step of the way. That was an amazing upbringing and I look back at it now just in awe. I mean to be a youth hockey player and to be able to hang out in the locker rooms of the Gophers, Olympics and New York Rangers, wow, what can you say? It was amazing. I think I was the luckiest kid in the world for that 15 year period when I followed my dad, literally, around the world.

"You know, the last time I saw him, it was a typical Herbie moment. He came over on a Saturday morning a couple weeks prior to the accident and, in a classic Herbie blue collar wannabe moment, he brings me a new spade shovel and a pair of saw-horses. Now, I have a nice new house, with a pretty small yard, and I don't do any yard work or anything like that. I mean I am not a fix-it guy. I even hire someone to mow my lawn. So, he brings this stuff over and I am giving him sh-- about what in the world I was going to do with this stuff! Well, he just wanted me to have it, just in case. That was my dad. So, those are hanging in my garage right now as a lasting reminder of him. I have to laugh every time I look at them and think of my dad. You just never know, I can still see him now as he left that day. So, what do I want to say to him? I don't really know. I know that my dad loved me and I know that he knew that I loved him deeply. Do I really want to say good bye? I don't think I really need to because I know and he knew. I had a great life with him and the memories I have, no one can take away from me. Not a day goes by that I don't think of him. You know, my mom just gave me a picture of him where we is sitting out on the end of our dock and I am floating in an inner-tube. I was home from college at the time and it was late in the afternoon with the sun shining and we were out there just talking. He was probably telling me stories of John Mariucci and I was listening to him in awe, like I usually did. I am going to have that picture blown up so that I can share it with my kids. Those are great memories. I will never forget him."

MEMORIES OF HERBIE
FROM HIS DAUGHTER, KELLY

WHAT DID YOUR DAD MEAN TO YOU? "He was just my dad and I loved him so much. He was my protector. He took care of me. And now I feel like that person who always, no matter what, watched over me, is gone. He was always there for me. You know, for me, my mother is my hero. My dad, he was so many other people's hero, and that was OK, because to me, he was my rock. He made sure that I had my oil changed or that I locked my door at night. Even today at 31 years old, he would come over and ask if I had taken my vitamins! That was my dad. It was his way to make sure everything in my life was OK. He didn't think of himself all the time, he always made sure that I was OK. I was his little girl. The day I got married, he was so nervous and so was I — not to marry Marc but to walk down the aisle with my dad. I wanted to be his little girl forever... I was at the church getting ready. My best friend was outside waiting for my family. She told me later that as I was walking out of the dressing room my dad was entering the church. She told my that he stood there motionless, looking at me in my wedding dress from down the long hall way. He burst into tears and left. I guess I never knew how much he loved me. That night he told me he hoped that my wedding was everything I wanted and how proud he was of me. I will never forget that night with him."

ON FATHERLY WISDOM: "Every now and then my dad used to write me letters and they were so special to me. He was just so amazing the way he could say things. His notes were not long-winded, they were to the point and so meaningful.

Here is part of a letter he wrote to me in September of 1990: "You have worked hard to get to where you are today. Don't change...stay on course. Many want to succeed but not all prepare to succeed. Determination has always been a strong point for you and me. That's more important than anything. Your reward will be peace of mind. Feel good about yourself for you have every reason to do so...Your values and principles must be above reproach. There are 10,000 plus laws on the books of society to cover the 10 Commandments!"

"It was tough being Herbie's only daughter. My brother, Danny, got away with a lot more than I did. He would say, 'You're equal…but different.' So, now that I too have a boy and a girl, I am going to use that line on my own kids. We laughed about all of his players who joked about his 'Herbieisms,' but hey, I got them too!"

WHAT'S THE BIGGEST THING YOU LEARNED FROM YOUR DAD? "To be honest, respectful and modest. He was the most honest and straight forward person. He was not a flashy man, he would prefer to wear Wrangler Jeans and drive a pick-up truck. He instilled respect inside of me for all people around me and most importantly, I really respected my parents. I never wanted to let my father down. I never drank, never got into trouble and never got bad grades. I just didn't want to disappoint my dad. Who would want to disappoint him? Not me! He would tell me not to be fooled by the 'now' society and that hard and smart work coupled with a sound code of conduct will last and endure. He told me to stand tall...and be strong."

WHAT ARE YOU GOING TO MISS MOST ABOUT YOUR DAD? "One of the first things that I thought of when I found out my dad died was my boys. He taught me so much in life that I wanted him to teach them. Boys are boys... and I knew that he would be able to teach them to uphold their name with dignity, integrity and class. He was a loving disciplinarian. He was a different person around his grandkids, it was amazing. And they loved him so much. It is so sad now. They still talk about 'Papa Herbie' all the time. When we say our prayers at night, we talk to Papa Herbie, and they know that he is in heaven. When we go visit him at the cemetery they talk to him and they miss him. My daughter, Olivia, has an angel next to her bed and another one that she keeps in her pocket. She tells everyone that Papa Herbie is her angel watching over her. Every time I start to cry she looks at me and asks me if I miss Papa Herbie. It is so sweet and I think that is what keeps me going. My son, Tommy, who is a twin, is really my dad's twin. My dad's baby pictures look just like my boys. Tommy has the same assertiveness, motivation, stubbornness and I can already tell that he will be a leader. Joe (the other twin) has my dad's athletic abilities, his eagerness to be a winner and his desire for knowledge. I tell them that they remind me of Papa and they just get a twinkle in their eyes. I want them to know his legacy and I know that they will some day make him proud. I think I am going to miss the way he taught Danny and I, because I wanted him to teach his morals and values to my kids. That will be rough. He was just the greatest guy."

WHAT IMPACT DID YOUR DAD HAVE ON YOUR LIFE? "He made me want to work hard with everything I did. I worked so hard in school. I knew I could do it and I just did it. I graduated from Denver University in just over three years and went to work right away because I had a lot of self confidence, and a lot of that came from my dad. He wrote to me in college and said, 'Remember, obstacles exist to be overcome...that is how life is...will be...has always been. There will be obstacles between your dreams and hopes and the actualities and realities of life. Do your best.'

"Then, it was all the little things. I am just like him in so many ways. I mean, my husband laughs at me all the time over things that I do, like the fact that I never sit still. I don't sleep in, I am just go-go-go. The minute I get up I am working, just like my dad. We even have the same funny little habits. And I can be a little serious at times too. Luckily that part of him will always be with me."

WHAT IS THE ONE THING THAT YOU WOULD WANT YOUR DAD TO KNOW ABOUT THE WAY THAT YOU FELT ABOUT HIM? I wrote him a letter when he died. I wanted him to know the way that I felt about him and how much

I loved him. He was not a lovey-dovey type of person, so his way of telling you that he loved you was by showing you. He took care of you, he provided for you and just did wonderful things for you. He was my protector, and my inspiration. So, I would just want him to know that I loved him and I would also want him to know that I know how much he loved me."

WHAT WAS YOUR DAD'S BEST QUALITY? "He was honest. He had integrity. He was a leader. He was a motivator. He was a lot of different things to a lot of different people. I don't know if he had a best quality, he was just amazing at so many different things. Maybe that was his best quality."

WHAT WAS THE SECRET TO YOUR DAD'S SUCCESS? "I honestly think he was born successful. He worked hard at whatever he did. I don't think people are born with a blank slate, they are born with their personalities... and my dad was really just a one of a kind. He also knew how to give credit to people who helped him succeed. He gave a lot of credit to my mom for being such a good mother and role model, and for raising Danny and I while he was coaching. My mom is my absolute best friend in the world and I love her so much. She was always there for us and still is today."

WHAT IS YOUR DAD'S LEGACY GOING TO BE IN YOUR OPINION? To me, he was the most brilliant man I have ever known. That was my dad, he was the best. I am just really going to miss him. We are all going to miss 'Papa Herbie.' He once wrote to me: 'After all is said and done, hopefully you'll have life's greatest reward...peace of mind, knowing that you lived by high standards.' "

FUNERAL PALL BEARERS

Steve Badalich
Butch Bloom
Dave Brooks
LeRoy Houle
Lou Nanne
Warren Strelow
Roger Wigen

**HONORARY
PALL BEARERS**
Dean Blais
Jack Blatherwick
Bill Butters
Paul Coppo
Lou Cotroneo
Craig Dahl
Mike Eruzioune
Ken Fanger
Wayne Ferris
Nick Fotiu
Gary Gambucci
John Gilbert
Chuck Grillo
Sid Hartman
Larry Hendrickson

Paul Henry
Clayton Jacobson
Doug Johnson
Paul Johnson
Art Kaminsky
Dave Knoblauch
Greg Malone
John Mayasich
Frank Messin
Joe Micheletti
Paul Ostby
Bob Paradise
Craig Patrick
J.P. Parise
Noel Rahn
Tom Reid
Bob Rink
Dr. Richard Rose
Don Saatzer
Neil Sheehy
Glen Sonmor
Bruce Telander
Tim Tyson
Lou Vairo
Charley Walters
Murray Williamson

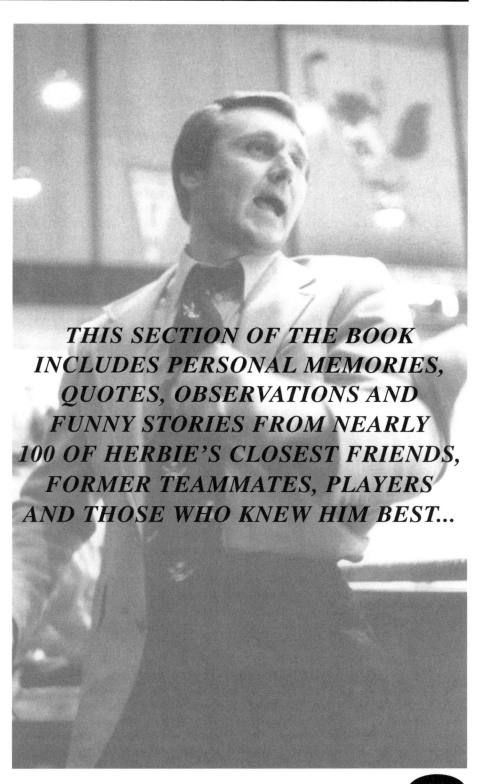

THIS SECTION OF THE BOOK INCLUDES PERSONAL MEMORIES, QUOTES, OBSERVATIONS AND FUNNY STORIES FROM NEARLY 100 OF HERBIE'S CLOSEST FRIENDS, FORMER TEAMMATES, PLAYERS AND THOSE WHO KNEW HIM BEST...

WHAT DID HERBIE MEAN TO YOU?

"I was starting out as a reporter in the mid-1960s, about the time Herb was starting out as a coach, and our rapport was something special from the start. We developed a mutual trust, off the record and in and out of hockey, and we often shared our innermost feelings with each other. He was bold and determined to pursue his ideals, with no regard to political correctness. As a reporter, I've always had a reputation of pursuing stories with determination, so maybe we were on the same wave-length. It's been said that I was a 'booster' of Herbie's coaching, but I also was usually his only critic, and we frequently clashed in the process, but always with mutual respect. In hockey, I always admired innovation, and Herbie was the greatest innovator in the history of the game." — *John Gilbert, former Star-Tribune hockey reporter and long-time friend*

"I knew Herb and really admired him, he was a great, great man. I got to know him and was very impressed with him. He was not at the University of Minnesota when I was there, but we got to know each other later on. We were in different activities together over the years and had a lot of mutual friends as well. He is one person who I really and truly enjoyed thoroughly. His passing was a real tragedy." — *Lou Holtz, Former Gopher Football Coach*

"Herbie was a good friend, and that certainly goes without saying. The hockey part of our relationship was one thing, but his concern for me as a person was above and beyond anything I ever expected out of a guy who had achieved so much success in his life. He always asked me about my family and about my kids, and was always genuinely concerned about me as a person. I can see how as a motivator he could use those same things with his players when he was coaching to become not only their task-master, but their mentor." — *Mike Sertich, former UM-Duluth Head Coach*

"Herbie certainly had a very positive impact on me and helped mold my whole profession. He was the one who was directly responsible for me getting into coaching. When I got done playing pro hockey Herbie called and asked if I wanted to be his assistant at Minnesota. At the time, they had never had a full-time assistant, so I was really honored and flattered that he would ask me to do that. I had so much respect for him, so I jumped at the opportunity. I spent six years working with him and when he went off to coach the Olympics, he really pulled for me to get the Gopher head coaching job. From there, we became great friends and it developed into a life long relationship. We were just very close and I always kept in touch with him on a pretty regular basis through the years. I am going to miss him." — *Brad Buetow, former Gopher Head Coach*

"You know, I still haven't even totally accepted the fact that he is gone yet. It is still such a shock to me. Since he has passed I think about him every day and I still can't really believe it happened. I was thinking and reflecting about the people in my life who have had a positive influence on me and who have really helped me, and I can't think of anybody who has had more of an impact than Herb Brooks. As far as why I do things and how I do things, I can't think of anyone who has had a bigger influence in my adult life than him. So, what he meant to me was immeasurable. We were such good friends. Our families spent a lot of time together, and we used to go camping and just had so much fun." — *Larry Hendrickson, former area high school hockey coach and longtime friend*

"Herbie was obviously a great friend. I think I learned every day from him that if you want things to be better, then you just have to work at it. He reminded me that there are no other answers to problems other than getting busy and working hard. So, besides losing a great friend, I have lost a great part of my motivation." — *Jack Blatherwick, Brooks' former strength & conditioning coach and longtime friend*

"Herbie was a man of uncompromising principles. That's who he was. He had high standards, and he held to them. He gravitated towards people who weren't phony and could smell out a phony very easily. He was a guy who wasn't impressed with his own accomplishments but used those accomplishments to push others to succeed." — *Neil Sheehy, hockey agent and close friend*

"Herbie was a very serious, dedicated person. He frustrated very easily if things weren't to perfection and he had a problem with that. Herbie was a straight arrow. He was also a man possessed with crusades. He would go out in search of a cause and would focus on that cause with all his heart. He was very dedicated to what he believed in. He was very politically astute too when it came to getting something that he had a goal to get. He could also burn a lot of bridges in the process as well. I remember once he told me that he didn't burn bridges, he blew them up! That was Herbie. You know one of the biggest voids in all of the discussions and articles following his death was his playing career. While the 'Miracle on Ice' and his coaching endeavors were well documented, I think more people need to know that Herbie was a great hockey player. He was a good, consistent team player and his teammates respected him. He was my teammate for four years at the University of Minnesota, and he then played on four U.S. National Teams under me as well. So, as a teammate and player, we became great friends. I will never forget after he won the 1980 Olympics he sent me a letter which read 'Without your leadership, this never could've happened.' That meant a lot to me. You know, I was the last coach he ever had. I am going to miss him." — *Murray Williamson, former Gopher teammate and 1972 U.S. Olympic coach*

"Herbie was a great example and a great mentor to me. The way he approached not only coaching, but life in general was amazing. When I was a young coach he took me under his wing and he would check up on me and he would give me advice. Once in a while he would get after me too, to tell me that I had to do this better and that better, and what have you. He really taught me the value of hard work and intelligent work. Those were the two models that he really strived to instill in those who worked and played for him." — *Craig Dahl, St. Cloud State Head Coach and former Brooks assistant*

"I think Herbie was a great motivator and tactician. We always knew that he would be competitive and that is why we enjoyed playing for him." — *Tom Vanelli, former Gopher player*

"I played for Herbie in juniors and then again with the Gophers and he just taught me so much. He was tough though too. As most of the guys will tell you, there was no loafing in practice. I can still remember if we didn't play well in a game we would skate for what seemed like an eternity without pucks, and that was just Herbie being Herbie. Really though, he was a fabulous coach. I would say he was the motivator of all motivators. I was his captain during my senior year and that was an honor, but also a tremendous responsibility. Herbie leaned on me hard to be the liaison between him and the team and that was tough. If someone stayed out late on a road trip or if we didn't play well, I was usually the one that was going to hear about it first. I was even responsible for bed checks on the road, and boy was that a tough job! He just had high expectations and demanded a lot of success in whatever he did." — *Pat Phippen, former Gopher player*

"He was the best coach I ever had, that was for sure. I learned a lot from Herbie. I learned what it took to be a success in hockey and what it took to be a success in life. He pushed his players hard and taught them that their limits were actually farther than they ever originally thought. He challenged us and he showed us how to be successful. He was just a big influence on my life in hockey and I look back upon those experiences, both successes and failures, and I use those today to make decisions on both my personal and professional life." — *Robb McClanahan, former Gopher & Olympic player*

"Herbie meant a lot to me. He had a great influence on my life and really impacted me as a person. He taught me how to be a man. He gave a 17-year-old kid from Babbitt a chance to play college hockey and I will never forget that. I won a national championship with him and I won an Olympic gold medal with him, so he meant a great deal to me." — *Buzz Schneider, former Gopher & Olympic player*

"He meant an awful lot. He recruited me out of high school and really took my hockey career to the next couple of levels that I would never have imagined. We won national championships at the University of Minnesota and an Olympic gold medal in 1980, so we had a lot of success together. He brought to the table a lot of passion, dedication and conviction. Hopefully he passed a few of those traits on to me and I can go about my life and use those characteristics as well. He always used to say that he minded more if we made mistakes out of the act of omission versus commission. That was Herbie." — *Phil Verchota, former Gopher & Olympic player*

"He meant a lot, and not just in hockey either. We still kept in touch even after my playing days and he was not only a great coach, but a good friend. He was somebody you could call on and know that he would be there for you. He was truly like a father figure to me." — *Mike Polich, former Gopher player*

"To me, Herbie was not only my coach, he was a guy who cared for me. I knew over the years that he cared for me as more than just a player, he cared about my well being. So, to me Herbie was not only a great friend, he was a father figure. My parents divorced when I was four years old, so most of the coaches I had in my life were pretty important to me. Herbie and I's paths crossed when I was a young guy and I really looked up to him. He did so much for me and taught me so much about life. He told me where I stood, what my strengths were and how to become a better player. A lot of people thought he played mind games, I never did. He evaluated your talent and told you what he thought of you. I respected his opinion obviously, so when he told me that I wasn't a very good hockey player, that didn't bother me at all because I knew I wasn't. I knew that I had a role on the team and that he expected me to run into people out there and play physical hockey. As far as character building, that is what Herb Brooks was all about. He had a passion for the game and he saw that despite the fact that I didn't have a lot of talent, I too had a passion for the game." — *Bill Butters, former Gopher player*

"You know, I grew up in a Polish neighborhood on the East side and his father got me to come over and play hockey for him at Phalen. Herb and I later became linemates on our Johnson High School team and I even became his son's godfather, so we were very close. I even used to tell my kids, 'don't turn out like me, turn out like Herb Brooks.' He was just a great person and a great friend, I am going to miss him. He was probably the best confidante I ever had and I think he felt the same way about me." — *Roger Wigen, former St. Paul Johnson High School Hockey teammate*

"I probably owe him a little more than other players who might have played for him because my career might have fizzled after college if it wasn't for him. He gave me the opportunity to play on the Olympic team and then gave me the opportunity to play for him in New York, so I am grateful to him. He was just a great coach." — *Mark Pavelich, former player on 1980 U.S. Olympic Team & NY Rangers*

"He meant a lot to me. We had a tremendous friendship and I will miss him dearly. We argued a lot but we loved each other. You know, now that he is gone I just feel like hockey has been cheated. I mean he still had so much more to give." — *Steve Badalich, longtime friend*

"I first met Herbie shortly after the 1980 Olympics at the old 49 Club bar. He had just moved into a new house next door to a friend of mine, so he introduced me to him. You know, when I first met him he asked me what I did for a living, and I told him: 'anybody I can and the easy ones twice!' He got a big kick out of that and just laughed like hell. I told him that I did tree trimming and stump removal, so he hired me to come do some work for him at his new house. From there, we just became really, really close friends. I loved the guy. We just clicked. I would have done anything for him. Anything. I just loved him. He was just so God damn nice, I thought the world of him. He was just one hell of a guy. He just sort of grew right on me and we spent a lot of time together hanging out and doing work in the yard." — *LeRoy Houle, longtime friend*

"I really feel blessed to have known him. He was just the most phenomenal guy I have ever met in my life. He had a way with people that was unreal. We loved to give each other heat and we just had a great time together." — *Butch Bloom, longtime friend*

"I first became acquainted with Herbie when I was playing at the University of North Dakota and he was playing at the University of Minnesota. As a player, Herbie was very solid and obviously had talent because he went on to play on several U.S. National and Olympic teams. From there, Herbie and I became colleagues within the hockey industry. He was someone I respected a great deal and someone who did a lot to grow the game. Herbie was very popular, very well received by people, very well known and he was just liked — as evidenced by the number of people who were at his funeral service. You know, Herbie and I traveled in different circles, but he certainly did his part to help expand hockey in Minnesota and I appreciated that. I remember when he made a flat-out statement that Minnesota should have more division one teams, and specifically, that Bemidji, St. Cloud and Mankato should be playing at that level. To think that we have five division one schools here now is wonderful. We have come a long way since our playing days back in the 1950s, when college hockey was pretty spartan. Much of that is due to the efforts of people like Herb Brooks, who, among others, worked very hard for not only the American player, but the Minnesota player. He really became known for his excellence as a coach. I mean his three national championships at Minnesota and the gold medal in 1980 were outstanding achievements and really did a lot for hockey in Minnesota." — *Bob Peters, longtime Bemidji State University head coach*

"I think whatever Herbie did, he did it with a passion. More than anything else though, he loved the game of hockey. He would drive people to make themselves better. He got the most out of people and could get them to do things that they never thought they could do. He was just a great hockey mind. He also gave people a lot of direction in their lives, not only in hockey, but outside of hockey as well." — *Tommy Reid, former North Star & current Wild radio analyst*

"Ever since I was a senior in high school and I got that recruiting letter from the University of Minnesota with the big 'M' on the envelope and Herb Brooks' name signed at the bottom, I have been a fan of his. His reputation before that was impressive to me and I couldn't wait to play for him at the U of M. Playing for him had a great affect on my life and he was really like a father figure to me. He was a real mentor to me both at the University and then again with the Olympics. I just felt very fortunate to have had him as an influence on my life for the four years that I did." — *Steve Christoff, former Gopher & Olympic player*

"You know growing up here I always wanted to play for the Gophers and I will never forget getting that first recruiting letter from Herbie with that raised letter 'M' on the envelope. I really looked up to him at that point and was thrilled to get the chance to play for him. I mean in college hockey at that time, Herbie was the man. He put that program on the map. I remember later having an NHL scout refer to the Gopher program at that time as the 'Montreal of college hockey,' and that said a lot. So, to play for him and to get to know him meant a great deal. He was a great coach and a great person, I will miss him." — *Reed Larson, former Gopher player*

"He meant a lot to me and I respected him a great deal. Our friendship was always strong through the years and I will miss him. He was such a smart guy and always made you think better. The more time you spent with him, the more you walked away feeling like a better person." — *Greg Malone, Pittsburgh Penguins head of scouting*

"Herbie and I played on the 1968 Olympic team together and that is where I first got to know him and became friends. He was a great hockey player, and when he skated he was just smooth as glass. From there, my son later married his daughter, so we shared grandchildren together. He was always a very good friend and someone I really admired." — *Bob Paradise, former teammate & father-in-law to his daughter*

"I knew Herbie for a long time but really got to know him when I played for him at the 2002 Olympics. He really inspired me. Even when I played against his teams that he was coaching in the NHL, I always tried to play as hard as I could. He just motivated me to do my best. Maybe it was a Minnesota thing, I don't know, but I really respected the guy and tried to give it my best whenever I was around him. Herbie meant so much to U.S. hockey, and you really don't know how much of an impact it had when he won the gold medal back in 1980. I mean that opened so many doors for American players, and I am very grateful to that." — *Phil Housley, former 2002 Olympian under Brooks & former NHL All-Star*

"To me, Herbie was the ultimate coach that you wanted to play for. When I was growing up it was the heyday of all-Minnesota kids winning national championships at the U of M. I was fortunate enough to win one with him as well, and that is something I will never forget. Herbie, to me, was just what stood for Gopher hockey, and I really respected the guy. He was the kind of person who, when he walked into a room, everybody knew that he was there. He just had a real presence about him. I will never forget when he came to my house to recruit me. He was real up front with me and told me that he didn't have any scholarship money left. But, he said that if I walked on and made the team that he would buy me a pair of skates. I did, and he bought me a new pair of skates. I will always remember that. He was just the kind of guy that you had the utmost respect for. Even later on, you sort of always had that player/coach relationship with him. You just had that total respect for him and wanted to do whatever you could to make your coach happy. You just never wanted to disappoint him. He was a great guy." — *Steve Ulseth, former Gopher player*

"You know, the only time I really spent any time with Herbie was at the 2002 Olympic pre-camp try-outs, but what he means to me is immeasurable. I don't think that I would have had the opportunities that I have had over my career without him. I mean, he put St. Cloud State Hockey on the map, and that is where I got my start. I had one scholarship offer out of high school and that was at St. Cloud State, so without that I don't know where I would be. So, if it hadn't have been for him going up there and turning that program into a division one school, who knows what would have happened. Herb was committed to having more kids playing hockey in Minnesota and I was a direct result of that vision. So, I thank him every time I lace em' up, because where I am today was a direct result of his efforts back then. I was a St. Paul guy and he was a St. Paul guy and I think we had that connection. He was a great person and someone that I really looked up to and respected." — *Bret Hedican, current NHL All-Star*

"Herbie touched my life on so many levels and for so many years. First and foremost, Herbie was somebody who came into my life when I was in high school up in Hibbing and gave me the opportunity to play college hockey at the University of Minnesota. Later, he became completely entrenched in not only my life, but the lives of my entire family, and that meant the world to me. He really became like a part of our family. You know, nine years ago, when my father died, we were at the wake up in Hibbing. Well, there was a classic Minnesota blizzard going on outside at the time, but Herb still made the four hour trip up through the blizzard to be there for us. Then, when my mother died this past Spring, Herb came from a scouting trip in Montreal to be at that funeral as well. So, he has meant a great deal to me and my family and I just can't say enough nice things about Herb Brooks. He was such a decent, wonderful human being, and I will miss him." — *Joe Micheletti, former Gopher player & current Fox Sports TV hockey analyst*

"Herbie was a winner and just an unforgettable person. He represented the old fashioned ideals of loyalty, commitment, integrity and hard work. If anybody would paint a story of him it should be someone like Norman Rockwell, who represents the history of what made our country so great. That was Herbie." — *Noel Rahn, longtime friend*

"He meant an awful lot, that was for sure. We were great buddies. He was probably the best coach I ever knew and certainly one of the best people that I ever knew. Herb was just a great guy." — *Paul Johnson, former Olympic teammate and longtime friend*

"Herbie meant different things to me at different points in my career. When I was a 17-year-old freshman at the University of Minnesota I was in awe of him. I mean he just had that certain mystique which made him kind of intimidating to be around. He just knew how to push the right buttons to get you to play the way he wanted you to play. I mean Herbie was someone who could take young players and mold them into what he wanted them to be. For me, I was fortunate enough to play for Herbie with the Gophers and then on the 1980 Olympic team, and those were great memories. From there, I was able to have a long career in the National Hockey League and now I am an assistant coach with the Wild. Herbie was just sort of with me every step of the way. I learned a great deal from him and have applied a lot of the things that he did to my own coaching style now. You know, more recently it was fun, because I got to enjoy him. We had that mutual respect for one another and it was much different. It was great because I could talk to him about coaching and our conversations were wonderful. So, our relationship really came full circle, and that was special."
— *Mike Ramsey, former Gopher & Olympic player and current Wild assistant coach*

"Herbie was someone who I leaned on quite heavily, especially early in my career as a player. I only had the opportunity to play for him for one year at the University of Minnesota, but it was a year that I will never forget. Then, he was very helpful to me during my first few years in pro hockey after that. I just respected him a great deal and really valued his opinion and advice." — *Paul Holmgren, former Gopher player & NHL player and coach*

"Herb was great. He always left you with something to think about. You might not know exactly what he meant at the time, but within a short period you usually did. He always had something there to give you. He just loved hockey. He loved talking hockey. He loved being with people and he loved life. He was just one step ahead of the next guys' thought process, he had a real gift that way. Then, you know, Herb was also a very good player and a very crafty, creative player. He was very slick with the puck and just came to work every day. He was always well prepared and was just a real good teammate." — *Larry Pleau, former teammate on 1968 Olympic team & current St. Louis Blues GM*

"Herb was one of the most complex, intelligent, interesting and courageous people that I have ever known. He was absolutely fearless in offering his opinion on issues and that was a really important attribute. We have got to have debate and as long as that doesn't turn personal, it is real healthy — be it politics or sports or what have you. That is what has made our country such a great place to live, and Herbie was a champion of that. You know, I respect the fact that Herb fought to keep the professionals out of the Olympics for so many years, but then, as soon as he lost the debate, he got on board. It didn't matter anymore to him. He had made his point and he lost. But he was eager to do his part and it was great to see him out there again when he coached the 2002 U.S. Olympic team in Salt Lake City. You know, I agreed with him on issues like that. But, we disagreed on a lot of things too, and we even went a few years without talking to one another. But we got past it and hockey was what always brought us back together. Herb wasn't always easy to deal with, but I grew to just really like and respect him. I especially liked what he had developed into that last several years. You know, he was really enjoying, and I hate to use the word, his legacy — because he would be offended by that. But it was the truth. He was starting to appreciate and enjoy some of the things that he had done in the world of hockey. Most of all though, he was really enjoying his time with his family. For me, personally, I am going to really miss him. He is gone now, he is at peace and with loved ones. But it is his family who is suffering and that to me is the biggest tragedy of his passing. It has nothing to do with sticks, skates or pucks, it has everything to do with his wife, children and grandchildren. He was just thoroughly enjoying his family and appreciating them. So, as soon as I got over the initial shock of hearing the news that he had died, his family was the first thing that I thought of." — *Lou Vairo, head coach of 1984 U.S. Olympic team & assistant under Brooks on the 2002 U.S. squad*

"For me it starts with excellence, and that was in everything he did. Certainly, his coaching was unparalleled at the collegiate level. He just had such a passion for the game of hockey and for life. He loved the game, had great ideas and was a very progressive thinker. He will be missed." — *Don Lucia, Gopher Hockey head coach*

"Herbie was a friend first and foremost. He was also a great coach who taught me a lot about commitment and work ethic in order to be successful in any endeavor that I did. Then, he was a great motivator for me. The things that he taught me and the values that he instilled in me are things that I will carry with me for the rest of my life." — *Mike Eruzione, former 1980 Olympian*

"I first met Herb when we worked at Ken Yackel's Hockey School over at Braemar Arena in Edina. He was just a young assistant coach under Glen Sonmor at the University of Minnesota at the time. We had a lot of fun together. I could see right away that he was a very intense coach and really knew the game. He could really teach and the kids listened to him. You could just see early on that he had a gift. I also respected the fact that Herb wanted to work with the kids who were not very good, which was oftentimes a tough thing to do at camps like that. He just felt it was important for those kids to get the attention they deserved and I think that said a lot about him. Then, from there, we just became good friends over the years. He was one of the great ones and I really enjoyed him. He always made time for me and was just fun to be around. He was a very intense coach, but after the battle he loved to sit down and have a beer, and that was great." — *Willard Ikola, former Olympian and longtime Edina High School Hockey Coach*

"He meant a lot to me. He was not only a great coach and a great motivator, but he was a great teacher. I learned so much from him both in hockey and in life. He was just a great person to be around. Sure, sometimes he was hard to be around, because he demanded so much, but that was his style. He made you work very hard, but he was a winner and you wanted to work hard for him." — *Eric Strobel, former Gopher & Olympic player*

"Herbie watched over my career and always offered me his advice or opinion along the way. I used to love it when he would come down before a game and visit with me. He was always so positive and really cared about what I was doing. So, he meant a lot to me and he meant a lot to the sport of hockey. He just always had time for me and was a real mentor to me." — *Dean Blais, former Gopher player & current head coach at the University of North Dakota*

"Herb was the best coach that I ever had. He was so good with motivational things, tactical things, strategy, preparation and hard work. There was just nobody like him. As for me, I have been coaching college hockey for 20 years now, and I draw much of my style from him as well. I know that from playing for him on the 1980 Olympic team that if my teams now work hard, good things will happen and that sometimes dreams can come true." — *John Harrington, former Gopher & Olympic player*

"Herbie was just a very special friend. It was such a tragedy, I am still struggling so much with it. I go to mass every morning to pray, but it is so tough. That kid meant the world to me. I remember, I used to call him 'Peter Puck' and he would call me coach. We met a lot privately over the years over coffee and we just talked about life. Sometimes we would talk about hockey and other times we would talk about politics. People don't realize just how close he was to running for public office. Then, when he left, it was always a handshake and a hug. I will cherish our friendship for the rest of my life. We had a beautiful relationship and he meant a great deal to me. I just have a big hole in my heart and that will take time to heal. He was family to me and I am going to miss him dearly." — *Lou Cotroneo, former St. Paul Johnson High School hockey coach & longtime friend*

"I don't think words can ever explain what he actually meant to me. He was my best friend. We grew up together as kids. He helped me so much in my career that I wouldn't even know where I would be today without him. I mean he believed in me and gave me so many opportunities to coach with him, and I will just never forget him." — *Warren Strelow, former goalie coach under Brooks and longtime friend*

"It was real obvious the things he did for me on the ice, but I think it was the things that he taught me off the ice that I will remember most about him. Things like knowing the meaning of hard work, dedication and what it takes to become successful. He taught me that in hockey and he taught me that away from the rink as well. I still use a lot of that today in my profession and I owe a lot of that to Herbie. He was a tough coach and you really grew up a lot under him. He stood up for what he believed in and I had the highest respect for him." — *Bill Baker, former Gopher & Olympic player*

"Herbie meant a whole lot to me. You just can't put into words what he meant. I mean he gave me the chance to play college hockey and then selected me to be a part of the 1980 Olympic team. So, from there it was just history. He really showed me the way both on and off the ice and just taught me about life. You know, when I first met him I was scared to death of him, but when you got to know him you realized that underneath that tough image he was really just a softie. He certainly played a big part in my success and I will never forget him." — *Neal Broten, former Gopher, Olympian and North Star under Brooks*

"The first word that comes to my mind is inspiration. He was just a very inspirational human being. You know, I knew Herbie before he was famous and he was every bit as inspirational as a human being as he was as a coach. We were teammates and roommates together on a couple of U.S. National teams and even there, he was so inspirational. He just always knew what to say to you and was always there for you when you needed him. You know, when I came down from Hibbing to play for the Gophers I knew all about Herb Brooks. Then, when I met him, he welcomed me to the team and made me feel like a million bucks. Herbie had great respect for the Iron Range and for Iron Range people, and a lot of that probably came from John Mariucci. He just loved that blue collar work ethic that was so prevalent on the Range and that was Herbie — just down to earth as can be. So, he was a great person, a great friend and he will dearly be missed. I just totally loved the guy. He was my idol, and not because he won national championships or gold medals, but just because he was such a great human being. I just really respected his character and his heart." — *Gary Gambucci, former Gopher and teammate on two U.S. National teams*

"Herbie was the ultimate definition of what passion was about. He had a passion for

everything and was someone who was constantly trying to be better. He just had so much passion and integrity. You know, I don't know if he was ever fully satisfied with any game he ever coached. I mean even after they won the gold medal in 1980, he was happy, but still knew that his team could've played better. He was just always in search of that perfect game. He was so driven, and just did not yield. That is what made him tick and that was what was so unique about him. He certainly inspired me to get into coaching, and that is something that I have been doing now for 25 years."
— *Craig Sarner, former Gopher and player under Brooks on 1979 U.S. National Team and in Europe & longtime coach at various levels*

"The thing I admired most in Herbie was that he was his own guy in the truest sense. He just did things his way and did whatever he felt was right. I think they could've used Frank Sinatra's motto of how 'he did it his way' on Herbie's tombstone, he was just that special type of person. He succeeded under his own terms without having to play any games and didn't care about public relations. I mean he probably could've coached a lot longer than he did in the NHL if he wasn't so strong willed about doing things his own way. But, that was Herbie. My guess was that he certainly could've had the New York Rangers job if he wanted it this past year and who knows, maybe he could've been the Wild coach had things turned out differently there as well. Herbie was just an autocrat, it was his way or no way. And fortunately for Herbie he was close with Craig Patrick, in Pittsburgh, who understood that to a degree. He recognized how bright he was and was willing to bend to allow him the latitude to express himself and make key decisions about the team's personnel. He was just a great coach and he was able to do things his own way, something most people could not get away with — and I respected that about him.

"Then, on the other side, I admired what a great competitor he was. He wouldn't give in to anybody. You know, I played professional baseball and I told Herbie that I would have enjoyed playing for him had he been a baseball coach. I did play for Billy Martin, when I was with the Twins, and I think those two were a lot a like with regards to how competitive they were. Herbie just had a great ability to motivate his players and had a 'win at all cost' mentality, and I admired that. He was a real winner.

"I would also add that I respected the fact that he was just a regular guy. I remember back a few years ago at the 2002 Winter Olympics in Salt Lake City. They had flown all the guys in from the 1980 gold medal team to light the Olympic caldron and it was a pretty big deal. But, Herbie had already committed to being at a retirement dinner for one of his old pals at a VFW in North St. Paul. So, rather than being on world-wide television in front of billions of people with his players, he spent a quiet evening with his buddies here in St. Paul. That was Herbie, he never forgot where he came from. He was just a common guy and was so loyal to his old friends.

"I remember he used to always tease me about being from Northeast Minneapolis. He was from Payne Avenue in East St. Paul and always used to say that the Payne Avenue guys were so tough and how they could kick the hell out of the Northeast guys. Stuff like that. You know, I am a Joe-six pack too, so we had that in common. My nickname is 'Shooter,' but he would always call me 'Floater,' just to tease me about 'walking away from my neighborhood and forgetting my roots...'. I remember one time I saw him wearing an expensive Polo Jacket, so I said, 'Hey Herb, from what store on Payne Avenue did you get that $500 jacket?' He got a kick out of that. So, I will miss the banter we had and just seeing him out at games. He was always a great quote and really a colorful character in the Minnesota sports scene. Herbie was just a one of a kind and there will never be another one like him. I still can't believe he is gone." — *Charley Walters, Pioneer Press columnist*

"Herbie made us all proud. He just did it all and was such a friend to the game of hockey. When you look back at all of his contributions, and not only the victories, but his expertise in so many areas outside of hockey, it was remarkable. I just consider it an honor and a privilege to have known him and to have been his friend. Whether it was through hockey or golf or whatever, we always had fun together. I will miss him." — *John Mayasich, former teammate on U.S. National Teams & long-time friend*

"When I think of Herbie I think of great leadership and of the great love that he had for the game. He would share his love and knowledge of the game with anybody who wanted to talk hockey, no matter who they were. And he was very opinionated too. He didn't care if people disagreed with him, he was just very principled and did what he thought was right. Period. He was really a great ambassador for the game of hockey and he will be truly missed. I considered Herbie to be a very good friend and I am going to really miss him. I think we will all miss him, he just did so much for the game of hockey." — *Jim Findley, President of the U.S. Hockey Hall of Fame*

"I was just a guy who knew Herbie from a whole different perspective. I didn't relate to him with hockey at all. We talked all the time, but rarely about hockey. In fact, if I would bring up hockey, he would change the subject. I mean with me he did not want to talk hockey. He just enjoyed being my neighbor and talking about totally different things. In that regard, even though he was a celebrity, we were good friends and really on an equal footing. You know, when he died I don't think anybody interview him because he loved to plant lilies of the valley in his yard, but that was how we related to each other. He was just a darn good friend and I will miss him." — *Bob Rink, next-door neighbor and longtime friend*

"He meant a hell of a lot. Herb was just a real class guy and a real class act. He never had a bad word to say about anybody. He was always coaching, especially out on the golf course! We just always had a lot of fun together and I am going to miss him. We had a lot of great memories together and he was just a great individual. He was a real first class guy and I was proud to have him as a friend for more than 40 years. I just loved the guy." — *Frank Messin, former hockey referee and longtime friend*

"Herb's dad and my dad were very close, so as a kid I got to watch Herb play high school hockey at Johnson, and then at the University of Minnesota. I later got the opportunity to coach with him as a scout with the 1980 Olympic team, and of course I got to coach against him for a number of years as well. Herb was just a great hockey mind and a great person. He was a good friend who was always there for you too. You could always call him and he would always give you his honest opinion. He just always made you feel important and that is the measure of a class person, and that certainly was what Herbie was." — *Jeff Sauer, former University of Wisconsin & Colorado College Head Coach*

"Herbie was born to be a coach, and I am sad that he had not been coaching for the past several years. That was where he was most at home, behind the bench, and it was too bad that things didn't work out with the New York Rangers this past year. It would have been great to see him get back out there again." — *Gregg Wong, former Pioneer Press columnist*

"Herbie was a tremendous dreamer in the world of hockey and he soaked up what he learned with all of his playing in international hockey. People don't talk much about his playing ability, but he was an outstanding player as well as a coach. He was just so determined. I remember when he was the last guy cut from the 1960 Olympic team. He didn't cry about it, he took it like a man, and then came back and played on the next several U.S. National Teams. Then, when I was the general manager of the 1964 Olympic team, he made the club with ease and was even named as one of the captains. So, that said a lot about Herb, he was determined and never gave up. We just later became friends and colleagues in the hockey business, and that relationship lasted more than 40 years. From him playing on my South St. Paul Steers team back in the 60's to the Olympics to everything now with USA Hockey, we have been through a lot together. Sure, we had our battles, but you had to respect Herb's passion for what he believed in. I enjoyed debating with him, he never called it arguing, and just really respected him. He had a dream of getting more kids playing hockey and his heart was always in the right place. You know, his candle burned out far too soon but his success will live on through the people he touched. He was just a very good, innovative coach and he will be missed." — *Walter Bush, Chairman of the Board, USA Hockey*

"Herbie did a great deal for me. We were both St. Paul guys and had played together on a U.S. National team, so we knew each other. As a player, Herb was silky smooth and really a tremendous athlete. Well, he really helped me out when he got me my first job coaching junior hockey with the Vulcans. And that was at a time when I had never even seen a junior game before. I was teaching at the time, but Herbie recommended me for it and that got me started in my coaching career, so I really appreciated that. I mean that job taught me how to be a coach and without it I would not have gone anywhere in the world of coaching. From there, we would go back and forth. I would feed guys over to him when he was coaching the Gophers, and it worked out well for both of us. Herbie loved the junior guys because they were a little older and had a little more muscle. Later, Herbie did a lot for me with regards to getting me the head coaching job at the University of Minnesota when Brad Buetow left. Herbie was originally going to come back to take the job at that point and have me serve as his assistant, but he dropped out at the last minute. Still, he and John Mariucci recommended me to Paul Giel, the athletic director at the time, for the job. So, Herbie did a great deal for me in my career and I will forever be grateful to him for that. As a person, I had a great deal of respect for him. He was a brilliant coach and tactician and worked very, very hard at whatever he was doing." — *Doug Woog, former Gopher Hockey Coach & teammate on a U.S. National team*

"Herbie represented excellence in hockey. That is what he stood for, bringing the game up to the highest level possible — an art form. I understand hockey more on an art form level than I do on an Xs and Os basis. I am a watcher of the game, not a player, and that is what I think of when I think of Herbie's teams — that they were elevated to a form of art. I just appreciated the way Herbie treated me and respected me through the years. We had a good professional relationship together and I will miss that." — *Frank Mazzocco, Gopher Hockey TV Analyst*

"I think about all of the people who I have met being in this profession, all of the stars who make sports headlines, but Herbie had an impact on an entire country. It wasn't just Herb Brooks winning a big game, it was what he did for the country in 1980 and then what he did for the sport of hockey from there. So, I consider it to be a privilege and an honor to have known him. We used to golf together and swap stories together and I will miss that." — *Joe Schmit, KSTP-TV sports anchor*

"Personally, Herbie meant a lot to me. I met him pretty early on in my career and, like a lot of people, was kind of intimidated by him at first. But as I got to know him that all changed and we became good friends. Certainly, being out at Lake Placid with him during the 1980 Olympics is something that I will never forget. Then, later, we worked together doing broadcasts at the State High School Hockey Tournament, and that was really fun too. Of course, he was just as opinionated about that as he was everything else, and that was another side of Herbie that was great to see as well. I mean he was just as excited about watching Warroad play Grand Rapids as he was the North Stars versus the Rangers. He just loved hockey and loved talking about hockey. He had an aura about him where if he spoke, you would just sit back and listen. I really felt a kinship with him, he was a great person. He had such a unique way of communicating with his players and making them believe in themselves. He could just get people to reach beyond their potential and that was special. He didn't accept anything less than the best from people and that was a big part of who he was."
— *Mark Rosen, WCCO-TV sports anchor*

"He meant everything to me, really. He gave me the opportunity to be a part of what he was creating. He appreciated what I brought to the team and that meant a lot to me. We won a couple of national championships at the University together and then he asked me if I wanted to come along to Lake Placid to be a part of the 1980 Olympics too, so that was a wonderful experience. It has opened so many doors for me and I am just very grateful to have been a part of it." — *Gary Smith, trainer under Brooks at the University of Minnesota and on the 1980 Olympic Team*

"You know, Herbie was just always there for you when you needed him. I run Olympic development programs for female hockey players and whenever we asked Herbie to help us out he was there for us. I just appreciated that so much. He would take time to talk to the young coaches and to the players and that meant so much to everyone. It was a wonderful learning experience for them just to meet him and ask him a few questions. I can remember taking him to a girls high school hockey game several years ago and asking him what things we needed to do to make these girls into Olympians. Well, Herbie came up with a detailed list of things and that immediately became the blueprint for how we designed the entire program. So, he had a lot to do with the success of women's Olympic hockey in America as well. He just had a real gift for helping others." — *Wayne Ferris, lawyer and business manager*

"I don't think that there was anyone who managed people better than Herbie. That was the genius of Herbie. He was just such a great person. He was really a builder of character and had very good values. I am just going to miss his energy. He was such a great friend." — *Dave Knoblauch, longtime friend*

"Herb was a great, very close personal friend. He did so much for me and for hockey. He had so many great ideas and had such a passion for what he believed in. Many of his ideas were radical and controversial too, but Herb stuck to what he believed in, even though he stepped on some toes along the way. I just really respected him as a person and as a friend." — *Don Saatzer, former Hastings High School hockey coach and longtime scout with the Boston Bruins*

"Herb was a real dear friend and we just hit it off from the very first time we met. We were roommates and linemates on the 1964 Olympic team and just had so much fun together. I will just miss him terribly." — *Paul Coppo, former teammate on several U.S. National Teams and longtime friend*

"My friendship with Herbie goes back a long way and he just meant a great deal to me. He appeared on the very first 'Let's Play Hockey' television show that I did on KSTP, that is how far back we went. Over the years we later did the state high school hockey tournament broadcasts together as well, and that was a lot of fun. You know, we were even together for the 1980 Olympics too, and there is a plaque on my wall which shows a bunch of hockey players raising the flag as though it were the World War II image of Iwo Jima. On the bottom of the picture it says: 'Thank you Bob, you made it all possible, the winning of the gold medal — your buddy, Herb Brooks.' So, that is how close we were." — *Bob Utecht, founder of Let's Play Hockey newspaper*

"When I played for Herbie with the Rangers it was a love-hate relationship, but as we got older we became great friends. He really trusted me and that meant so much to me. He was just a very good friend and we spoke on the phone with each other all the time, just talking about hockey and about life. I am just so sad to lose my friend. He was one of the only people who believed in me and I owe him so much. After our playing days in New York we just stayed in touch to the point where we became just the best of friends. I mean I was so humbled when he called me and asked for my advice when he was picking the roster for the 2002 Olympic team. That blew me away. I learned so much from him being his assistant during the team's training camp. You know, we especially talked a lot this past year. I really thought he was going to take the New York Rangers job and we were just in constant contact over it. He would ask for my advice and then tell me that 'he was trusting me with his life.' That was how we felt about each other, it was very special." — *Nick Fotiu, former New York Ranger under Brooks*

"Personally, I loved the guy like a father. I don't know if my bond with him was any bigger or better than it was with anybody else, but I just thought he was the greatest. My earliest memories of Herb Brooks are so vivid. Being from the east coast I will never forget what he did in 1980 with the Miracle on Ice. I was a 14 year-old kid at the time and was just in awe of what those guys did. I remember seeing Herbie and thinking what a dynamic, incredible character he was. Then, when I met him, I was even more impressed with him. He was just an amazing person. And he was just so gracious to everybody. He was truly a leader of the people, amongst the people. He treated the NHL All-Star the same way he treated his barber, that was his gift — he could connect with anybody." — *Brian Lawton, hockey agent and former North Star under Brooks*

"After my father, I would say that Herbie was by far the strongest male influence in my life, particularly at a time when I was looking for direction. What he did was to help me to mature into somebody who believed in himself and to understand the discipline it took to accomplish my goals." — *Jim Boo, former Gopher player*

"Herbie was just a wonderful friend. I knew Herbie, but never really got to know him until I started to work with him in 1987, when I was an assistant under him with the North Stars. It was one of the most wonderful years of my life, being with Herbie. I remember even after our first practice with the team, I came to my desk that next day and he had left me a nice note which read: 'Great start *Jeeper*, let's keep it going!' That meant so much to me. He gave me a lot of responsibilities with the team and treated me with nothing but class. He gave me advice not only about hockey, but about life. He was very astute and very smart. He really made my life better and cared so much about me. He was just a wonderful human being and I miss him terribly." — *J.P. Parise, former North Star player and assistant coach with the North*

"Herbie's practices? We used to say that if Herbie did this to a dog, the humane society would throw him in jail! But it taught us to keep pushing each other as teammates, and to be in shape that third period so we could win. You know, Herb wanted me to go to Canada for a year of juniors in return for a half scholarship at the U. Colorado College had offered me a full scholarship afterwards, but I told them I was committed to the University of Minnesota. I went to visit the campus one time, and I told him that even though I needed the full ride because my parents needed to save money for my other family members, that I wanted to go to college and I would accept the half scholarship. Herbie looked at me, smiled, and said, 'I'm proud of you for making the decision to come here on a half ride. I had a full scholarship waiting for you the entire time, but I wanted to see how badly you wanted to be a Gopher.' " — *Don Micheletti, former gopher player*

"Herbie and I struck up a real close friendship at the athletic department. When he came in he was totally lost. He didn't know what he was going to do and how he was going to do it, because he hadn't done it before. But, he took over and the next season he got his feet wet. His second season was one the University will never forget. It was the biggest surprise any of us could imagine, being national champs. Herbie used the Vulcans (junior team) as his farm club. He liked the older, tougher, hard-grinding players, who knew how to win and were more mature. Herbie was something else. I've never known anyone who fought as hard for his program as he did. Herbie was fun to be around, a fabulous coach, fun to travel with, and a whale of a nice guy." — *Tom Greenhoe, former Gophers Sports Information Director*

"Herbie was a symbol of Minnesota hockey and he inspired me to be a better person. I remember the first Gopher game I ever saw, I walked in to Williams Arena as a seventh grader and saw Herbie down on the bench. I went and bought a pair of maroon and gold wrist bands at the concession stand and I said to myself that someday I was going to be a part of that. And even though Elk River, my hometown, was just starting hockey at that time, there was never any doubt in my mind that that was going to happen. Well, I went on to play one year as a freshman under Herbie, on the 1979 national championship team. Even though I didn't get to play in any games that year as the third goalie, he had a big impact on my life. I later spent a summer in New York with him, trying out with the Rangers before I played on the U.S. National team, and I had forgotten how hellish his practices were! From there, we became business partners and great friends. Even today, I use a lot of his psychology in my own coaching style. In fact, I relate a lot of what I learned from him to the kids I work with now. Even more than that though, I just really valued his friendship and the advice that he gave me over the years. He was just always there for me when I needed him, on personal matters as well as on business stuff, and I just totally respected the guy." — *Paul Ostby, former Gopher player and business associate*

"Herbie was a very close, personal friend of mine for a very long time. We go way back. Our fathers worked together and we have just been close friends for many, many years. He was a dear friend and I will just miss everything about him." — *Bruce Telander, former Gopher Blue Line Club president and longtime friend*

"Herb was a very good friend and someone I greatly respected. He helped me when I needed it and I thought a lot of him. Between he and John Mariucci, boy did they do a lot for hockey. Losing Herb was a real blow for the entire hockey world, he will really be missed. You know, I haven't even been able to call Patti yet, I am just still struggling with it. I am just going to miss him. He was a good hockey man." — *Amo Bessone, former Michigan Tech Head Coach*

"I have known Herb for a long time and he was a dear friend. I played with him, I coached with him on several teams and worked with him for many years. Between the 1980 Olympics, the Rangers and the Penguins, we shared a lot together. He was someone who brought a lot of passion to our business and to our sport. I never met anybody who cared more about hockey than he did and he never let an opportunity go by where he could pass that passion on to someone else to try to teach them something. I admired him a great deal and will miss him very much. He was just born to teach and had such amazing God given talents. He was a special person. I am just so sorry that I didn't get a chance to say good bye to him." — *Craig Patrick, General Manager of Pittsburgh Penguins & longtime friend*

WHAT IS THE BIGGEST THING YOU LEARNED FROM HERBIE?

"Personally, I learned the most about hockey from Herbie. For example, I was amazed at the Russian hockey skills and I soon realized Herb was one of very few North Americans who wasn't timid about admiring the skills and creativity of the Russians and other European teams, from having played against them. I constantly quizzed him as I watched him assemble his own hybrid style with the Gophers in the '70s, and I got so I could anticipate his moves. I was coaching Squirts, Peewees, Bantams, and summer-league college guys at the time, as my two sons grew up, and I used what I learned from Herbie that the most creative styles aren't copied from tradition, but are what you might invent out of your own mind. He was the best there was at that." — *John Gilbert, former Star-Tribune hockey reporter and longtime friend*

"Everybody admired Herbie's success, but I don't think there were that many people who really realized how he did it. When I sat down and spoke with him way back in the early 1980s, he told me that I had to follow my heart and be my own person. He told me that I can't be something I am not, and to not try to be something I wasn't. I guess I never really realized everything that he had said to me and how much of an impact it had on me. Obviously, the Xs and Os are one thing, and the philosophical, technical and tactical things are another, but his message always came back to just being yourself and doing what you think is right. He used to say 'let your players be an extension of who you are,' and that message became pretty clear. So, I learned a lot from Herbie." — *Mike Sertich, former UM-Duluth Head Coach*

"I think I learned to give a sh--. I think I have learned to be able to sit down and be thankful for what you I been given. Now, I don't have the gifts that some people have, but I have some great gifts. Herbie would remind me that the good Lord had given me some gifts, and then he would challenge me to see what I would do with them. So, it goes from being thankful for having a gift, and then having a responsibility that goes with that gift — to try to give that back. Herbie brought that out in me. I am not trying to sound like I am Mr. Wonderful here or anything, but I knew early on that I had a talent to work with young people. I really like kids, and I can express that. I don't think Herbie could do that. He always felt like he had to wait until later, after they were no longer his players, to tell them that. When he was mad at a guy he would tell him that he expected more from him than he was seeing, and that was sort of a 'put-down compliment.' Herbie was the master of double-talk, where he had a little angle behind everything he did or said. I mean on one hand he was telling that kid that he was not playing at the level he thought he was capable of, but on the other hand he was telling him that he was good, and that he was capable. That was Herbie. He wanted people to work a little harder, listen a little more and give it just a little more effort. He made you think about every little thing he said to you. He wanted his players, his friends, his family, everyone, to get better — and he wasn't afraid to challenge them. He was tough on you, but you always knew that it was for your benefit. Only Herbie could do that. If I tried to do the things he did or say the things he said, I think the guys would leave! But, that was Herbie, he was the greatest. You knew that if he pushed you, that he believed in you, and that was one of his best attributes. He made you think that if you did things, and worked hard, then you could achieve anything. He subconsciously rose your expectations of what you thought you could do in your own life. That was amazing. The other thing with Herbie was that he reminded you that you couldn't do it by yourself.

"I remember one time when Herbie was coaching the Gophers and I was coaching at Rosemount. I asked him why in the world he would put Donnie Micheletti alongside Steve Christoff and Timmy Harrer on the same line? He had these two gifted scorers in Christoff and Harrer, and then he was putting Micheletti in there, who was not a goal-scorer. Herbie would tell me, 'that is the right line.' He just believed in it, and knew that they would all make each other better. Well, it worked. I mean by the time Mick was a senior he was scoring a bunch, and it turned out to be the perfect balance to that line. Mick kept them in line, protected them, got in front of the net and just made the other guys better. As a result, his skill level went up, he got better and the team got better. I joke about this with Mick all the time, he is one of my best friends, and he would say 'I had to get better, those guys were so damn fast, I was just trying to keep up with them!' Herbie just had that gift to be able to identify talent and to put the right combinations of guys together out there to work as a team. You know, even though Christoff and Harrer were both outstanding players, Herbie let them know that they weren't very good without Mick. He reminded them that he did things that they couldn't do, and that they needed him. He celebrated players' differences and used that to make his teams better. He didn't need 20 Mr. Hockeys who were all goal scorers, he knew that he needed a blend of talent to be successful and that is what he did. He knew that a Billy Butters, a tough, physical, character guy, was just as important as a Steve Christoff, a goal scorer, and that is why he won three national championships at the University of Minnesota. Herbie was the epitome of 'the name on the front of your jersey was always more important the name on the back.' Herbie reminded his players that no one person was ever the reason a team won, and visa versa, that no one player was ever the reason why the team lost. It was a team game and he reminded them that every player had a role on the team and that they won and lost as a group. Period." — *Larry Hendrickson, former area high school hockey coach and longtime friend*

"I don't know that I could limit it to just one thing, there were so many. First of all, I would say that he taught me that in order to do something well, you have to be totally prepared in advance. You just can't spend enough time in preparation, that is so key. Then, the answer to every problem is to just get busy and work harder. Finally, Herbie taught me by his example. He taught me how important it was to appreciate and stick with the values that you grew up with. So, no matter how much he was sought by people who were in the public eye, he always wanted to spend more time with the common person — a person like myself perhaps, or like the people from the East Side of St. Paul. You know, any youth, high school or college coach who had a question for him, he was there for them. So, being true to his own grass roots development really shaped a lot of his own philosophies for developing hockey in the country. He strongly believed in that." — *Jack Blatherwick, Brooks' former strength & conditioning coach and longtime friend*

"To stand up for what you believe in and to be passionate. Herbie was all about passion, in whatever he did. He loved to challenge people and find out where they were coming from. For Herbie it didn't matter how big you got or how good you were in anything, he never let you forget your roots and where you came from. He always described himself as a 'Joe six-pack' from Payne Avenue in St. Paul, yet he influenced a nation through the sport of hockey. Really, he influenced the game of hockey throughout the world. Not bad for a 'Joe six-pack' from Payne Avenue in St. Paul! And even though I am an attorney now, Herbie always reminded me that I was just a lunch bucket guy from International Falls. He's right, that is who I am and I am proud of that." — *Neil Sheehy, hockey agent and close friend*

"Perseverance, and maybe the fact that I shouldn't blow up so many bridges. There is a path to an easier life and it does not involve blowing up bridges and it is not taking on an adversarial approach almost every endeavor he got involved with. He loved challenges and I think he loved the battle which would ensue, and that is what made him so unique." — *Murray Williamson, former Gopher teammate and 1972 U.S. Olympic coach*

"I learned so much. His attention to detail and work ethic were two of the biggest things. He used to always say 'plan your work and work your plan.' So many things, he just taught me a lot about life. Herbie was a great teacher and he definitely taught me a great deal." — *Craig Dahl, St. Cloud State Head Coach and former Brooks assistant*

"I learned from Herbie that if you are prepared, give it an honest effort, play smart and play as a team, then you have a great chance to succeed." — *Tom Vanelli, former Gopher player*

"Herbie not only taught us a lot about hockey, he taught us a lot about life. He just did not put up with loafers and he didn't pamper anyone either. I remember one time I got my teeth knocked out in practice one day and so I was heading down to the locker room to get them checked out. Well, as I was skating off the ice, Herbie came over and said, 'get out here, we have another hour of practice left!' If you played for Herbie you just had to give 110% all the time, because if you didn't you were going to *A)* hear about it and *B)* ride the pines." — *Pat Phippen, former Gopher player*

"I learned how to set goals; how to have a plan to achieve those goals; to be aware that it is not easy... wait. Let me rephrase that. What's the biggest thing I learned from Herbie? I learned how to be a winner. Period. That's what I learned, plain and simple." — *Robb McClanahan, former Gopher & Olympic player*

"I learned how to be a man from Herbie. I loved hockey when I became a Gopher, and when I was done I loved it even more. He just took me to another level that I didn't think I was capable of getting to and that was incredible. He taught me how to achieve goals to be the best player and person that I could be." — *Buzz Schneider, former Gopher & Olympic player*

"I learned to prepare, to do my homework and to never get beat for a lack of effort. You know, even if you weren't the most gifted player, Herbie felt that you could make up for that with hard work and with preparation. That was what Herbie was all about, working harder than the next guy." — *Phil Verchota, former Gopher & Olympic player*

"The biggest thing I learned from Herbie that I was able to take with me into the real world was proper preparation. He used to always tell us that we couldn't just come to play on Friday and Saturday and turn it on like it was some kind of light switch. He really emphasized practicing and preparing. He told us that however well we were going to play on Friday and Saturday came down to how hard we worked and how well we prepared ourselves between Monday through Thursday. He was a firm, firm believer in that and he pushed us very hard to be our best. I even remember a saying he had, 'competition without preparation is suicide.' He pushed you almost to your breaking point because he wanted to get the most out of you. So, what I have learned from him is that if you work hard and prepare, then you are going to succeed. He taught me that nothing comes easy. You have to work hard and prepare hard, then you will do well." — *Mike Polich, former Gopher player*

"I would say it was to be a man of character. If your word means anything then when you shake somebody's hand, you look them in the eye and say what is in your heart, then you don't need a contract. You live by your word. I learned that from Herbie." — *Bill Butters, former Gopher player*

"Herbie had a favorite saying, 'don't prostitute your principles,' and that was something he believed strongly in. So I learned that, as well as honesty from him. He stood by his principles and he never wavered from them. I respected that greatly about him." — *Roger Wigen, former St. Paul Johnson High School Hockey teammate*

"You realized how much you didn't know when you spent time with Herbie. Playing for him was like a total enlightenment. He just made you better and was really amazing that way." — *Mark Pavelich, former player on 1980 U.S. Olympic Team & NY Rangers*

"I think that integrity and honesty are the two words that really come to my mind. I learned so much from him, but those two really stand out." — *Steve Badalich, long-time friend*

"Honesty and integrity. That is what I learned from Herbie because that was who he was. He was also right to the point and never pulled any punches. I mean if you were acting like an a--hole, he told you so. And he wasn't afraid to tell you that to your face either. He was just a straight shooter and I respected that about him. There was no bull-sh-- with him, he was just a man of his word." — *LeRoy Houle, longtime friend*

"The biggest thing I learned from Herb was that everybody had a story. Everybody, no matter who they are. Since his death I can tell you that I have become more tolerant, more patient and have become a lot more open to people — no matter who they are." — *Butch Bloom, longtime friend*

"To give it your best shot and never look back and say that you could've done a little bit more. You just can't rest on your laurels. It was like in the 1980 Olympics when they beat the Russians in the semifinals, he knew that they couldn't relax because that next game was going to be the most important one of their lives. They did, and they won the gold medal. I can still remember his statement of telling those guys that if they lost that next game they would all take it to the grave. He was never satisfied with just good enough, he always demanded that they do better." — *Tommy Reid, former North Star & current Wild radio analyst*

"I learned focus, determination, honesty and hard work. He taught me a lot. Maybe I didn't understand that early on in my playing career, but now I see that the things that he tried to teach me were all right on." — *Steve Christoff, former Gopher & Olympic player*

"Herbie was such a great motivator. A lot of people know Xs and Os, but knowing how to get guys fired up to play is something entirely different. I mean he put that psychology degree to work every day with us. He worked us hard when we were playing well and then backed off when we weren't. You know, we would sweep a series over a weekend and then he would skate us to death on Monday and Tuesday. Then, if we lost a series, he would take it easy on us. That was his style. He worked very hard and just demanded excellence from everyone around him." — *Reed Larson, former Gopher player*

"Persistence. Herb was a very persistent and determined guy. He was willing to stick to his principles no matter what, even if that meant costing him his job. If Herb had a point of view he was going to voice it and he was willing to take the consequences. I respected that." — *Bob Paradise, former teammate & father-in-law to his daughter*

"The biggest thing that I learned from Herbie was to remember to take time out for other people involved in hockey, to go out of your way to help organizations if they ask you to come out and to just be available to share your knowledge. Herbie was so knowledgeable of the game and just always went out his way to talk to people and to help them. I just respected him a great deal for that." — *Phil Housley, former 2002 Olympian under Brooks & former NHL All-Star*

"He taught me so much. In fact, I learned more about the game of hockey from Herb than from anyone else in my career, and I learned a lot about life from him as well. He taught me how to motivate, he taught me hard work, he just taught me so much. The thing that stands out here though, is the way he cared for people. He was tireless and went out of his way for people and that is what I learned most from him. Even now, as I work as a hockey television analyst, my understanding of the game goes all the way back to Herb and from what he taught me. So, he will always be with me, teaching me and encouraging me, even now that he is gone." — *Joe Micheletti, former Gopher player & current Fox Sports TV hockey analyst*

"I think I learned how to be a better person when I was around Herbie. He was just a great guy. I always thought that whatever he did was right. He could just do no wrong as far as I was concerned." — *Paul Johnson, former Olympic teammate and longtime friend*

"As a player with the Gophers, he prepared me for my NHL career. Then, I got to Buffalo and played for Scotty Bowman, who was similar in style to Herbie. So, that was an easy transition for me. Herb took me from a boy to a man, and I will always be grateful for that. Then, as a coach, Herb was very innovative and had a lot of different ideas. He was never afraid to express those ideas either, whether you agreed with them or not." — *Mike Ramsey, former Gopher & Olympic player and current Wild assistant coach*

"The importance of working hard all the time was first and foremost. He showed me that if you work hard towards your goals then you can attain them. Then, he taught me to play my game, and to just stick with who you brought to the dance. He also encouraged me to focus on my weaknesses so that I could work on them to get better. For me, that meant puck handling, and as soon as I got better at that, my confidence went way up in every other aspect of my game." — *Paul Holmgren, former Gopher player & NHL player and coach*

"To always believe that you can accomplish anything if you work for it." — *Mike Eruzione, former 1980 Olympian*

"I think communication was the biggest thing I learned from Herbie. You might not always agree with how he taught you different things, but you could talk to him and get things out in the open, no matter what it was." — *Eric Strobel, former Gopher & Olympic player*

"What it takes to win. There are a lot of little pieces of the puzzle that go into that, but he knew how to win and he passed that along to his players. He just hated to lose. The fear of losing was as great as the joy of winning with Herbie." — *Dean Blais, former Gopher player & current head coach at the University of North Dakota*

"I would say game management, which means getting the right people out on the ice and having a feel for whose hot. Certainly, there are pecking orders on any team and roles that certain players play, but Herb could recognize when guys were playing well and then go with those guys. Then, it was the ability to work the clock, to break periods down into pockets of time and to create line combinations. Finally, it was motivation, and Herb was the best at that, bar none." — *John Harrington, former Gopher & Olympic player*

"To be fair and to be honest, particularly when you are working with young people. That was Herbie." — *Lou Cotroneo, former St. Paul Johnson High School hockey coach & longtime friend*

"I learned to believe that through hard work and perseverance that anything could happen. I also learned a lot about motivation and gained a much bigger compassion for the game as well." — *Warren Strelow, former goalie coach under Brooks and longtime friend*

"I think discipline would be the biggest thing and then respect for my teammates would be second." — *Bill Baker, former Gopher & Olympic player*

"I learned so much from him, but the main thing was hard work and just being a team player. That was so important to him, that we worked hard and that we played together as a team." — *Neal Broten, former Gopher, Olympian and North Star*

"He taught me that you could have a lot of success in life and still be a regular guy."
— Gary Gambucci, former Gopher and teammate on two U.S. National teams

"As a coach he taught me to do things my own way. He knew that there were many different paths you could take to be successful and just felt strongly that you had to be comfortable in the path that you picked for yourself. He stressed that you have to coach to your personality too, that was important. Then, and maybe most important-ly, he taught me to never be satisfied and to always be reaching for more. So, I learned a great deal from Herbie, he was a great coach." *— Craig Sarner, former Gopher and player under Brooks on 1979 U.S. National Team and in Europe & long-time coach at various levels*

"I think I learned that sometimes it is great to be the underdog because that is really when you achieve. You have to give 120% when you are the underdog, but it is that much more rewarding and satisfying when you win." *— John Mayasich, former teammate on U.S. National Teams & longtime friend*

"How to keep people focused on what they are doing. I think his knowledge was transferable to all walks of life. He just had a blueprint for success and could then motivate like heck to get stuff done." *— Dave Knoblauch, longtime friend*

"To be creative in the game of hockey. I learned so much from him, both on and off the ice. He was such a great teacher. He taught me how to create and how to com-municate, to become a better person." *— Nick Fotiu, former New York Ranger under Brooks*

"That passion can carry you further than anything else in life." *— Brian Lawton, hockey agent and former North Star under Brooks*

"I learned that with the belief that we could win, and understanding what it took to do that, we could enjoy success." *— Jim Boo, former Gopher player*

"Herbie was huge in relating motivation to people. He was a coach to everybody: his teams, his friends, his business associates and his family. He was just always coach-ing in whatever he was doing. His methods of motivation were really unique too. You know, we have a tendency in our society as coaches and as people that when things are going well, we pat people on the back and say 'great job, way to go.' Then, conversely, when things are going poorly, we get real negative. Herbie was just the polar opposite of that. For him it was all about reverse psychology. So, when things were going well, that is when he put the heat on and asked for more — because that is when an athlete or a person is most receptive to that kind of psychology. Then, when things were going poorly, he would back off. Now, sure, sometimes you need a kick in the butt, but for the most part he would ease up on you when you were down.

   "You know, I remember one time when we were in business together, he and I got into a huge, face-to-face shouting f--- you match with each other. It went on and on and on until finally Herbie took a step back, took his glasses off and just looked at me with a grin. He said, 'That's it? That's all you can handle? Holy moly Jesus Jenny, I thought you were a competitor! That is the extent of your pressure tolerance? That is all you can take? You get pushed a little bit and you just snap? Oh my God, I thought you were a competitor, boy was I wrong!' So, Herbie saw that I was in a state that was beyond discussion and was all about emotion and anger. Well, he popped the balloon and got me to think in a different way. Right away he defused the

situation and took the air out of it. That was Herbie, he could get you to go outside of your comfort zone to reach you differently. I have always carried that with me."
— *Paul Ostby, former Gopher player and business associate*

WHAT ARE YOU GOING TO MISS MOST ABOUT HERBIE?

"The confidences and the knowledge that we could discuss anything and either agree or disagree but maintain a respect for each other's views. That included heckling each other and being able to laugh at ourselves. To this day, whenever I hear of some odd or ironic little thing in hockey, my first thought is, 'I've got to call Herbie and tell him this one.' That may never go away." — *John Gilbert, former Star-Tribune hockey reporter and longtime friend*

"I will miss the note here and there; the phone call here and there; and just the conversations here and there. Although we didn't talk and communicate regularly, it was always timely. And, when we did get together, it was always about helping other people. He always had an agenda for how he wanted to rally everyone together to help out other people, and I really admired that about him. He really touched me that way. I mean here was a guy who had such success in moving pucks up and down the rink and could still be so focused on the humanity of the sport. It just blew me away, and I will miss that about him." — *Mike Sertich, former UM-Duluth Head Coach*

"I think his vision. He was always thinking ahead and he just had a great passion for the game and for young people who wanted to get into the game. I think helping me was a prime example of that. I will miss so much about him, he was a great friend." — *Brad Buetow, former Gopher Head Coach*

"What was fun about having Herbie as a friend was that almost every time you spent time with him, you would talk about values. He was constantly talking about values — about what was important in life?; why do we live?; what is our objective?; are we working hard enough?; and what can we do to make it better? To me, to talk about those things was exciting. When you were with him it was always exciting. I just feel that he was a notch above me, but I loved him. It is so hard to explain. I remember one time when I was coaching the Apple Valley High School team and Herbie came out to one of our games. We were down by four goals to Bloomington Jefferson but came back in the last period and rallied to win. So, afterward, Herbie and I are sitting in this cheap 3:2 joint, "Sandy's Tap," on 67th and Penn, talking hockey. We just spent the night talking about what it takes to get your team to come back like that and to not quit. The lessons we talked about were life lessons, it was like sitting in church with him. It was just so fun to be with him. I mean we were eating crappy burgers and drinking watered down 3:2 beer, but those are the wonderful memories that I will never forget with Herbie.

"I remember another time, when his Gophers were playing at Wisconsin, he invited me to come along and stay in his room with him. I remember staying up all night and diagramming plays with bottle caps on the hotel room table, and just being in awe of him. It is all of those little memories that I will cherish forever. It was watching his kids, Danny and Kelly, grow up. I remember him buying that house on Turtle Lake and him being so worried that he couldn't afford it. Just to watch his whole evolution as a family man, as a coach and as a person was such a privilege to be a part of. Then, getting to know Patti, she is such a wonderful person. What she has done behind the scenes for charity and for her friends, it is so neat to be a part of that too. The whole family, they are such first class people. Really, Herbie's passing is just a hell of a loss." — *Larry Hendrickson, former area high school hockey coach and longtime friend*

"Certainly his love, kindness and loyalty. There was no more loyal person than Herbie. I think his love and kindness very often were hidden in the way he expressed himself. He grew up in a generation where showing affection was not something that adult males did very often. So, he showed his respect and his love by constantly raising the bar for people who he thought had potential. For players, he raised the bar every single day of the year, and that was oftentimes painful; for friends, it was not always comfortable; and for anyone who sat in a position of authority to help youngsters, it could be a nightmare." — *Jack Blatherwick, Brooks' former strength & conditioning coach and longtime friend*

"I will miss his companionship. I think that over the last eight years or so, aside from the people I work with and my family, I probably spent more time with Herbie than any other person on the planet. He was a great friend. I will miss our conversations and the way he always challenged and needled me. He never gave you any slack and was always pushing you to be better and to never be satisfied with where you were at." — *Neil Sheehy, hockey agent and close friend*

"His friendship, and really that was more off the ice than it was hockey related. We were just good friends." — *Murray Williamson, former Gopher teammate and 1972 U.S. Olympic coach*

"I ask myself who is going to carry to torch for all of his 'radical ideas' about making U.S. amateur hockey better. He had a tremendous influence on changing things and was hard at work right up until the day he died, trying to get the entire USA Hockey youth program restructured. And it wasn't just about kids either, it was about developing coaches too. Herbie always talked about broadening the base of the pyramid, and that was a vision which needs to be carried out for the good of the game. His theory was that if you give more kids an opportunity to play and give them good coaching, then you are going to have more and better players down the road — as opposed to just picking out a select few and concentrating on them. I agree with all of that. In fact, I don't think we should even have any traveling teams until after Christmas. They should all have to play in a house league with the better players having to play with the not so good players. That will make them all better over time. Herbie had so many great ideas and I think we will all miss his passion to make change and do what he felt was right for the game." — *Craig Dahl, St. Cloud State Head Coach and former Brooks assistant*

"I will miss the confidence of knowing that hockey was in good hands with Herbie. He did so much for the game and we should all be grateful for that." — *Tom Vanelli, former Gopher player*

"We are all going to miss him so much. It is so sad that he is gone and it is really a tragedy. He was such a great person and great coach, and I will never forget him. He was just like a second father to all of us. If you needed some good advice after hockey was over, he was always there for you. When you played for him he was tough, but afterwards, he was great, and I will just miss talking to him and having a beer with him the most. We could talk about anything. He was such a neat person." — *Pat Phippen, former Gopher player*

"I will miss giving him crap whenever we got together, something we didn't have the ability to do 25 years ago when we were too young to know better. It was great to get together with him later in life though because it was fun to see him. We had such good interactions with each other and I am going to miss that. You know, playing golf and giving him a hard time, that is what I will miss most." — *Robb McClanahan, former Gopher & Olympic player*

"I am just going to miss having him around. You know just seeing him and saying hello and finding out what is new, that is what I am going to really miss. Whenever I would talk to him he was always analyzing every team, every coach and every player that he was watching at that time. He was always coaching, right up until the end." — *Buzz Schneider, former Gopher & Olympic player*

"I am just going to miss the opportunity to sit down and actually just visit with him about anything and everything. You know, we never really developed a relationship beyond coach/player, and unfortunately we won't ever get that opportunity. I envied a lot of other guys, guys like Billy Butters for instance, who were able to connect with Herb on a friendship basis. I wish I could've had that, but I am just grateful to have known him and played for him nonetheless." — *Phil Verchota, former Gopher & Olympic player*

"I am going to miss just seeing him on the golf course and talking to him. My kids played junior hockey and sometimes I would call him to run some things by him and he was always there for me. Even though he was so busy, he would always call me back very quickly and say 'Michael, here is what I would suggest...'. He was a sort of sounding board for me and I was able to use him as a tremendous resource to advise my own kids. That was invaluable because I looked up to him so much for his advice. And with Herbie, a lot of times he wouldn't tell you what you would like to hear, he would tell you his opinion with brutal honesty, whatever it was. I respected that and valued that. In fact, we even spoke recently about getting together with my son, who is going to play hockey at Colorado College this Fall, for breakfast, to just talk hockey. I was really looking forward to that, and my son was so excited about it too. I will miss that breakfast with my old friend. I will miss Herbie." — *Mike Polich, former Gopher player*

"I will miss his phone calls and just hearing his voice. I knew that I meant something to him and wasn't just some guy. I mean with a lot of hockey people you could be talking to them and if somebody more important walked by they will leave you to talk to them. That was not Herbie. He would spend time with even guys like me and that was special. I will miss driving up north with him or seeing him in Rochester at a hockey game, or whatever. So, I will miss that time with him." — *Bill Butters, former Gopher player*

"I am going to miss the every other day phone calls that said, 'Hey Roger, what's going on?' Just the little stuff, that is what I am going to miss. He was just a special person. He went far beyond just being a good friend. Whenever there was something that you thought was bad, he would turn it into something good." — *Roger Wigen, former St. Paul Johnson High School Hockey teammate*

"Herbie was constantly coaching, in whatever he was doing, whether it was hockey or golf or just life in general. And he always had an opinion, boy did he have an opinion!" — *Steve Badalich, longtime friend*

"I am going to miss having my best friend around. You know, I sell dirt. And Herbie was always planting something or tinkering with something over there at his house. Well, I always knew when he came over to take my dirt because there was always several little holes in my dirt pile. I knew it was him. He would come over with his five gallon pails and take a bunch of dirt and then take off. I would call him that night then, and say 'You son of a bitch, you were in my dirt pile again weren't you?!' And he would laugh and laugh! He would say 'You owe me that dirt from the other day when I helped you.' He used to just love to come and help me trim trees and work with me. I would be trimming trees and he would come with and be my ground man on the job. He just loved it. He just did it because he loved it and because he liked to hang out with me and get dirty. He really helped me out a lot over the years. Hell, he even helped me paint my house. Three days in a row he came over here, that was the kind of guy Herb Brooks was. So, I am going to not only miss my friend, I am going to miss finding those holes in my dirt pile and knowing that Herbie had been there." — *LeRoy Houle, longtime friend*

"I am going to just miss having him around. We spent a lot of time doing a lot of different things together and I am just going to miss having him around to give me a hard time. We used to get together and laugh like hell and I am going to miss that. He was the world's greatest chain-jerker. He loved that and he made life fun. You know, he was also such a kind person and would go way out of his way to help anybody. And he was always checking up on people to see how they were doing and to see if he could do anything to help them. Then, he would follow up with a warm note, or a call, just to let them know that he cared. He was a special guy." — *Butch Bloom, longtime friend*

"The thing I will remember most about him was that whenever something happened, good or bad, in someone's life, they got a note from Herbie. He never forgot to send you a little note to congratulate you or to say some kind words about you. He did that with so many people and I tell you, when you got a note from Herbie it was really something special. Those little things made such an impact on people's lives. He just had a way of reminding people how important those things were in his life and that you accomplished things and were doing OK. I will miss that." — *Tommy Reid, former North Star & current Wild radio analyst*

"Herbie was the leader of our hockey teams and I am going to miss him. I just totally trusted the guy and really believed in him. So, now that he is not going to be around any more, that is just a very sad thing." — Steve Christoff, former Gopher & Olympic player

"You know, as I got older I was able to get to know him better as a friend. Before it was on a different level, as a coach/player, but later on it was just as two hockey guys — and that was neat. Later, it was just fun to see him with that big smile on his face and seeing a different side of him that wasn't so intense. He was actually a pretty funny guy, and not a lot of people saw that side of him." — *Reed Larson, former Gopher player*

"Herbie was a great mentor for me. I had so many questions and he would always give me great advice. We spent a lot of time together out on the road seeing players and going to games. Those were the best times because we could just relax and visit. I really enjoyed our friendship. He had so many great stories to tell and I could just listen to him for hours on end. So, I will miss talking to him and just being with him." — *Greg Malone, Pittsburgh Penguins head of scouting*

"I used to love seeing him at my son's house, where he was always doing projects. He loved that kind of stuff. Then, he used to love to play with the grandkids. I think that is what I will miss most, seeing how happy he was being with them. I am just so sad that he won't be around to see those little guys grow up. They meant so much to him. He was just a wonderful grandpa." — *Bob Paradise, former teammate & father-in-law to his daughter*

"I will miss the conversations and just being around him. He was such a great guy. He was witty and quick with the one-liners, and really just fun to be around." — *Phil Housley, former 2002 Olympian under Brooks & former NHL All-Star*

"Herbie was the consummate promoter of his sport. He was such a neat guy to just sit and talk with too. You learned so much from being around him. His ability to speak what he thought was great and he was such an honest and sincere guy. You know, both my parents went to St. Paul Johnson High School, where Herbie went, so Herbie knew that I had East side roots and we sort of had that special connection." — *Steve Ulseth, former Gopher player*

"There is just going to be a big void in a lot of different areas. You know the thing about Herb was when you talked to him or were just around him, there was an instant inspiration of some sort. He was like a walking shot of adrenaline! Some of it was just a sense of you have to keep doing something with your life, meaning don't get lazy and keep accomplishing your goals. He didn't have to tell you that, but he sort of inspired you to be your best, no matter what you were doing. He just always wanted to accomplish things and was such a motivating factor to do well. He also had such a passion for everything he did, whether it was hockey, or with friendships, or just in life — he was so passionate. And, he always wanted to help people and to be there for them. That truly inspired me and I will miss that about him." — *Joe Micheletti, former Gopher player & current Fox Sports TV hockey analyst*

"Herbie was a reminder to me that the ideals which he stood for were always present and whenever I talked to him it brought me back to my basic value system." — *Noel Rahn, longtime friend*

"I am just going to miss my old friend, he was a great person." — *Paul Johnson, former Olympic teammate and longtime friend*

"I will just miss seeing him at games and the banter that we used to have back and forth with each other. You know, as a young player you could never do that with him, but later it was totally different and so much fun. So, I will definitely miss that." — *Mike Ramsey, former Gopher & Olympic player and current Wild assistant coach*

"Herbie was Minnesota hockey. Period. The entire hockey world will miss him tremendously. He was a real figure head for hockey not only in Minnesota, but in the United States. He will never be forgotten by many, many people. Personally, I will miss bumping into him at an odd game and talking about hockey and about the old times. You know, we were both from the East side of St. Paul and we loved to talk about that too. He was just a great man." — *Paul Holmgren, former Gopher player & NHL player and coach*

"I will miss his passion for the game. The love of the game that he had was unparalleled. Certainly, he had his own ideas about how he thought the game should be played, whether that was here in Minnesota or with USA Hockey, and sometimes he was controversial. But he always had his heart in the right place and did things which he thought would better the game. The thing that really set him apart was that he was never afraid to let you know what he thought. He wore everything on his sleeve and didn't sugarcoat anything. He stood for what he believed in and I respected that." — *Don Lucia, Gopher Hockey head coach*

"I will miss the friendship the most. You know, just the little things, like the phone calls to see how I was doing or running into him somewhere on the road at a hockey game. I will just miss having him around, he was a great, great man." — *Mike Eruzione, former 1980 Olympian*

"I will miss him as a coach and as a person. He was always so nice to me and my family. I mean he came to both my parents funerals and that meant so much to me. Sure, there will be a void with him gone, but a small part of him will live on in all of us who knew him." — *Eric Strobel, former Gopher & Olympic player*

"Herbie was a good friend and I will miss him. I will miss seeing him at games, I will miss his phone calls to see how I was doing, and I will just miss the little things like that. You know, if I ever lost a couple games in a row, I would always get a little inspirational note from Herbie in the mail. He was just great that way and I will really miss that." — *Dean Blais, former Gopher player & current head coach at the University of North Dakota*

"I will miss his convictions for what he believed in. Herb could certainly get up on the soap box with the best of them, but he would always be definitive and decisive in what he said and in what he believed. He just believed in what he said and made sure people knew what his message was. Then, it was the little things, like the odd note here or there, and stuff like that. He just never forgot his former players and I will miss that." — *John Harrington, former Gopher & Olympic player*

"I used to talk to Herbie about every other day, so I am going to miss him terribly. We used to love to talk about hockey and about life. Herbie will still be with me every day because I think about him all the time. He just meant so much to me, I still can't believe that he is really gone. I was so close to him, but I don't think I ever felt as close to him as I feel right now. He was just such an amazing person." — *Warren Strelow, former goalie coach under Brooks and longtime friend*

"You know, after the Olympics, we became friends and every time I would see him I would just get a shot of adrenaline. Just seeing him gave me such a rush and I am going to really miss that." — *Neal Broten, former Gopher, Olympian and North Star*

"Just knowing that he was there and that you could count on him for whatever it was that you needed him for, that is what I will miss most. You know, seeing him at games or playing golf, that kind of stuff. Herbie just personified what Gopher hockey was all about. It was the people and the relationships. It also meant that you were tied into a business network too. And Herb was great to me there as well, always trying to throw me new business here and there, and I always appreciated that. I just felt bad calling him because I knew that so many people called him and were tugging at him all the time. Everybody wanted a piece of Herbie and that was tough for him sometimes I think. But, overall, I will just miss my old friend." — *Gary Gambucci, former Gopher and teammate on two U.S. National teams*

"I will miss the rare times when he would let his hair down. I think some of the best times I ever had with Herb were when we actually didn't talk about hockey. I mean he was very smart, very well read, and was always interested in everything from politics to the economy to gardening. He was also the consummate tinkerer, and was always looking for new ways to do things. Then, I will miss the long phone conversations which seemed to carry on for hours. But, they were never dull, and you always learned something too. So, I will miss all that, but mostly I will just miss him. He was a great person and a great friend." — *Craig Sarner, former Gopher and player under Brooks on 1979 U.S. National Team and in Europe & longtime coach at various levels*

"He just left us too early. He set such high standards not only as a player and coach, but as a person, and I will miss that. We were just good friends and I will miss him. It was such a tragedy." — *John Mayasich, former teammate on U.S. National Teams & longtime friend*

"I will miss my visits and chats with him. We have had some great conversations together over the years and that will be hard to let go of. Probably my most memorable conversation with him happened a few years ago. I was sitting here at my house watching the pre-game show for the Pittsburgh Penguins and my phone rang. It was Herbie, and he had just thought about something that he wanted to tell me regarding the Hall of Fame and wanted to visit. I asked him, 'Herb, aren't you coaching the game tonight?' and he said 'Yeah, I am in the locker room right now.' So, I am watching on TV as the players are starting to head out onto the ice to start the game, and I said 'ah Herbie…' and he says, 'Yeah, I gotta run, I have a game to coach.' That was Herb. He was just always thinking about hockey. You know, his support for the Hockey Hall of Fame was just the greatest. Whatever he could do to help the Hall, he would do, and we appreciated that so much." — *Jim Findley, President of the U.S. Hockey Hall of Fame*

"I will miss talking over the back fence about his garden or sitting on our back porch talking about our kids. He used to take my kids out for Dairy Queen and make them promise that they wouldn't tell us because he knew that we would kick his butt. You know, we used to see each other quite a bit up at Shadow Ridge, this little driving range in the neighborhood. I remember one of the last times I talked to him, we were hitting balls and he said that he was considering becoming a left handed golfer. He thought that if he worked at it over the Winter that maybe that would be the cure to his golf game. And do you know what? He probably could have. He just worked so hard at things and was so determined in whatever he did. He just felt that if you did your thing, and did it well, then you would be a success, regardless of what that was. So, I will miss his friendship and I will miss his determination." — *Bob Rink, next-*

door neighbor and longtime friend

"Just being with him and listening to him talk. We loved to talk hockey and I was always fascinated every time we spoke. Once you got him started talking, well, then you knew that you were in for the long haul. He was just a great person, and I will miss him dearly." — *Frank Messin, former hockey referee and longtime friend*

"You know, it was the little things with Herb that made such a difference. I remember a few days after I won the national championship with Wisconsin in 1990, I got a really nice note from Herbie telling me what a great job I did and that he hoped I had a great Summer. Then, a few years back when my father died, who shows up? Herbie. I really appreciated that so much. We were both St. Paul guys, and we respected each other a great deal. He was just such a thoughtful person and I thought the world of him. He was one of those guys who was bigger than life and I still can't believe that he is gone." — *Jeff Sauer, former University of Wisconsin & Colorado College Head Coach*

"I will miss his brutal honesty. Herbie always spoke his mind and never pulled any punches." — *Gregg Wong, former Pioneer Press columnist*

"I am going to miss seeing him at games and then wondering what his next project was going to be. Herb was a character. Sometimes he spoke before he thought with regards to the state of hockey, and that got him into hot water every now and then. So, I will miss seeing him get out of all that from time to time too. You know, the entire hockey world will miss him, he was just a real innovator." — *Walter Bush, Chairman of the Board, USA Hockey*

"I will miss the excellence that he stood for and the dogged determination that he had. You know, there was Herb's philosophy and there was USA Hockey's philosophy, and he had his differences with some people at the 'U,' but I can't argue which one of those was any better than the next. But the fact that here was a real strong man who had these beliefs and then stuck by them, I mean we will miss that kind of leadership." — *Frank Mazzocco, Gopher Hockey TV Analyst*

"You know, Herbie golfed in my charity tournament every year and was very loyal. In typical Herbie fashion he would always tell you that he couldn't let you know if he would be there until like a day or two before the event, but sure enough he would be there on the first tee with all the guys telling stories. So, I will miss that." — *Joe Schmit, KSTP-TV sports anchor*

"I will just miss having him around. You know, I saw him a few weeks before the accident and we talked a lot about the new movie coming out. He was so genuinely excited about being a consultant on it and was really looking forward to having the story told on the big screen. He opened up about the Olympics to me for the first time that night and that was neat to see. I just think he was in a good place right now and was really enjoying life. That is what makes the whole tragedy even more sad." — *Mark Rosen, WCCO-TV sports anchor*

"I will miss the calls, from wherever he was at the time, Saskatchewan or Manitoba or wherever. And whenever he would call that would mean that there was a project that he was working on, and that was exciting. So, I relished those calls and I will miss talking to him." — *Dave Knoblauch, longtime friend*

"I will miss seeing him, calling him and just laughing with him. We had so much damn fun when we were together. We were such great friends and I am going to miss having my friend around. But, I have wonderful memories and that is how Herbie will stay with me." — *Paul Coppo, former teammate on several U.S. National Teams and longtime friend*

"I will miss those late night phone calls once a month or so. Whenever the phone would ring that late I would look over at my wife and say, 'that's Herb…' and an hour and a half later we would get all caught up over what was wrong in the world. We were friends, and I will miss him. We shared a lot of memories together and he just left us far too soon." — *Bob Utecht, founder of Let's Play Hockey newspaper*

"I will miss his friendly smile, the kind words and the sincerity that he always displayed towards myself. I never ever felt like he was B.S.ing me, and I never felt like he didn't have time for me. He made time for everybody, no matter who you were, and that was special. He was a friend, and I will miss him." — *Brian Lawton, hockey agent and former North Star under Brooks*

"I lived pretty close to Herb so I got a chance to see him pretty often. I was lucky in that I was able to be become friends with him after my playing days and I will miss that. He helped to mold me into a man and really helped to define who I am as a person. Herb Brooks was just one of the most exceptional people in the hockey world and we will all miss him." — *Jim Boo, former Gopher player*

"There is an old quote that I think sums up Herbie pretty well and it reads: 'He was willing to do what had to be done, sacrifice what had to be sacrificed and give what he had to give.' That was Herbie to me, he was just that kind of a person. He was a missionary and an apostle. I am going to miss him and hockey is going to miss him." — *Bob Peters, longtime Bemidji State University head coach*

"I will miss the little things that he would do. He would just send you little notes or articles out of nowhere, for no reason, other than to say hello. He was very thoughtful. I remember being at a funeral this Summer and seeing Herbie in the lobby of the funeral home. I didn't know that he was going to be there, but when I saw him he ran out to his car and came back with a North Dakota tee shirt for me. My son, Zach, plays there now, and Herbie was up there scouting or something and thought I would like it. He just did little things like that and that meant the world to me. I mean, when I became an American citizen he threw me a big party out at his house. I just loved the guy." — *J.P. Parise, former North Star player and assistant coach with the North Stars under Brooks*

"I am just going to miss his friendship. Sure, he was an unbelievable coach, but to me he was also a friend." — *Paul Ostby, former Gopher player and business associate*

"How do you replace a person like Herbie who was a one of a kind and who was obviously loved by a great number of people? You can't. Watching him as he maneuvered through the minefields of life, that was the other side of Herbie. The 'adventure of Herbie' was always there and I will miss seeing that. Herbie was just a great friend to me and to my family, and we loved him.

'We just had so many great times together. I remember back in 1974, when the Gophers won their first national championship out in Boston. I was at the game with a couple of very close friends of ours, George Lyon and Bill Hurley. Well,

George did a lot of business out in Boston and knew the area, so he made reservations for a victory party at this Italian place called Dom's, before the game that night. Now, he didn't even know if we were going to win at that point, but just in case we did, he got them to stay open for a post-game celebration. So, we win the national championship, and after the game Bill, George, Paul and Nancy Giel, Herb and Patty Brooks and myself, all went back to Dom's. We didn't get there until two in the morning, but they stayed open for us and we partied till dawn. It was one of the great parties of all time, with a very select group of people who were very close to Herb. We just had so much fun. That party was obviously the beginning of a great run for Gopher Hockey, and to have been there and celebrated with those people under those circumstances is something that I will never forget. In fact, I was back in Boston just a few years ago and we went back to Dom's. And guess what, they remembered us! Thirty years later the owner's kid is now running the restaurant, but he still remembered that party!" — *Bruce Telander, former Gopher Blue Line Club president and longtime friend*

WHAT IMPACT DID HERBIE HAVE ON YOUR LIFE?

"Herb had an impact on my entire family. We watched each other's families grow up. He used to go to the clinic where my wife, Joan, was a physical therapy assistant, and he insisted she was the only one who could relieve the pain he might have in his shoulder or back. He asked my older son, Jack, to be stick boy, and he still has rich memories of Herb's first three Gopher teams. And he put my younger son, Jeff, into his Squirt (9-10) hockey school when Jeff was only about six, and he loved it when Jeff socked a big kid who was pushing him around. And for me, personally, I lost a trusted friend who was more than just a friend. I don't know if there was a topic so personal we didn't share with each other, and we felt free to offer advice to each other, and we both respected whatever we heard." — *John Gilbert, former Star-Tribune hockey reporter and longtime friend*

"I think in a lot of ways Herbie helped me to understand myself and what I was about. I think that a lot of young coaches get caught up in that. I mean one day they want to be like Bob Knight and the next day they want to be like Bobby Bowden — instead of just being themselves. Herbie taught me that I think. He was a great teacher and he showed me how to be a teacher." — *Mike Sertich, former UM-Duluth Head Coach*

"He certainly helped me as both a hockey player and as a coach. He helped me get into a profession that I have loved for more than 30 years now, so I am very grateful to him for all that he did for me. I have been able to make a good living doing what I love to do thanks to Herbie, and that is an amazing thing." — *Brad Buetow, former Gopher Head Coach*

"That is immeasurable. I knew him and worked closely with him with him for 25 years, and like anybody who has ever played for him or worked with him, they too would probably never have achieved anything like what they would have achieved had they not had Herbie's constant prodding and interest in their lives." — *Jack Blatherwick, Brooks' former strength & conditioning coach and longtime friend*

"Herbie was a man of uncompromising principles. One thing I always said to Herbie was that I would never ask him to compromise his principles, just the strategy on how he attained them. He liked that one! You know, I wrote something for the funeral that Bill Butters read, and I would like to share it because I think this is what captivated who Herbie was: 'Coach, mentor, teacher, counselor, confidante, motivator, friend — Herb Brooks was many things to many people and what he shared with every one of us was magical. His magic was captured by a nation through a hockey game in 1980, but those of us who knew him and lived with him experienced his character and his magic with each passing moment shared with him. Herb Brooks is one of those few truly remarkable people who walked this earth among us. His brilliance as a man and in hockey was only surpassed by his uncompromising principles from which he could never waiver, even to his own peril. Without hesitation, he always told us where he stood, which is why we followed. Simple yet complex, bullheaded yet compassionate, famous yet never forgot his roots, Herb Brooks impacted our lives as he gave of himself daily. He challenged us not to be ordinary, but to make a difference in our lives and become extraordinary.' That was Herb Brooks, and I will never forget him." — *Neil Sheehy, hockey agent and close friend*

"Let's put it this way… without Herbie I wouldn't be where I am today. I certainly wouldn't be coaching at St. Cloud State, and our program would never be to the point where it is now, having gone to four straight NCAA Tournaments in a row. That was his impact on me and on this program for starters. He had faith in me and he believed in me. Then, he set an example for me to follow and I will forever be grateful to him for that." — *Craig Dahl, St. Cloud State Head Coach and former Brooks assistant*

"He clearly made me understand that you have to work for what you get. And, aside from the championships, he left us all with a lot of life lessons that we were able to take with us after hockey." — *Tom Vanelli, former Gopher player*

"Herbie showed me how to be a winner and helped to set the process for me to be successful not only in hockey, but in life after hockey." — *Robb McClanahan, former Gopher & Olympic player*

"It was tremendous. I learned how to act as a person, how to treat people, how to be treated, how to strive to achieve goals and how to work hard. He just had a big impact on me in a lot of ways." — *Buzz Schneider, former Gopher & Olympic player*

"Hardly a day goes by where the 1980 Olympics doesn't come up, and I am reminded of that on a regular basis. Herbie is just always right there with me." — *Phil Verchota, former Gopher & Olympic player*

"Herbie really liked the players who worked hard for him. I worked hard for him, and I think that is why we were close even after hockey. That work ethic that he instilled in me, drives me to this day in my own life and in my career. If you work hard, if you prepare and you are humble, then you will have success. What you put into it is what you are going to get out of it. If you work hard then you will have great dividends. It is up to you, and Herbie impacted me greatly on that. He just had a great work ethic. You know, Herbie hated prima donnas — guys with lots of talent but never used it. He would much rather have a bunch of guys with less talent but worked hard. That foundation is the impact Herbie had on me.

"I remember one time between periods during a game. Herb singled me out in front of the everybody and said 'Polich, you're supposed to be a leader on this team! You're the most selfish player and biggest prima donna out there!' Well, the younger players eyes were wide open and they were just in shock at that point. Then, he leaves and slams the door behind him. So, just before the period starts he comes back in and as the players are filing out to hit the ice, he comes over to me and puts his arm around me. 'Now, Michael,' he says, 'show these guys how to play the game.' That was Herbie, he would break you down and then build you right back up to make a point to the entire team." — *Mike Polich, former Gopher player*

"In hockey, when I wasn't playing well or as aggressive as I could've been, Herbie used to always tell me to remember what got me here. Even later, when I was thinking of leaving Hockey Ministries, he told me that he thought I was right where God wanted me to be. So, whenever I was at a crucial point in my life, I would bump into Herbie and he would always have the right words to say to me every time I needed someone to speak truth into my life." — *Bill Butters, former Gopher player*

"He gave me a never-give-up attitude. I wound up working as a manager with 3M and the persistence I learned from Herbie drove me to be successful. He impacted my entire life a great deal, both professionally as well as personally." — *Roger Wigen, former St. Paul Johnson High School Hockey teammate*

"Herbie taught me how to win and that was probably the biggest thing. It was an interesting transition to play for him on the Olympic team and then again with the Rangers. It was a very different situation and I think that Herbie might have had a hard time adjusting to that level. He didn't have as much control over his players at that point, so he had to change his coaching style to make up for that. But he did it, and was successful there too." — *Mark Pavelich, former player on 1980 U.S. Olympic Team & NY Rangers*

"Just knowing him has meant so much. I was very close to his entire family, they are just wonderful people. Now, my wife, Gretchen, and Herb's wife, Patti, are the best of friends, so we were all very close with one another." — *Steve Badalich, longtime friend*

"Well, I know damn well that I am going to miss him, that was his impact on me. We just grew to be great friends and I don't know why, but I loved him. I would do anything for him and I know that he would do the same for me." — *LeRoy Houle, longtime friend*

"Herbie made me a better person. He forced you to think things through, and I just learned a great deal from him. Then, for me personally, I am very grateful to him. He was one of the main reasons why the Penguins drafted my son, Ryan. He helped him up at St. Cloud and took him under his wing a little bit. So, when someone of Herbie's stature comes along and takes the time to spend with your son to help him in his career, that is very special. So, He had a very big impact on my life, both professionally as well as personally." — *Greg Malone, Pittsburgh Penguins head of scouting*

"I was so lucky to get to play for him so late in my career. I had always hoped to play for him, and to finally get that opportunity in 2002 meant a great deal to me. He chose me to be on that team, and to be the only Minnesota player on the roster meant the world to me. He had to make some tough decisions and I was fortunate to be selected by him. It was a real honor. You know, when I scored the game-winner over Russia in the semifinals, it made me feel even better about the fact that Herbie had picked me and that I was able to be on his team. That was an unbelievable experience." — *Phil Housley, former 2002 Olympian under Brooks & former NHL All-Star*

"He was a guy who you would do anything for, and you would go through a wall for him. He just had that impact on me." — *Steve Ulseth, former Gopher player*

"Herbie taught me early on about the importance of teamwork and I have never wavered from that in my life. I will never forget him telling me that our team was a team of destiny. We were all Minnesota kids and that we were destined for greatness if we all worked together. I never forgot that and still apply that to my everyday life." — *Joe Micheletti, former Gopher player & current Fox Sports TV hockey analyst*

"Herbie was a very good investor. He was very well read and what people don't realize about him was how intellectual he was about our economic system and how it operated in the world. He had great political and geopolitical interests and observations which determined the direction of investments. He was also very interested in how certain companies were doing and how they were forecasting in the long term and short term. He read a great deal about that. So, whenever you talked to him you had better have been on your toes. I have been in the investment business for over 40 years and he was as smart as any investor that I have ever dealt with. I actually learned a great deal from Herbie over the years." — *Noel Rahn, longtime friend*

"He was so loyal. You know, if I ever asked him to come somewhere or do something, like play in my golf tournament down in Iowa, he was always there for me." — *Paul Johnson, former Olympic teammate and longtime friend*

"Herb gets a lot of credit for my success as a player and now as a coach in the National Hockey League. I just think that when he got a hold of me I was a boy and after playing for him, he turned me into a man." — *Mike Ramsey, former Gopher & Olympic player and current Wild assistant coach*

"Even though I only played for him for one season, he had a tremendous impact on my life as a player and as a person. He pushed me to do my best, to learn as much as I could, and to use my strengths to benefit the team. He was very dedicated to the game and I think he wanted to win more than his players did." — *Paul Holmgren, former Gopher player & NHL player and coach*

"I remember back in the '70s as a kid growing up in Grand Rapids and listening to the Gophers on the radio. I went to some games as a kid too and got to experience the passion of college hockey. Then, when he came to my house to recruit me, that was an incredible experience too. There was almost a sense of awe when you were listening to him talk, and that was a very memorable thing for me. So, Herbie was a part of all that, and certainly that fueled my own passion to play hockey and to later get into coaching." — *Don Lucia, Gopher Hockey head coach*

"He gave me an opportunity to compete in the Olympics and I will never forget that. I look at my life today and where it is headed and much of it is based on what happened to me back in 1980 as a member of Herb's team." — *Mike Eruzione, former*

"I think back to what happened back in 1980 and I will never forget that. Herbie made that all possible and I will forever be grateful to him for the opportunity to be a part of it." — *Eric Strobel, former Gopher & Olympic player*

"He had a big impact on my life. He gave me an opportunity to go back to the University of Minnesota and get my degree and to work with him to learn the progression of going from a player to a coach. You know, you watch players who played in the National Hockey League fail time and time again when they go right from playing to coaching. You just can't do it. There is a whole other way of thinking and planning and that takes time. You don't really learn the game until you start teaching it to others. And that is what Herbie taught me. He taught me how to teach the game, but only after I was able to learn as much as possible first." — *Dean Blais, former Gopher player & current head coach at the University of North Dakota*

"He certainly played a big part in my decision to get into coaching. I appreciated his time with me through the years too. He always made time for me and always let me run my ideas by him. He was just there for me and always gave me his honest opinion. He would give you some suggestions, but in the end he would always let you know that you had to do what you felt was right." — *John Harrington, former Gopher & Olympic player*

"I knew him for over 50 years, back to our days in the Phalen youth hockey system. We go way back, and I don't think anybody has had a bigger impact on my life than Herb Brooks. Not only was he a really good friend, he also put me into situations where I had a chance to achieve success. He was able to motivate me to be my best and I was able to apply that to my entire career." — *Warren Strelow, former goalie coach under Brooks and longtime friend*

"Herbie just taught me that if you don't have as much talent as the next guy then you have to out-work him. That is something that I use daily. I work hard and know what it takes to be dedicated to what I do and to stay focused. Herbie taught me that and it impacts my life every day." — *Bill Baker, former Gopher & Olympic player*

"I remember when he got the Gopher coaching job. I was playing in Cleveland at the time because the North Stars had just sent me down, but when I heard I was so excited. I sent him a telegram right away that read: *'The No. 1 man for the No. 1 job!'* I mean I never knew that he would become the icon that he would become, I just I knew him when he was an insurance salesman and a former Gopher. He certainly went on to make us all very proud." — *Gary Gambucci, former Gopher and teammate on two U.S. National teams*

"Just being his friend and observing what he accomplished had a big impact on my life. I think we all have learned and been enriched from our association with him. He was just that type of person. He personified the saying that if you put your mind to something and work hard then you can achieve anything." — *John Mayasich, former teammate on U.S. National Teams & longtime friend*

"Herbie just made me see things a little bit differently and he made me see things outside the box. He was someone who I considered to be a true friend and I will miss him. You know, you never knew what day, what time or where you were going to get a phone call from Herbie, but when it came, you felt like you were the most important guy in the world. He just had that impact on your life. He was a great, great man." — *Jim Findley, President of the U.S. Hockey Hall of Fame*

"We were just two 65-year-old guys who had raised their families together and were on to bigger and better things in life. So, did he impact me? Probably not, but he impacted so many others. You know, I was so amazed being at his funeral and seeing all the different people who were there, from the rich to the gifted to the famous. And then realizing that his best friend, of all those thousands of people, was LeRoy Houle, who trims trees. That was his best friend. That speaks volumes of who Herb Brooks was. I remember one day I saw Herb in the garage and he had some old clothes and boots on and as I was leaving for work I said, 'boy you are getting an early start today.' He said, 'Yeah, LeRoy has a big project going on and can't get anybody to help him, so I am going to work for him for a couple of weeks.' Herb Brooks, the famous coach and celebrity, went to work, probably for nothing I am sure, for two weeks trimming trees for LeRoy Houle. That is the kind of person Herb Brooks was. I have known a lot of famous and successful people over the years, and believe me, they wouldn't think twice about doing something like that. They would make a phone call or two to try to find somebody to help LeRoy. But Herb knew that his friend needed help and he was there for him. So, he put on his boots and went to work. That was the way he lived his life. He would do that for anybody. Yet, he was this tough guy who would holler at the refs during big games and things like that. Then, you would see him walking this little white dog down the street. So, there was an entirely different side of Herb Brooks that most people didn't know about. He was just a special person." — *Bob Rink, next-door neighbor and longtime friend*

"You know, I was in the trucking business and he was in the coaching business, but we were the best of friends. He was just a quality person and he meant so much to me. I looked up to him, even though I was taller and older than he was. I used to kid him about that! I just had all the respect in the world for him." — *Frank Messin, former hockey referee and longtime friend*

"He did more for my career than anybody and I can't think of anybody else who I owe more to. He gave me my first two coaching opportunities, with the Vulcans and then the Gophers, and that truly changed my life. Without Herbie I would probably still be teaching at South St. Paul High School. So, he had a huge impact on my life." — *Doug Woog, former Gopher Hockey Coach & teammate on a U.S. National team*

"Herb had a great impact on me as a player and as a person. He was always there for you when you needed him and he wouldn't think twice about coming all the way up here to Green Bay to help me out when I asked. We are trying to get hockey going up here and he has always done whatever we asked of him, he really cares about growing the game. So, not only was he a great friend to me personally, but he was a great friend to hockey." — *Paul Coppo, former teammate on several U.S. National Teams and longtime friend*

"He was just such a very, very good friend. My friendship with Herb would rank right up there with the likes of Hubert Humphrey, Harold Stassen and Orville Freeman — all close personal friends of mine. We shared a lot of great moments together and I will never forget him." — *Bob Utecht, founder of Let's Play Hockey newspaper*

"I cried so much when I found out Herbie died. I just cried and cried, it was so tough.

I don't know if anybody has had that much of an impact on me. He was just so special to me. I lost a real friend that day and it will take a long, long time to get over that." — *Nick Fotiu, former New York Ranger under Brooks*

"Herb got the most out of me by challenging me. Now, that wasn't always a comforting thought, but the growth that came along with that was priceless." — *Jim Boo, former Gopher player*

"Herbie helped me in so many ways. He gave me confidence. He also gave me a chance, as his assistant with the North Stars, and I will forever be grateful to that. Then, he helped my kids, they thought the world of them. He would go watch them in Waterloo, Iowa, when they were playing juniors and that was very special. He just went out of his way to make them feel special and to compliment their games. He also told them things that they needed to work on too, and they appreciated that. He was just a tremendous person and I feel very lucky to have known him." — *J.P. Parise, former North Star player and assistant coach with the North Stars under Brooks*

"Through hockey he inspired me. He was the driving force behind the American hockey movement and he really believed in Minnesota players. So, because of his success and dedication, many of the things that I have done in my life are because of him. He had an incredible impact on me to be a better hockey player and he had an incredible impact on me to be a coach." — *Paul Ostby, former Gopher player and business associate*

WHAT IS HERBIE'S LEGACY GOING TO BE IN YOUR OPINION?

"Everybody's got ideals, dreams for a perfect world for themselves, and goals they hope to accomplish. Herbie had loftier ideals, and his idea of perfection was to improve everybody's status. He also was stubborn, could be tough and intimidating, and he made some mistakes along the way, such as feeling strongly enough about his objective that he might seem insensitive to others. But he was right most of the time. His greatest legacy is his constant attempts to improve things, and the fact that he did it his way." — *John Gilbert, former Star-Tribune hockey reporter and longtime friend*

"I think the majority of the people who will answer this question with answer the 1980 Olympics. But I would instead say the love that the people who worked for him and played for him showed to him would be his legacy. I think long beyond the miracle of 1980 it will be the people who went to battle with him at the University, or at New York, or at New Jersey, or at Pittsburgh, or here with the North Stars. I think those are the people whose lives he touched and whose attitudes he influenced. That, in my opinion, will be his legacy." — *Mike Sertich, former UM-Duluth Head Coach*

"I would say his effectiveness to get people to follow him. He was such a great leader and had so many outstanding leadership qualities. He could really get people to believe in one thing and have one common goal, and that is what made him so suc-

"That is the question that everybody is asking these days, and I think there are many. I think Herbie wanted American hockey to become No. 1 in the world. To do that, Herbie's theory was that we had to expand the base of the pyramid. That involved putting things into two categories: rural and urban. In rural hockey, *A)* we have to go new areas, like Pierre S.D., and help them any way we can to get hockey started there. *B)* We have to go to traditional places that are now having economic issues, like Hibbing for instance. At places like that, you help them to keep their hockey going strong. They have the tradition there, they know what to do, they just don't have the resources because of economic changes. Then, in urban hockey, *A)* we have to expand in the inner city and attract minority athletes to take up the game of hockey. That is new hockey. *B)*, we have to protect the communities within the city whose programs are down, such as the St. Paul Johnsons and Minneapolis Southwests for example. Those are dynamic powers with the tradition, but also have some economic issues. So, by building the base of our athletes, we will build the base of our pyramid. That will grow the game and make it stronger for the next generation.

"I also think that Herbie always felt that the players were much more important than the coach. We have good athletes, and Herbie could put them together, but he felt that we needed more people to chose from. Herbie also felt that hockey was just a fun, great game, and the more kids that played it would be that much better off in life for having done so. Sure, if they go on to play in college, or the Olympics or in the pros, that was great, but for him, it was more about getting players to play the game and enjoy it." — *Larry Hendrickson, former area high school hockey coach and longtime friend*

"It has got to be that one man had such an incredible impact on so many people, both in hockey and outside of hockey, and that was because he was a non-stop work-a-haulic. So, in 66 years, he spent many more hours than the average person might on projects that he thought were important. He still could not have had such an impact on as many people if he didn't really love and respect the common person who wouldn't often get recognized by someone as big as Herbie." — *Jack Blatherwick, Brooks' former strength & conditioning coach and longtime friend*

"His legacy is that he broke down the barriers for Americans to play in the National Hockey League and got them to be respected as hockey players throughout the world. I mean he did that single-handedly with a group of 20 college kids 23 years ago. I don't think Americans were ever respected in the game prior to that, and certainly not the American college kid. I also don't think that there were too many NHL teams that ever scouted U.S. colleges prior to the 1980 Olympics, but that all changed after that. Now, they all have two or three guys that do nothing but scout college hockey as well as junior and even high school hockey. Herbie had a lot to do with that, and that is a big thing. He really helped to promote hockey in this country, and was so passionate about the American hockey movement. I think as of late, his ultimate passion was to work with USA Hockey on a broader scale. That was his ultimate passion and really what he wanted to do was to help grow the sport for American kids." — *Neil Sheehy, hockey agent and close friend*

"It would have to be the 'Miracle on Ice.' I mean had that not happened I don't know what Herbie would have been doing right now. Sure, he won three national championships, and that sometimes gets overshadowed, but the 1980 Olympics really defined him. That was the peak of his mountain I think. I also think he realized the importance of junior hockey, and in developing guys like Paul Holmgren through it. That was how he had so much success at the University and that was significant as well." — *Murray Williamson, former Gopher teammate and 1972 U.S. Olympic coach*

"He left a legacy of helping people and of demanding that they strive to be the best that they can be. He demanded excellence. It wasn't always about winning and losing either. I mean he was totally satisfied if he felt that he had gotten the best effort out of his team or out of a person, because then he could build on that. He was a builder and he loved to take incremental steps with you and teach you how to be the best you could be. He was demanding from that standpoint but sometimes he could push you farther than you thought you could be pushed. You know, Herbie just left a tremendous legacy, to so many people. He was a great mentor to me and really showed me the way you are supposed to live your life and how to do things. Sure, Herbie had his faults, but you can't argue with what he did and for what he stood for. The man was a legend and I was very proud to have known him. I loved him." — *Craig Dahl, St. Cloud State Head Coach and former Brooks assistant*

"I think Herbie would downplay the impact that he had on the game, but I think it was obvious when people paid tribute to him on how powerful he actually was and how much they respected him as an innovator, motivator and guiding light to the game." — *Tom Vanelli, former Gopher player*

"I think more so than anything the 1980 Olympics will be what Herbie is probably most remembered for. What he did best though, was formulate a team. In other words, he knew everybody so well. He knew what your strengths were and he knew how to get them out of you. That was his forté. He knew what you were really good at and he knew what you weren't really good at. Then, he used that to put together lines and a team, and that is how he found success. He could just get the most out of people, and that didn't necessarily mean he was going to do that in a real nice way either. But in the end, you would do what he wanted you to do and he would smile at you. One thing about Herbie, psychologically, he would figure you out and he would also figure out how to beat any opponent. The guy was just brilliant." — *Pat Phippen, former Gopher player*

"Herbie was a winner. He was able to bring a hockey player of less than stellar talent and show them the road as to how to succeed in the game. He was a lunch-pailer's coach. He also didn't always go with the majority. He had opinions and generally stuck to them, even if he was the odd man out. And, in so doing, he created rifts amongst some of his peers." — *Robb McClanahan, former Gopher & Olympic player*

"I would say that he is the best American hockey coach ever. He was respected around the world and that is something he worked very hard at and really earned." — *Buzz Schneider, former Gopher & Olympic player*

"Herbie has been the innovator of so many hockey related issues in the United States. He has blazed a trail for players in the U.S. to further their careers from college to Olympics to professionals. He brought to the game an open mindedness, which the game really needed. He also taught us that there are other ways of playing this game, whether that involved the European style or the Russian style. He was just an innovator and wasn't afraid to try new things if he thought it would improve the game. He always questioned the status quo, and you need people like that. Then, you have things like what he did in St. Cloud, to get that school up and running. He did so much for Minnesota hockey and for American hockey, his legacy is incredible." — *Phil Verchota, former Gopher & Olympic player*

"Certainly the Miracle on Ice will always be something he will be remembered for. But beyond that, Herbie touched a lot of people in a lot of different ways. He was very, very humble in anything he did. He did not like arrogant or cocky people, and I think people will remember him as a person of character and dignity. He just emphasized the fact that if you prepare hard and you work hard, you will have success — then when you have that success, be humble about it and appreciate it. In my opinion that will be Herbie's biggest legacy." — *Mike Polich, former Gopher player*

"I think his legacy is his family. And not only his immediate family, but his hockey family too. You know, to me Herbie's legacy is the fact that he always had time for everybody. Everyone at Herbie's funeral thought that he was his best friend, and to me that is something that I would like to aspire to." — *Bill Butters, former Gopher player*

"An undaunting psychology about winning." — *Roger Wigen, former St. Paul Johnson High School Hockey teammate*

"Obviously he is an icon in hockey at all levels and so forth, but outside of hockey it was just being Herbie. That is legacy enough, just being Herbie. He was a one of a kind." — *Steve Badalich, longtime friend*

"In my eyes he is going to be remembered as one hell of a fine man. I'll tell you that! He was just an honest, straight-shootin' guy. That was it. That was Herbie, and he meant one hell of a lot to me." — *LeRoy Houle, longtime friend*

"I think it will be a long time before someone comes along and takes his place as far as hockey is concerned in Minnesota, that is for sure." — *Butch Bloom, longtime friend*

"More than anything else Herbie was a man who prided himself on doing his very best. The success he had as a college, Olympic and NHL coach — I think he brought the game to a new level. He showed that even though you are an underdog, you can still be successful in what you do. Then, I think that another thing he was responsible for was the fact that so many Olympic sized sheets of ice have been built since the 1980 Olympics. Herbie saw the benefits of the European style of hockey, on that bigger sheet of ice, and was very influential in getting a lot of them built in order to help the American kids progress. He just had a vision and that big sheet of ice allowed that vision to come true. He felt that the extra space out there let kids be creative with the puck and it got them away from all the clutching and grabbing that you see on the standard sized rink." — *Tommy Reid, former North Star & current Wild radio analyst*

"I believe he was the best college hockey coach in the country when I was playing and I never understood why he never came back to the U of M to finish his coaching career to tell you the truth. But, he was just a great coach. Period. He really had a big influence on my life and his legacy to me will be that." — *Steve Christoff, former Gopher & Olympic player*

"I would say as somebody who just did it his way. Whether it was right or wrong, he stuck to his beliefs. He just stuck to his word and if he made you a promise you knew he would follow through on it. Then, certainly the Olympics will be the thing he is probably most remembered for. I will tell you this though. The 2002 team, which he coached here in Salt Lake City, was probably the best group of American players ever assembled. In fact, I would say that they were the best team in the world at that time, bar none. So, when they lost to Canada in the gold medal game, I thought that was just a down game for them. They were tired and feeling sick and just couldn't get it done that last game, that's all. I talked to Herbie privately about this and he really wanted to win that one. So, I guess it was neat that he got to finish out his career with the Olympics because that was something he loved as a player and as a coach." — *Reed Larson, former Gopher player*

"Whenever his name comes up the first thing people think of is hockey, so that is first and foremost. You know, he was also the first guy who ever had the courage to establish a European style of hockey into the National Hockey League. That was revolutionary at the time. He initiated that style way back when and now that is the way everybody plays. So, he was really responsible for a revival or regeneration of hockey in North America. It is a much, much better and more exciting game that way, and the kids are much more skilled now than they were back in the 1960s and 1970s. The credit for that really has to go to him, and that is oftentimes overlooked I think. Then, the 1980 Olympic team will forever be linked with him. What he did with those kids was remarkable." — *Bob Paradise, former teammate & father-in-law to his daughter*

"The 1980 Olympics were the single greatest thing to ever happen to American hockey, it just grew from there and Herbie was a huge part of that. That was one of the biggest upsets ever in the history of sports and was such an amazing thing. So, Herbie's legacy will include a lot of things, but I think that the Miracle on Ice will be the biggest." — *Phil Housley, former 2002 Olympian under Brooks & former NHL All-Star*

"He was just hockey Minnesota. You know, John Mariucci gave Minnesota players the opportunity to play, and then Herbie made them champions." — *Steve Ulseth, former Gopher player*

"The Miracle on Ice will be a big part of his legacy, for sure. That was an amazing thing and really helped to grow American hockey. I know that as of recently he was more determined than ever to get more kids into the skill development aspect of the game and that was great to see. He recognized the differences between North American and European hockey and tried to incorporate them together to get the best results for kids, and that was significant." — *Bret Hedican, current NHL All-Star*

"You know, Herbie died so young that I am not sure it is even done being written. I think when it is all said and done, and all the stories are told, there will be a picture there of Herb that will emerge. It is just so many things — from college championships to the Olympics, to the NHL, to working with kids, to caring for people. The man just did so much and had so much energy for so many causes that he believed in. His causes changed as he changed over the years too. I mean he first proved to the world that he could win a national championship with all Minnesota kids. Then, he proved to the world that he could win an Olympic gold medal with all college kids. I just think that he was the champion of the underdog and he just did it his way. You know, whatever Herb's legacy will be, I know this for sure, his heart was always in the right place. To me, that, more than anything, will be his legacy." — *Joe Micheletti, former Gopher player & current Fox Sports TV hockey analyst*

"He was a guy who stood up for what he thought was right and was not influenced by others. His commitment to tell people what was on his mind and not backing down because of peer pressure was incredible. He was just his own person when many people were, politically, trying to influence his decisions. I respected that a great deal about him." — *Noel Rahn, longtime friend*

"He was an innovator and somebody who was a little bit ahead of his time. He was definitely outside the box and he just stuck to his convictions. He had some great ideas and was able to implement them, and that is why he had success. Herb's name is just synonymous with hockey and he will never be forgotten, I can certainly tell you that." — *Mike Ramsey, former Gopher & Olympic player and current Wild assistant coach*

"It is hard to look much further past the 1980 Olympic team. But beyond that, he was just an incredibly hard worker and was a winner." — *Paul Holmgren, former Gopher player & NHL player and coach*

"To me, he always left you with something, and it was always meaningful. And, it was not just about hockey, it was about life with Herb. He was just a great, great hockey man, and will surely be missed by many." — *Larry Pleau, former teammate on 1968 Olympic team & current St. Louis Blues GM*

"Herb could have been anything he wanted to be. He could have been the governor of Minnesota, or the president of the United States. He was smart enough to do any of those things. His legacy will be a lot of things, but particularly the 1980 U.S. Olympic team. I don't think that team would have won with any other coach. In my mind he was just the right guy for that particular team at that particular time. He and those players were the perfect marriage and that was special. So, his legacy in that regard was that he renewed the American spirit. As a country we were in trouble at that time and that event, the Olympic hockey team, was a very big deal. We were losing our pride, what with everything going on in the world at that time, and Herbie helped to get that back." — *Lou Vairo, head coach of 1984 U.S. Olympic team & assistant under Brooks on the 2002 U.S. squad*

"He will probably be most remembered for the success he had with the 1980 Olympic team. But more than that, he was just one of those giants in the game of hockey not only within our state, but also on the national scene as well. He really helped to put hockey on the map for a lot of people, and I think that all goes back to 1980. Prior to that hockey had really only had a regional following, but after the success he had with the Olympics that all changed. That event really not only opened the door for the sport across the country, but it opened the door for U.S. players to get into the National Hockey League as well." — *Don Lucia, Gopher Hockey head coach*

"He orchestrated the greatest sports moment of the 20th century. That is a pretty good legacy! Then, what he has meant to the sport of hockey is really immeasurable. He was just so ahead of his time. He was a great innovator and a great motivator. He was an icon in the state of Minnesota and was somebody who young kids looked up to and admired because of his accomplishments. He was very successful in everything he did in life and just stuck with his convictions. He truly believed in his systems and in his players and he was greatly respected for that." — *Mike Eruzione, former 1980 Olympian*

"To me, even in the early days, he always had opinions on things he felt strongly about. He really believed strongly in the European style of hockey and that too will be something that he will be remembered for. It was a unique style, what with the circling and regrouping, and was really revolutionary at the time. You know, in order for that type of hockey to work over here, you had to have really good kids who were in really good shape. So, Herbie made it a point to make sure his kids were in top physical condition, and that afforded him the opportunity to run that system." — *Willard Ikola, former Olympian and longtime Edina High School Hockey Coach*

"He was such a great ambassador to the sport of hockey. He just lived it every day of his life. Then, he always had his opinion, and he never really varied from that opinion. What you saw was what you got from Herbie. He was a one of a kind and he will be missed." — *Eric Strobel, former Gopher & Olympic player*

"You know, most people will refer to the Miracle on Ice, but he was so much more to so many people. Herbie always had time for everyone, he did a lot of volunteering and did so much good for hockey. He was the guy who was concerned about the game, first and foremost, and then the people in it. It really wasn't always about winning and losing with him, he wanted to make sure that the players were getting better and were developing. That will be Herb's legacy in my eyes." — *Dean Blais, former Gopher player & current head coach at the University of North Dakota*

"Herb always gave 100% to whatever he was doing, whether it was in coaching or in his personal life, and that is what I think he will be remembered most for. He just instilled a sense of knowing that through hard work and sacrifice, good things could happen. He was able to get people to believe in what he was trying to do, and that was why he was so successful." — *John Harrington, former Gopher & Olympic player*

"Herbie knew what was first and what was best. So, he always put his family first. From there, he did what was best for his community, his school and for his friends. To me, that will be his legacy. You know, after I had some heart troubles I coined the phrase, *'everyday is a bonus.'* So, even today, when people ask me how I am doing, I tell them that everyday is a bonus — because God never promised tomorrow to anybody. Herbie's death was such a tragedy, and you just never know when your time will come. So, you do what you can on this earth to make a difference while you are here. And Herb Brooks made a big difference. Life is so fragile, but his time with us, every minute of it, was a bonus." — *Lou Cotroneo, former St. Paul Johnson High School hockey coach & longtime friend*

"His compassion for people was what I will think of most. He had time for everybody, he believed in people, he had strong convictions and he worked very hard. Then, he was just a white collar worker with a blue collar lunch pail style. There will never ever be another Herb Brooks. He was just a one of a kind. And he had such an impact on so many people. It didn't matter how big or how small you were, he respected you. I mean if he was in a room talking to someone and someone more important came in, he wouldn't leave that person to go talk to the more important person. He would continue talking to you. That was Herbie. He never forgot his East Side roots. That is where he learned his values. You know, Herb used to say that your legacy is what people have to say about you after you die. So, his legacy will be a lot of things to a lot of people. But for me, it will be our friendship and that will be with me forever." — *Warren Strelow, former goalie coach under Brooks and longtime friend*

"Herb just did things his way. You didn't have to agree with him, but you had to respect his convictions. He just stood up for what he believed in and then took that as far as he could, in whatever it was that he was doing." — *Bill Baker, former Gopher & Olympic player*

"After the 1980 Olympics hockey just grew as a sport, not only in Minnesota, but all over the world, and Herb had a lot to do with that. The guy was just a legend and did so much to grow the game. I think that will be the biggest thing." — *Neal Broten, former Gopher, Olympian and North Star*

"Herbie put USA Hockey on the map. Period. I mean they did not have a pot to piss in before the 1980 Olympics. So, winning that gold medal in 1980, he won that for so many of us who had played on U.S. teams and had gotten the sh-- kicked out of us by the Russians, Czechs and Swedes through the years. That was just wonderful. He gave American players so much credibility and that alone did so much for the advancement of the game here in the United States. He just really validated the American hockey player at a time when we were not taken seriously, and for that he should be given a sincere thanks." — *Gary Gambucci, former Gopher and teammate on two U.S. National teams*

"I don't know if it is legacy as much as it is a void. Because what Herb leaves behind is a huge void. Somebody of his stature and credibility fighting for the right things in the game is not on the horizon and I don't see any college or USA Hockey people who have that stature to bring those ideas to the forefront. That scares me. Then, I just think that the 1980 Olympic team will always be associated with him and for what it did to spawn the growth of American hockey. I mean that single event did more to expand hockey across the country than any one thing or person in history. Look at how the NHL expanded after that. There was a hockey boom in the 1980s following that, and much of that credit goes to Herb. So, there is a void now, and that will be tough to replace." — *Craig Sarner, former Gopher and player under Brooks on 1979 U.S. National Team and in Europe & longtime coach at various levels*

"I think it would just be all of his accomplishments within the sport of hockey. That will never be approached by anyone." — *John Mayasich, former teammate on U.S. National Teams & longtime friend*

"I think his legacy was that if you were willing to be a human being and you wanted to succeed and you wanted to dream, then you had to just work hard and go after it. He showed us all that dreams can come true. He had great success at whatever level he was coaching at and he just did so much for the game. Herbie really studied the game and just worked extremely hard. Nothing came easy for him and I respect that about him. He will never be forgotten, that is for sure." — *Jim Findley, President of the U.S. Hockey Hall of Fame*

"Herbie's legacy will be different to different people. You know, he had us believing in miracles 23 years ago. And in my opinion those same miracles were happening at his funeral. I mean there were little kids, dads, the rich, the famous, the poor and just a real dichotomy of people who were there. So, his legacy might be the fact that he was able to bring together a wide variety of different people with the same spirit and dedication, and unify them towards one common goal. I don't know. Sure, some will say his legacy was the Miracle on Ice, or the national championships at the University of Minnesota, and those are great things, but I think it was about his ability to unite people from all different walks of life. He just related to people on all levels, that was his charm. It mean it didn't matter if you were a hockey player or just his neighbor, he was the same way to everybody. Then, he was very determined, very bull-headed and very committed to what he believed. Herbie had a lot of determination and did everything to its fullest. He was a very unique person in so many ways." — *Bob Rink, next-door neighbor and longtime friend*

"I think he will go down as one of the most outstanding coaches of all time." — *Frank Messin, former hockey referee and longtime friend*

"I think the 1980 Olympic team will be on the top of that list when it is all said and done. He also had a lot of success at Minnesota, and in such a short period of time, and that was very impressive. Then, for him to go up to St. Cloud on John Mariucci's request, that was just a tremendous gesture on his part. So, to see the success that they are having now, a lot of that goes back to Herb. More importantly though, I would say his legacy included the way he did things his own way. He also made time for young coaches and did his part to help them. He was very outspoken, of course, on things he felt strongly about and that was impressive too. He wasn't afraid to express his opinion and when he did he stuck by it. His contributions to promote the game not only in Minnesota but all across the country, that will be the biggest thing." — *Jeff Sauer, former University of Wisconsin & Colorado College Head Coach*

"His legacy will always be the 1980 Olympics. The three national championships at Minnesota are wonderful, if you are from Minnesota, but on a national scale, it will be the Miracle on Ice. And really, it wasn't so much beating Finland for the gold, it was more about beating the Russians in the semifinals. Then, people will always remember too how after the game, when all the players were celebrating, he slipped into the locker room and disappeared. He wanted his players to enjoy the moment and didn't want to get in their way." — *Gregg Wong, former Pioneer Press columnist*

"I think it will always be the 1980 Olympic team. There is no way to get around that. Those who knew him well, however, might say it would be his never ending fight to make hockey better. He was very passionate. He was someone you had to listen to, and I certainly did. You know, Herb was a lot like John Mariucci in that he came up with a lot of great ideas, but it took a lot of people and a lot of money to implement them. One thing that he was passionate about was creating regional camps for our elite kids, and that is something that USA Hockey will try to do. We all have the same goal of putting the best American players on the ice and being competitive world-wide. He played a big part in international hockey and did a lot for the development of the game." — *Walter Bush, Chairman of the Board, USA Hockey*

"He did it his way. You know, I remember one time I asked him for some help and advice on something when I was just starting out coaching the Gophers. And he said no. He told me to build my own mouse trap because when it breaks down, then I would know how to fix it. That was Herbie. He would help you with some things, but he really wanted to help you help yourself to be successful." — *Doug Woog, former Gopher Hockey Coach & teammate on a U.S. National team*

"The 1980 Olympics were probably the biggest thing. That was more than a sporting moment, it was a social moment and a political moment. It was just such a powerful thing. I mean, beating the acknowledged leader in skilled hockey, the Russians, at their own game, with a system that he believed in, was incredible. You know, because Herbie believed in that system so deeply and then succeeded with it, I think that is a great part of his legacy. A lot of us have dreams, a lot of us have beliefs and a lot of us have ideals, but to stand behind them and then pull off excellence — there are few people on the planet who could do that. That was Herbie. Then, I would also say that the three NCAA championships at the University of Minnesota will be a part of his legacy too, because they were the only ones in history up until that point, and the next wouldn't come for another 23 years. Lastly, I would say that the growth of college hockey in general throughout the United States is a part of his legacy as well. Herbie championed the college game. I mean the success that St. Cloud enjoys can directly be attributed to Herbie, and as a side benefit, Mankato and Bemidji are now doing well at the Division One level because of his hard work too. So, Herbie followed John Mariucci, and hopefully others will follow Herbie." — *Frank Mazzocco, Gopher Hockey TV Analyst*

"I think those who knew him best will say that he always put hockey first. Aside from his family, his whole life was about promoting hockey. He wanted to not only get more kids playing the game, but he wanted them to play it the right way. That was so important to him. And he wasn't just concerned about the superstar in the NHL, it could be a five year old kid, he just cared." — *Joe Schmit, KSTP-TV sports anchor*

"Obviously, it starts with the 1980 Olympics, but it doesn't end there. I think his legacy from a hockey standpoint is just the opportunity that kids now have to play the game with the same passion that he had. I mean the number of rinks that have opened because of him, directly or indirectly, is amazing. Then, too, the fact that American players now have more opportunities in the National Hockey League is a part of his legacy as well. He just instilled a level of pride into everything he did and was really the gold standard for our state when it came to hockey. Everyone who ever played for him didn't want to disappoint him and they all wanted to make him be proud of them. He left generations of players understanding what hockey means to this state and then just how much hard work is involved in achieving success." — *Mark Rosen, WCCO-TV sports anchor*

"He really knew how to motivate people to get them to perform beyond their wildest dreams, and my God, it will never happen again — someone taking a bunch of kids and beating what would be the equivalent to the Gophers beating the Vikings in football, only on the biggest stage in the world. So, yeah, the Miracle on Ice will always be with Herbie and that was history. I am just glad that he made me a part of it, it was something I will never forget." — *Gary Smith, trainer under Brooks at the University of Minnesota and on the 1980 Olympic Team*

"I think Herbie will just be remembered as one of the greatest coaches of all time. I also think he could do more with less material than maybe anyone, and he knew how to put that material together to be winners too." — *Wayne Ferris, lawyer and business manager*

"To dare to dream, that was Herbie. You know, Herb was never comfortable being a celebrity, but he used that celebrity as a powerful tool to get things done to better the game of hockey. I totally respected that about him." — *Dave Knoblauch, longtime friend*

"He will go down in my opinion as the No. 1 all-time hockey coach in the United States. He was such a dynamic person and had such a passion for hockey. His knowledge of the game was second to none and I think he observed the coaches as much as he observed the players. He was just a one of a kind person and will dearly be missed." — *Don Saatzer, former Hastings High School hockey coach and longtime scout with the Boston Bruins*

"You just can't say enough about what he accomplished. He was a fantastic coach and was a hell of a player too. Sure, the 1980 Olympics will probably be the biggest thing for him, but he did so much more. Whether it was at the University of Minnesota or at St. Cloud State or with the New York Rangers, he just did so much to improve the game. He was the ultimate team player and always put his teams before individuals. Herbie was just an icon. He worked so hard at whatever it was that he was doing and just wouldn't quit until it was done. And then he would move on to the next project. That was Herbie." — *Paul Coppo, former teammate on several U.S. National Teams and longtime friend*

"I don't think there will ever be another person like Herb Brooks. Sure, the 1980 Olympics and national championships at the University were all a part of it, but for me it was the little things that he did to grow the game. For instance, I remember when Somerset, Wis., a little town of just 900 people wanted to get an ice rink built. Herb and I made several trips over the border together to sit in their high school and show them how to get it done. Well, they did it, and they got their rink built. You see, Herbie wanted to build the game from the ground up and knew that building arenas was the first step towards getting more kids playing the game. He was very special that way." — *Bob Utecht, founder of Let's Play Hockey newspaper*

"The hockey world lost a great person when Herbie died, but his legacy isn't finished. I know that I am going to now do whatever I can to continue it. He will be with me forever. Everywhere I go and every game I see, Herbie will be there with me. So, it is not over. You know, I have even got the *'Herbies,'* where I find myself doing the little things that he used to do, like diagramming plays on napkins or on tablecloths in restaurants. He is just a part of me now." — *Nick Fotiu, former New York Ranger under Brooks*

"His legacy to the public will be that of an incredible coach and motivator. His legacy to me, however, will be as an incredible person." — *Brian Lawton, hockey agent and former North Star under Brooks*

"He will probably be remembered most for the 1980 Miracle on Ice, but he did so much more than that. He had success at a number of different levels and really, his legacy was that he was a winner. He was just a legend." — *Jim Boo, former Gopher player*

"Herb covered every gamut of the game. I mean he played in high school, college, national and Olympic teams, and semipro teams, and then he coached in the junior ranks, in college, in Europe, and in the National Hockey League. He was even involved with player-personnel, so he really just did it all. I mean that was quite a broad brush and not many people can say that they have done all that at so many levels. His legacy? I would probably say the 1980 Olympic team. That event had a profound impact on the growth of the game in America and will forever be linked with him. Herbie had always been a proponent of Minnesota hockey and for hockey throughout the United States, and that was at the root of his philosophy I think. He championed that and encouraged it any way he could." — *Bob Peters, longtime*

Bemidji State University head coach

"I think everybody will paint that with a different brush. For me I think his legacy will be his family, first and foremost, because Patti, Danny and Kelly are just incredible individuals. Danny is one of my very best friends and that legacy speaks for itself. Then, as far as hockey goes, his legacy would be that he was a grass-roots hockey person. That is what he was. Then, whether it was the Gophers, the Olympics or in the pros, Herbie was always rooting for the underdog. He loved guys who maybe didn't have as much talent as the next guy but who worked hard and had character. You know, Herbie always looked towards people who didn't have as much and then tried to help them. He didn't bail them out or anything like that, he helped them to help themselves — and there is a big difference. His generosity was incredible and he enjoyed helping others to be better. Herbie had a lot of humility too. Rarely did he ever call attention to himself unless he had a specific reason, it wasn't because of an insecurity. He was just so humble too. I don't think I ever heard him say 'I did this or I did that.' And that was from a guy who did more than all of us combined. He was just a special person and will forever be remembered as one of the greatest coaches of all time." — *Paul Ostby, former Gopher player and business associate*

"Herbie obviously leaves a legacy of tremendous organizational skills and the ability to build and put together things that had an impact on a lot of lives — whether that was winning national championships at Minnesota or winning Olympic gold medals. His ability to formulate a plan and set goals and then implement them to accomplish things was amazing. What he accomplished in his life was unbelievable. I always knew that he would be successful, but then to see it all unfold in front of your eyes makes it even that much more special." — *Bruce Telander, former Gopher Blue Line Club president and longtime friend*

"Herbie will go down as one of the great American hockey heroes. He was one of the best." — *Amo Bessone, former Michigan Tech Head Coach*

"I think his legacy will be his love for his family and for the sport of hockey, and then for teaching about those two loves." — *Craig Patrick, General Manager of Pittsburgh Penguins & longtime friend*

WHAT IS THE ONE THING THAT YOU WOULD WANT HERBIE TO KNOW ABOUT THE WAY YOU FELT ABOUT HIM?

"I totally admired and respected him in everything he did, even when I disagreed with him in some lively debates. Sometimes he was totally off-base, in my opinion, but even then I admired him for sticking to his guns and insisting on doing things his way, or not at all." — *John Gilbert, former Star-Tribune hockey reporter and longtime friend*

"How much I deeply appreciated him. He wasn't the kind of guy who would go around talking about that kind of thing, but I hope he knew how much I cared about him and how much I appreciated him as a person." — *Mike Sertich, former UM-Duluth Head Coach*

"I believed in him and he knew that. He entrusted me to make a lot of decisions, particularly in recruiting, and I would like to think that I had a big impact on our team's success." — *Brad Buetow, former Gopher Head Coach*

"That I recognized perhaps how much he loved me and how much he loved his family. Herbie just wasn't the kind of guy who would tell people he loved them, cared for them, or that he wanted their lives to be better. But he never stopped working towards that end." — *Jack Blatherwick, Brooks' former strength & conditioning coach and longtime friend*

"That I loved him. I loved being with him every chance I had. I was never able to tell him that, but I think he knew it." — *Neil Sheehy, hockey agent and close friend*

"That I respected him as a coach and as a person." — *Tom Vanelli, former Gopher player*

"You know I really respected him. I think one thing that people don't realize about Herbie is that he didn't listen to all the big money backers from Minneapolis. That clique had a lot of influence when Herbie first got there on who played and didn't play, and Herbie just did his own thing. He played the kids who he thought should play and didn't let politics enter into it. I totally respected him for that. Not all coaches can say that, but Herbie was true to himself and that went a long way for me." — *Pat Phippen, former Gopher player*

"That I respected him as a coach. I can't say that we were friends, because he was my coach — and that was the way Herbie handled relationships and such. That was the relationship that he wanted. Now, that was just me. For others that might have been very different." — *Robb McClanahan, former Gopher & Olympic player*

"That I cared about him and respected him. He treated me like I liked to be treated and I felt that I did the same for him. I also really cared about his family, they are wonderful people. I just loved the guy, he was a great man." — *Buzz Schneider, former Gopher & Olympic player*

"That I appreciated his style and that I appreciated his confidence in me. I would also like to thank him for the opportunity to play for him as well." — *Phil Verchota, former Gopher & Olympic player*

"I have told Herbie how much I respected him and how much I loved him. The one thing that I would like to tell more people is that if they feel something about someone then they should not be afraid to tell them how they feel – because you never know if they will be there tomorrow. So, I was glad that I got to tell Herbie how much he did mean to me." — *Bill Butters, former Gopher player*

"I think his wife, Patti, summed it for me when she sent me a card after the funeral. She said, *'Herbie loved you and so do I.'* So, I guess I would like him to know that I loved him and appreciated everything he did for me through all the years." — *Roger*

Wigen, former St. Paul Johnson High School Hockey teammate

"That I really respected him — not to the point of where I was in awe of him, like some other guys, but just that I appreciated what he did for the game. Knowing that we both came from similar blue collar backgrounds in St. Paul, we just had a connection I think. He never forgot where he came from and I admired that." — *Phil Housley, former 2002 Olympian under Brooks & former NHL All-Star*

"That I had the utmost respect for him." — *Steve Ulseth, former Gopher player*

"That I loved him, I cared for him and I deeply appreciated what he did for this country when we needed a shot in the arm." — *Noel Rahn, longtime friend*

"Just how much I thought of him and that he could never do any wrong in my eyes." — *Paul Johnson, former Olympic teammate and longtime friend*

"How much I respected and admired him. When Herb was inducted into the Hall of Fame he asked me to be his presenter. Clearly Herb had that kind of respect for me, and I would like him to know that I felt the same way about him. You know, I remember being at his house with the rest of the 1980 Olympic team for our 10 year anniversary. Herb was out on the lake in a paddle boat with a bunch of the kids and wives having a ball. And I just sat there and said to myself, 'that cannot be the same guy who coached us!' So, there was a totally different side to Herb. He was a very straight forward, in your face kind of a guy on the ice, but off the ice, he was a great family man." — *Mike Eruzione, former 1980 Olympian*

"That I was his friend and that more than anything else I respected him." — *Dean Blais, former Gopher player & current head coach at the University of North Dakota*

"That I appreciated everything he did for me as a player and then later as a coach. Now, whenever I am trying to accomplish things as a coach, I think about how he would've handled certain situations." — *John Harrington, former Gopher & Olympic player*

"I would want him to know that I loved him very much. He was a good friend and I appreciated everything he did for me. I just miss him very, very much." — *Warren Strelow, former goalie coach under Brooks and longtime friend*

"I would want him to know how much I respected him. I would also want him to know that I appreciate what he did for me. He took a raw high school kid and gave him the opportunity to play college hockey at the best place in the country. There, I got to win a couple of NCAA championships and become an All-American. Then, I got to win a gold medal on an Olympic team, so he did so much for me and I appreciate it all." — *Bill Baker, former Gopher & Olympic player*

"You know, Herbie was so grounded and so down to earth. I think the least impressed person in the world about Herbie Brooks was Herbie Brooks. He didn't have to drive a big Mercedes or anything like that. That stuff didn't mean very much to him. Oh, he could afford it, no question, but that was not him. He never forgot his St. Paul roots and that is why people respected him so much." — *Gary Gambucci, former Gopher and teammate on two U.S. National teams*

"I didn't always agree with him, but I certainly respected him. In fact, the only other person who I respected more in my life was my father." — *Craig Sarner, former Gopher and player under Brooks on 1979 U.S. National Team and in Europe & long-time coach at various levels*

"I was a great admirer of Herbie's. In fact, I would have liked to have played for him, he was a real winner. I would add, however, that I wished I could have had a few more yes' or nos from him instead of so many maybes along the way. He was always on the go and had a full agenda not matter what he was doing. You were just lucky if you could set a time and get him to commit to it. He was just so busy and was wanted by so many, and that had to be tough. He was very generous with his time and when he did commit to something, he made the most of it and always had a good time. We just enjoyed being around him, he was a lot of fun to be with." — *John Mayasich, former teammate on U.S. National Teams & longtime friend*

"One day I got a picture in the mail of the 1980 Olympic Team. Underneath the picture it said, *'Jim, thanks for all your hard work, commitment and dedication to the great game of hockey…'* and it was signed, Herb Brooks. I didn't know it was coming, I didn't expect it, but it meant the world to me. So, I would just want to say to Herb that it meant so much to me. It is something that I will treasure even more now that he is gone." — *Jim Findley, President of the U.S. Hockey Hall of Fame*

"I would want Herbie to know that I appreciated his friendship and the way he looked after people who were less fortunate than he was." — *Paul Ostby, former Gopher player and business associate*

WHAT WAS HERBIE'S BEST QUALITY?

"His inventive mind, and his stubbornness. He was always working, always plotting, always a mental jump or two ahead of everybody around him. But if stubbornness was his greatest flaw, it might also have been his singular best quality, because it was his stubbornness that drove him to express his inventiveness rather than fit into somebody else's mold." — *John Gilbert, former Star-Tribune hockey reporter and long-time friend*

"I would say his best quality was his integrity and his honesty. He never sugar-coated anything. If he had an idea or feeling, he spoke to it — right, wrong or indifferent, he said it like it was. Hey, I didn't always agree with him. But, his whole life was about honest opinions, honest thoughts and honest feelings. He had no agenda. With Herbie, it was just out there for everybody to see. Whether he was at Schweits' Bar or at Rockefeller Center, he was just Herb Brooks. I don't think Herb ever forgot where he was from either. I mean he could go into Vogel's Bar as the head coach of the New York Rangers, but as far as they were concerned he was just another East Side patron. Those guys kept him grounded. He always told me that too. He told me to always be proud of the fact that I was from the Iron Range. He said to never make excuses for what you do or where you are from or where you have been. I will always remember that about him." — *Mike Sertich, former UM-Duluth Head Coach*

"He was a great evaluator of talent. I mean even with me, he converted me from a defensemen to a winger during my senior year. Now, I had prided myself on being a good defenseman but he thought I would be better as a forward. At the time I was furious with him, but I ended up playing pro hockey as a forward — which was something I don't know if I would have been able to do as a defenseman. He just had a vision for his players and wanted to help them, particularly if that meant being able to play at the next level." — *Brad Buetow, former Gopher Head Coach*

"He was just one of the guys. I will never forget his Fourth of July parties, with all of his old Johnson High School buddies, those were just special, special memories. When Herbie would let his hair down and let his high school pals give him some crap, that was great. I think Herbie had more fun with who I would call hard-hat, lunch bucket people, than he did with the hockey royalty. I mean he has met presidents and danced with dignitaries, but he was in his element with the regular old fellas from the neighborhood. He never forgot where he was from, and I respected that about him.

"You know, I remember being at the wake, the day before his funeral, and going through the line to pay my respects. I saw this kid go through the line by himself and then went back to the pews and started crying. I didn't think anything of it at the time, but about 45 minutes later I see the kid still back there crying. So, I went over to talk to him. I introduced myself and told him that I knew he felt bad. I just wanted to see if he was OK and if he wanted to talk about it. The kid then proceeded to tell me that one day he was having breakfast at a restaurant, and that at the time, he was going through a tough time and was going to drop out of school. So, he sees Herbie sitting there eating, and he goes up to him and introduces himself to him. He said, 'Mr. Brooks, I was wondering if I could just meet you.' Herbie says, 'sure, sit down and have breakfast with me.' Well anyway, they got talking for an hour and he said by the time they were done the kid was totally committed to going back to school and getting his life back on track. He said that out of nowhere, Herbie took the time for him and really made a difference in his life. And, by the way, he said Herbie even bought him breakfast. I mean that was Herbie to a tee.

"I remember speaking at his funeral and just looking up through those thousands of people and seeing so many spheres of life. You could see guys in nice Italian suits, and you could see guys in golf shirts and jeans. There were all races and religions and that was the impact he had. He crossed borders and touched everybody in some way. I mean he could speak to the executive from IBM one day at a speaking junket, and speak to a guy on the street the next. That was just natural for him and that is what made him so unique." — *Larry Hendrickson, former area high school hockey coach and longtime friend*

"Loyalty. For people he loved and respected, he would do anything. And, he would never stop because it was a lifetime commitment with him." — *Jack Blatherwick, Brooks' former strength & conditioning coach and longtime friend*

"Passion and intelligence. You know, he was an extremely intelligent man. The two of those qualities together, along with his work ethic, made Herbie who he truly was." — *Neil Sheehy, hockey agent and close friend*

"His brutal honesty. He was a very principled guy and had a lot of integrity, honesty and tenacity. He was also very politically astute when he had to be. He was also very serious and was always worrying about something too. If he didn't have something to worry about, he would go out and find something to worry about." — *Murray Williamson, former Gopher teammate and 1972 U.S. Olympic coach*

"Herbie was very intelligent. He could've been a tremendous businessman if he would've wanted to. That is one thing. Then, he was very honest. He used to always tell me that when he was a young guy he would watch the older guys to see what they would do. He used to look for the guys who were up to shenanigans, or who were cheating, or cut corners. Herbie never did that, and was determined never to do that. So, you combine his honesty and values with his work ethic, and it was a recipe for success." — *Craig Dahl, St. Cloud State Head Coach and former Brooks assistant*

"He just got the most out of his players, he was amazing that way." — *Tom Vanelli, former Gopher player*

"You know, Herbie was just a common guy who never let his ego get the better of him. I actually ran into him out on the golf range just a couple of weeks before the accident. He was telling me that he plays in a bunch of celebrity golf tournaments nowadays. Well, at one of the tournaments, the announcer introduced every player at the first tee and then said where they were a member at. So, he would say 'Lou Nanne — Spring Hill,' and 'so and so from Interlachen,' and everybody was from some really nice, expensive course. Well, they introduced Herbie as 'Herb Brooks — Shadow Ridge.' Little did anybody know, but Shadow Ridge is his golf range! That was Herbie. I mean even after the Olympics, when he was a big-time celebrity, he used to even be in a pool league up by where I live in this little town of Centerville with the local patrons at Kelly's Bar. He was just one of the guys, and that was Herbie. What can you say, the guy never forgot his roots. He was just a pretty normal guy from the East side of St. Paul. He could relate to anybody, from presidents to bikers at Kelly's Bar in Centerville. He liked guys like that. I mean look at the guys who were at the 'U' when I was there, not one of them came from a dime. Herbie could see that and went after kids who were blue collar workers, much like he was." — *Pat Phippen, former Gopher player*

"He got the most out of his players, whether it was done in a good fashion or not I can't say, but he got the absolute most out of his players." — *Robb McClanahan, former Gopher & Olympic player*

"I think his best quality was his ability to motivate his players and get the most out of them. He got them to take that extra step to get to the next level and was just able to push certain buttons in order to get them to achieve their goals. Some guys he yelled and prodded at, and other guys he coddled, but he knew how to motivate each person at their own level." — *Buzz Schneider, former Gopher & Olympic player*

"I would say honesty. He also had conviction and a passion for life. Once he made up his mind, it was going to get done. His straight-forwardness to the point of bluntness was what he was all about. That approach was what made him unique and what also made him successful both on and off the ice." — *Phil Verchota, former Gopher & Olympic player*

"Honesty and integrity. He would tell you things that maybe you didn't want to hear, but he was honest with you. Then, he was such a great motivator. I can still remember and even get goose bumps thinking about winning that first national championship. I remember him telling us that this was going to be one of the biggest days of our lives and that we would remember this 30 years from now. He was right. His speeches just totally woke you up and made you realize things that you never realized." — *Mike Polich, former Gopher player*

"Herbie's best quality and his worst quality were probably the same. He was a man who was committed, even to the point of driving some people away. He had a vision, he had goals, he had things in his life which meant something to him, and that was Herbie. He was so intense and so committed, and for some that was a deterrent. But not for me, that was an attraction. I am drawn to people like that. He was such a passionate person and very committed to his ideas. You know, most people tell you what you want to hear, but that was not Herbie, he was brutally honest and told it to you like it was. I respected that." — *Bill Butters, former Gopher player*

"Honesty was his best quality. No matter how small a guy you were or how big a guy you were, there was nothing that mattered more to Herbie than to be honest." — *Roger Wigen, former St. Paul Johnson High School Hockey teammate*

"I would say his tenacity I suppose. He was an intense guy and was really determined to win. He was a winner." — *Mark Pavelich, former player on 1980 U.S. Olympic Team & NY Rangers*

"I never met anybody who didn't immediately like him. He was just so nice to everyone. He just fit in with anybody and everybody, I don't care who it was. You could walk out of a joint some night and there could be a bum sitting on the corner and Herbie would talk to him. That was just the kind of guy he was. He was so dedicated and he just did what he thought was right. He was never going to be a 'yes man,' he was just his own person." — *LeRoy Houle, longtime friend*

"Herbie could wine and dine with kings and then talk to a guy with nothing, and fully understand what that guy was all about. That was a gift and in my opinion, his strongest suit." — *Butch Bloom, longtime friend*

"I would say honesty and integrity. Then, he just had an amazing ability to really know everything about his players so that he could motivate each one of them individually to be their best. He had a real vision. I also think that he was good at using his wit to get his point across to people. I remember one time at a practice he told me that the puck was not my God. That was all he said to me and I didn't know what he meant at the time. But later I figured out that he was trying to tell me to not worship the puck so much and to pass more. He wouldn't just say 'you have to pass the puck more,' or whatever, he would find a clever way to get his point across to you without rubbing you the wrong way." — *Steve Christoff, former Gopher & Olympic player*

"His fire and enthusiasm, that is what made Herbie, Herbie. Of all my coaches, and I played for a lot of years in the NHL, Herbie gave me the most. He was a great, great coach. You know, I would also say that there was one thing that made him different from a lot of other coaches, the fact that he didn't hold grudges. I will give you an example. Herbie, obviously, had his issues over the years with Badger Bob Johnson (the former head coach at Wisconsin). Still, despite that, Herbie chose his son, Mark Johnson, to be on the 1980 Olympic team. Mark Johnson was a great player and Herbie knew that. He wouldn't be the kind of guy who would take something out on him because of his feelings for his father. Herbie was fair, and that is something that people oftentimes overlook and don't talk enough about." — *Reed Larson, former Gopher player*

"He was unique in that he could hang out with owners of teams and people of authority in one minute, and then hang out with Joe six-pack the next. That was a very special quality that he had and I respected that a lot about him." — *Greg Malone, Pittsburgh Penguins head of scouting*

"In addition to his persistence, I would say it was just that he was a real, regular guy. He was a terrific person and never forgot his Payne Avenue roots. You know, if Herb knew you, or knew your father, or grandfather, or anybody, he would treat you like a king. He had such respect for people and for their families." — *Bob Paradise, former teammate & father-in-law to his daughter*

"He knew what to get out of every individual player. He knew and studied their personalities and could motivate 20 different players 20 different ways. That was his biggest quality." — *Phil Housley, former 2002 Olympian under Brooks & former NHL All-Star*

"His ability to speak out and to get the best effort out of people. He was very unpredictable too. When you expected one thing from him you would get the other, and that would always change the mindset of the team to get them refocused. He kept us on our toes, that was for sure. I mean if we won he was much tougher on us than if we got beat. There was just no room for let-down with him." — *Steve Ulseth, former Gopher player*

"Herb had so many great qualities. First and foremost was his heart. He was just a winner and got people to follow him so that they could become winners too. You know, Herb did so much for the American hockey player. He felt that they were overshadowed by Canadians in Canadian systems, and what have you, and was a strong advocate of the American hockey player. He also felt strongly about the way the game should be played. He respected the game and that is really going to be missed. He always took the road less traveled so to speak with regards to issues as well. He always spoke up for what he thought was right and that will me missed." — *Joe Micheletti, former Gopher player & current Fox Sports TV hockey analyst*

"His intellectual integrity. Whatever it was that he stood for and what he felt was right, he just did not back down from that." — *Noel Rahn, longtime friend*

"Loyalty. Herbie was loyal to everybody he liked. If he didn't like you, then he was against you completely. So, he had a lot of friends and he had a lot of enemies, but he was very loyal to those who supported him and were loyal to him." — *Paul Johnson, former Olympic teammate and longtime friend*

"Herb was his own man, and he was just a special guy. You know, if his players said that they liked him all the time, they were full of it, because there were times when his players absolutely hated him. And I think he did that by design. There was always a method to his madness I think. But the guys always respected him, that was for sure." — *Mike Ramsey, former Gopher & Olympic player and current Wild assistant coach*

"His love of the game. I think deep down that was just a love of life. Hockey was his profession in life and if you enjoy your profession to the degree that he did, then that usually meant that you were enjoying life." — *Paul Holmgren, former Gopher player & NHL player and coach*

"His honesty. He would tell you exactly what was on his mind and sometimes that got him into trouble, but that was Herb." — *Mike Eruzione, former 1980 Olympian*

"Herb was a teacher of the game of hockey at all levels and he spent time with you if you asked for it. He just always remembered you and never forgot the little people. Sometimes as coaches move up they don't have time for the common guys, but that was not Herbie. Whenever he saw you there was a warm conversation and a sincere effort on his part to do what was right. He was a coach's coach and I respected that." — *Willard Ikola, former Olympian and longtime Edina High School Hockey Coach*

"He was a great teacher. You know, a lot has been made of how demanding he was as a coach. But, if he blew the whistle and tried to correct what you were doing wrong, you could actually disagree with him and talk to him about it. Then he would come back with another way for you to do it where it would really make sense to you. That was one of his best attributes I think. Herbie just always kept you on the edge of your seat, and that is why guys played so hard for him. I mean if you were doing well he would scream at you and if you were doing poorly he would pat you on the back, you just never knew." — *Eric Strobel, former Gopher & Olympic player*

"Herbie had a great personality. He could laugh at himself and I don't think he ever took himself too seriously. Sure, when he was coaching he was intense, but when he was scouting or something, he was just a totally different person. I think that if he looked back on his life I don't think he would change a thing. He had success, he had happiness with his family and he had fun." — *Dean Blais, former Gopher player & current head coach at the University of North Dakota*

"Herbie was very direct. He told it like it was and a lot of times people did not want to hear that, but that was his style." — *John Harrington, former Gopher & Olympic player*

"I think Herbie was a better teacher than he was a coach. His best days were at the University of Minnesota and then with the 1980 Olympic team. He was dealing with amateurs at that point and Herbie could teach them, and mold them. They really listened to him. I think it was tougher for him at the professional level because he didn't have that same type of relationship. So, I think he was happiest when he dealt with the kids, the amateurs, because he could really teach and that is where he really made a difference in my opinion. I just don't think he had as much fun coaching the pros. I don't think he had the same smile on his face that he did when he was with the Gophers. So, I just thought he was a great teacher, and I really respected him." — *Lou Cotroneo, former St. Paul Johnson High School hockey coach & longtime friend*

"His ability to get people to do their best. His motivational skills were just outstanding. Then, he had such a great knowledge of the game. He was able to make adjustments during game situations and was just a brilliant tactician. He never got too close to his players either, because he wanted to be able to make objective decisions about them when he had to. That was very important to him. He just was able to get people to overachieve and that was amazing. I mean what he did with that 1980 Olympic team was unbelievable.

"Herb was great with the college and Olympic kids, but when he got into the pros it was different. I think that even though he didn't have as much success in the pros than he did elsewhere, he was still a very good pro coach. He did have that one year in New York where they scored close to 100 points and then lost to the Islanders in seven games. But, I think if Herb could have been the coach as well as the general manager or director of player personnel, he would still be coaching in the NHL right now. I mean in college he could go out and get the players who he wanted, but in the pros the players were assigned to him. So, if he would have been able to sign guys and trade for guys to get just the right mix that he wanted, he would have won a whole bunch of Stanley Cups. Even in New Jersey, he complained and complained about his centermen. He just thought that they couldn't compete with the centers that he had. I was with him as an assistant and I heard this from him all the time. I mean our number one guy would be number four anywhere else. We just did not have good centermen at the time. Well, he leaves that next year and wouldn't you know it, management changes everything that next season, brings in some different centermen and they win the Stanley Cup.

"You know, Herbie had some really different ideas in pro hockey. One of them was to take all the coaches, scouts, trainers, support staff and everyone else, and give them a five year contract. Then, if they don't win in five years, you get rid of all of them. It made sense. He had so many innovative ideas. I mean when he went to the NHL he was light years ahead of anybody else. People used to tell him that his ideas wouldn't work at that level, but he proved them wrong. He truly changed the game." — *Warren Strelow, former goalie coach under Brooks and longtime friend*

"As a coach his best quality was a toss-up between being very innovative and being an exceptional motivator. His talks between periods and before games were just phenomenal. Even after being with the guy for four, five and six years, those talks still got the best out of me. He was able to come up with different twists to things and could just motivate us in so many ways." — *Bill Baker, former Gopher & Olympic player*

"He got the best out of his worst player and he got the best out of his best player. That was Herbie. He could just get guys to give more than they ever thought that they could give and then he could motivate them to give a little more." — *Neal Broten, former Gopher, Olympian and North Star*

"Herbie was the most principled person I ever met. I mean I look back just a few years ago to when he quit as the head coach of the New Jersey Devils. That probably cost him three to four hundred thousand dollars. Yet, out of principle he said good bye I am out of here. I mean he could have gotten himself fired and collected the rest of his paycheck via a severance clause in his contract, but instead he quit on his own terms. That was Herbie. How many people would do something like that? I don't know too many. There were other things too, like when his son, Danny, decided that pro hockey wasn't necessarily for him. Herb said that was fine, come on home, but give back your signing bonus money. Again, how many people would do that? He was just so principled and would never waiver from what he believed in." — *Gary Gambucci, former Gopher and teammate on two U.S. National teams*

"I would say commitment. Once he committed to a cause, he was determined to see it through and he gave it his all. Then, I would say that Herbie clearly had a special talent of getting the best out of everybody, not to mention himself." — *John Mayasich, former teammate on U.S. National Teams & longtime friend*

"Herbie was very forthright and didn't B.S. you. If he liked you as a person, he would just about do anything for you. But, if he thought you were trying to take advantage of him, then he would have no time for you." — *Bob Rink, next-door neighbor and longtime friend*

"Just being Herb Brooks. He never forgot where he came from and he meant something to everybody he touched base with. He helped so many people during his life and he was always trying to help people to better their lives. He used to call me to get his players jobs working on my docks at my trucking company. It was a great situation for both of us, and Herb really appreciated it if you could help him out. Everybody who knew him respected him in one way or another. He was just that kind of guy." — *Frank Messin, former hockey referee and longtime friend*

"Herb was really a student of the game. He was consumed with hockey. He would talk about it, sleep it, eat it, drink it and just be consumed with it. The convictions that he had about the game of hockey were really his strength. The way he would select teams and the types of players that he would pick for his systems was also extraordinary. He had a real gift to motivate people of all types and get them to buy into his systems. I am sure that he went head-to-head with a lot of general managers in the National Hockey League over which players he thought he could coach to be successful. His philosophy was unique and that is what made him a winner." — *Jeff Sauer, former University of Wisconsin & Colorado College Head Coach*

"Herbie was so focused on hockey and on winning, that it was his best quality and it might have also been his worst. He was just so focused and hockey was his life. He was an outstanding coach, but it got to a point where I thought he missed out on things because he was so driven to be successful. Then, he always spoke his mind and never backed down. I remember he had the opportunity to coach the 1992 U.S. Olympic Team, but he said he would only take it if he could have the 1994 job as well. In a lot of ways that made sense, because they had that staggered two-year deal going on at that time, and Herbie wanted to keep the team together for both Winter Games. But, USA Hockey didn't want to commit themselves to that and Herbie was adamant about it, so it fell through. It was 'my way or the highway' with Herb, and that could be good and bad I think." — *Gregg Wong, former Pioneer Press columnist*

"Herbie was a white collar guy who wanted to be a blue collar guy. He was just a very hard worker. He also had a very complex personality too. You know, Herbie recognized his accomplishments, but he never really wore them on his sleeve and ran around bragging about what he did. That wasn't him. Then, he was a great motivator and could really get into the coaches and players heads." — *Walter Bush, Chairman of the Board, USA Hockey*

"One thing about Herb was that he was always looking ahead to new things. I remember about a week after the 1980 Olympics he came down to our newsroom here at the station and I told him that I had some great footage of him at the Olympics that I thought he would love to see. So, I tell him to come over and look at it and he says, 'Na, not interested.' I just thought to myself, wow, he is already moving ahead. For Herbie it was like, been there done that, and it is time to move on. He just didn't care about patting himself on the back, he wanted to look ahead to keep fighting for hockey and to do what he loved to do — coach." — *Mark Rosen, WCCO TV sports anchor*

"Herbie always considered himself to be a lunch pail kind of a guy. He always took care of the little people — the bus drivers, equipment managers, trainers, janitors or what have you. He had a tremendous compassion for the job that they did and appreciated them as people. I remember during the Olympics sometimes we would be in the locker room hanging gear until like two or three in the morning, and when we got back to the hotel there would be sandwiches there waiting for us with a nice note from Herb. He just appreciated the little things and as a result, we all wanted to do our best for him. He gave us a lot of responsibility too. For instance, it was my job to tell him when the end of a penalty was coming up or if we were on a power play. Then, I just did what I could to help out the team. I remember every now and then if we were tired and needed a rest, I would hop over the boards and tell the ref that one of our guys had lost a contact lens. So, I would be down on all fours looking and looking and finally I would spit out a lens that I had had in my mouth the entire time and pick it up for him to see. Little things like that sometimes went a long way and Herb appreciated that stuff. You know, sometimes the fringe people get left behind with big name coaches and what not, but not with Herbie. We were just as important to him as his top centerman, or at least that was how he made us feel." — *Gary Smith, trainer under Brooks at the University of Minnesota and on the 1980 Olympic Team*

"Herbie was a detail guy and a real creature of habit. I remember one time I went over with my wife to have dinner with he and Patti. Well, as my wife and I were in the car with Patti, we were waiting for Herb before we could leave to go out to eat. So, Patti, jokingly says, 'Watch this, Herb will go over and make sure that Kelly's car is locked,' and sure enough he walks over and locks the car. 'Now he will go down to the beach house and make sure it is locked,' and sure enough that is what he does. 'Then, he will go back into the house to make sure that the lights are turned off,' and like clockwork, back he goes. 'Now, he will go down to make sure that the second garage is locked,' and that is exactly what he did. 'Lastly, he will go back and make sure that the house is locked,' and she was right on. Finally, after doing like eight things right on cue, by the time he got to the car we were all laughing so hard that we were speechless. He couldn't figure out what the heck we were laughing about, and we never had the heart to tell him!" — *Wayne Ferris, lawyer and business manager*

"Honesty. Herb was so up front about things it was incredible. He didn't B.S. anybody and had so much integrity." — *Bob Utecht, founder of Let's Play Hockey newspaper*

"Herb was an outstanding public speaker. He could've been Patton, what, with his ability to rally people around what he believed in. His motivational skills were incredible. He was such an intellectual, dynamic thinker. He very easily could've been a politician. That was the truth. He could speak to a group like no one I had ever seen before. He could just connect with people, whether that was one on one with somebody or in an auditorium in front of a thousand people. So, for me it wasn't that he was a wonderful tactician or a great hockey player as a young man, it was his people skills. He was the best." — *Brian Lawton, hockey agent and former North Star under Brooks*

"Herbie never lost sight of his east side roots. He was a champion of the little person and just rooted for the underdog, no matter who that was. That was an endearing quality, and that was Herb to a tee." — *Jim Boo, former Gopher player*

"Herbie was very determined and wanted to make a difference. I would suspect that he had the same attitude that I had with regards to *'That is where we were, look where we are today, where can we be 25 years from now?'* I would also say that he and I were both on the same page in terms of wanting to see growth, development, improvement and changes to the game, particularly at the high school level with regards to numbers of games, lengths of periods and that type of thing. We were both strong proponents of hockey throughout our country and that is what we had in common. You know, Herbie was always thinking ahead and always had his heart in the right place I think, and that was to help advance the sport of hockey to new people and in new areas. Both he and John Mariucci would travel miles and miles to promote the game and encourage people to play and to help communities build rinks. That was what it was all about for Herbie." — *Bob Peters, longtime Bemidji State University head coach*

"Herbie was very straight forward and he wasn't afraid to tell you things that you didn't necessarily want to hear. He was very, very honest. For example, when my son, Zach, was deciding which college to go to, we asked Herbie what he thought. He was just so helpful. He did a bunch of research for us and told Zach which schools would be the best fit for him. I mean, he said that if he were making the same recommendation for his own son, and he wanted to know where he thought he should go, then he said he would go to Harvard. They have a good hockey program and it is the best school in the country. Then, the number two school that he recommended was Notre Dame. From there, he went on down the list. Well, Zach chose North Dakota and Herb supported that decision too. So, we appreciated that a lot. Herbie was just a very considerate person who helped people when they needed help. He was truly a marvelous friend." — *J.P. Parise, former North Star player and assistant coach with the North Stars under Brooks*

"Herbie loved the underdog and was so loyal to the Minnesota guys, and not just the hockey players either. I mean, I think back to the interview he gave to Ed Karow immediately following the victory over Finland to win the gold medal back in 1980. I could only imagine how many national and international reporters were trying to talk to him at that moment. But, he cleared out of there and wound up in some small school in Lake Placid to give Eddie the exclusive interview. That was typical Herbie, always pulling for the underdog.

"I had heard another story one time when Herbie was coaching the Rangers, and it was the last pre-season game of the year. Well, Herbie went with an unknown Minnesota kid in goal that night. So, Craig Patrick asked him why he would go with that guy in that situation. And Herb said, 'Because he was a Minnesotan.' That summed it up for Herbie. He was from Minnesota and he was going to catch his break as long as Herbie saw to it." — *Paul Ostby, former Gopher player and business associate*

"Herbie had a lot of qualities. What Herbie said he was going to do, Herbie did. That was first. Then, you could always depend on him. He was someone who never forgot people and someone who remembered his roots. And, he was very quick to embrace people and thank them for anything that they did for him." — *Bruce Telander, former Gopher Blue Line Club president and longtime friend*

"Communicating and teaching. Herbie could communicate with people all over the world at all levels of life. He just had a gift. He was also very caring. I think he wanted us all to be like him and care as much as he did about the things he cared about." — *Craig Patrick, General Manager of Pittsburgh Penguins & longtime friend*

WHAT WAS THE SECRET
TO HERBIE'S SUCCESS?

"He had an amazing ability to attempt the most abstract concepts while remaining totally organized in the basics. I used to tell Herbie that while he had some far-out and totally liberal ideas for how his Gopher teams should play, he also was so conservative he'd have preferred uniforms with button-down jerseys and wing-tip skates. He loved that. In recent years, there have been rumors that he was approached to run for political office, but not many people realize he got approached by both the Democrats and the Republicans." — *John Gilbert, former Star-Tribune hockey reporter and longtime friend*

"Obviously, Herbie knew the game, tactically, very well. He understood the whole game, and how it should be played. But I think his ability to get the most out of everybody and to reach in to that individual and push the right button to get him to achieve more than what he thought he was capable of achieving was his forté. I am also not sure he was so hung up on the superstar player either. He was more concerned about the total team and the team always came first with him. But that pretty much reflects his attitude about his family, about his friends and about the game." — *Mike Sertich, former UM-Duluth Head Coach*

"Herbie was able to read people, read situations and had great insight. He was also such a great motivator and used so many different ways to motivate people. I mean some of those ways weren't the most pleasant, but they were very effective." — *Brad Buetow, former Gopher Head Coach*

"Herbie never surrendered. Once he got a goal in his head, it was going to be accomplished. He never got discouraged, he just got pissed off. I mean if he had a goal in his mind to do something, and he truly believed in it, he got a plan and then just did it. Nothing was going to stop him! Nothing! He was smart enough politically to know how to get the right guys on his side; he was tough enough to go in and tell a guy off to his face; and he was honest too, which was just an amazing combination for success. I will give you an example, 'over-speed skating.' How does he invent this? He goes to legendary Gopher track and field coach, Roy Griak, and asks him how he develops speed. Roy had this interval idea where you are always sprinting guys when they are rested. So, he applies that to hockey. Then, he brings in Jack Blatherwick, who has without a doubt, spent more time with Herbie on developing new training techniques than anybody. The two of them would then research things, and implement a plan. Herbie studied the Europeans, the Russians, the Scandinavians, he wanted to know what everybody was doing and then apply it to his own guys, only better. He would take all of these ideas and then surround himself with experts, like Roy and Jack, and hammer out a plan to get his kids into world class shape. Herbie would have the concept, and then he would have Jack do all the work — he was also a master delegator. Then, he would tweak it, and implement it right away. Things were just going to get done with him, and if you weren't with him, then you were in his way, and he would run you over to get it done. If that meant telling this guy off and lining up his ducks over here, then that was all part of it. He would take on anybody, it didn't matter to him. He would fight and kick and eventually get whatever it was that he wanted to do, that was Herbie.

"I tell you what. There was not one kid on that 1980 Olympic team who thought they could win the gold medal. Herbie knew though. He just willed them to win. He had a plan and he executed it. He wanted them bigger, faster, stronger and worked them very hard. You know, the world is filled with dreamers. But Herbie could execute those dreams, and that is what made him so different. His work ethic was unparalleled and he was just a winner in every sense. He let his players know that they had a gift, and that they had a responsibility to use that gift. He was just so intense, and I am even getting intense just talking about him!

"You know, 1980 was such a fun time. I remember Herbie was set up at the Met Center at that time, but wanted his own space, so he moved everything over to the Civic Center. Well, he didn't have any money for anything, so he begged, borrowed and stole everything he could. Do you know where he got his weight room? From my garage! I always had a lot of great weight training equipment, so I let him have it all. One day some pickup trucks came over and we loaded it all in and off it went to the Civic Center. Then, he raised some more money to buy some more things to get his kids into shape. That was very important to him, that his kids were strong, and were in great physical shape. Nowadays the players have everything top of the line, but back then it was on a shoestring. I mean the kids played on the team because they loved it and because it was a great honor. At the time, being on the Olympics meant that you were one of the top college players in the country. So, behind that humble setting at the old Civic Center, and with my weights, he put that team together. Wow, what a story that was. And that was Herbie. We all just pitched in. I remember we would have that entire team over to our house all the time for dinner. My wife would cook like four turkeys and we would all get together and eat. We didn't have a lot of money for stuff, so we rallied behind each other and just got it done."
— *Larry Hendrickson, former area high school hockey coach and longtime friend*

"His uncommon drive. Herbie was a multi-tasking kind of guy and he just never rested. He was just constantly on some kind of project, whether it was working on his own yard, or building a deck, or whatever, he was still always thinking about hockey while he was doing those things. He was relentless. His life was just one steady stream of projects, and that is what made him so successful I think, both on and off the ice. The funny thing about all the decks he used to build was the fact that he could never just sit down to relax and actually enjoy them. He just liked having a project to do, that was Herbie." — *Jack Blatherwick, Brooks' former strength & conditioning coach and longtime friend*

"Herbie would do whatever he believed in and was passionate about it. He would never compromise on his principles, but he would on the strategy to achieve those principles, that was Herbie. Herbie always thought that coaching was like tying a string around somebody so that you could pull the talent out of them. Then, after you pulled it out, that string became like an iron rod, and then you could push them. Everything with Herbie was knowing when to push and when to pull, that was his secret, and he was the best at that. It was all about getting people out of their comfort zones and then getting them to do things that they didn't think they were capable of doing." — *Neil Sheehy, hockey agent and close friend*

"I would say it was his intensity, his obsession with achieving goals, his attention to detail and his fear of failure." — *Murray Williamson, former Gopher teammate and 1972 U.S. Olympic coach*

"He just had that special personality. He was so intelligent and persuasive in his arguments and he just had a tremendous amount of energy too. Then, he paid a great attention to detail, and he was really good at delegating authority. Now, he would drive you nuts in the process because he would keep checking on all the details all the time, but that was Herbie. All of those things went into his style, and that is what I think made him so successful. I will give you an example. One time when I was working with him here as his assistant at St. Cloud, he asked me to make a couple of calls and check on a couple of things. So, a few days later he follows up and asks me where I was at with that stuff. Well, I told him that I hadn't gotten around to it yet. Whoa! He chewed me out something fierce! He said, 'Listen, if I wanted to do it myself I would've done it, but I wanted you to get this job done, and I didn't mean three days later!' So, from that point on he never had to ask me twice about things. He just sort of put that fear into you. I am sure General George Patton was the same way. Leaders just have those qualities and can get things done. Sometimes he felt that he had to ruffle feathers, and he was never afraid to do that — that is for sure."
— *Craig Dahl, St. Cloud State Head Coach and former Brooks assistant*

"Herbie knew how to push everybody's buttons at the right times to get them to be successful as a team. Herbie knew when to light us up and when to pat us on the back. You know, a lot of the things that Herbie did back then, just wouldn't fly today. I mean back then, if there was a problem, you could buy a couple cases of beer and leave the room so that the guys could work it out amongst themselves. Nowadays a coach would get fired for that. I remember one time when I was a sophomore and we were playing up at Michigan State. Well, Herbie walked into the locker room and just ripped Mike Polich a new you-know-what right in front of all of us. I was just in awe of the fact that here was our best player and the coach was just laying into him like that. But Herbie knew that deep down Polich could handle it and that he would probably get mad about it and play harder as a result. Then, because everyone else was so intimidated, that we would go play harder too! It was classic Herbie. He knew when, where and why to vent, in order to get the entire team fired up. And, he wasn't afraid to lay into one guy if he felt it would benefit the entire team." — *Tom Vanelli, former Gopher player*

"Herbie was so smart. I mean he was head and shoulders above any other coach when it came to intelligence. He could out-think anybody and that was why he was so successful. You know what though, there was another wild side to Herbie too. I mean I remember once during a game back when I was playing for him in junior hockey, he picked up our entire bundle of extra sticks and threw them at the ref. So, he could cut loose if he wanted to. And, usually if he did do something like that, it was to make a statement to his players to get them fired up. It didn't happen very often, but when he did, watch out!" — *Pat Phippen, former Gopher player*

"Herbie never picked the best players, rather, he picked the players he felt would make the best team. There is a big difference. In doing so, it shows you that the players he picked for his teams were winners before that, and they carried that torch in endeavors after that. All Herbie did was to verify or validate the processes that each individual had, whether it was a work ethic, or belief or something that we went through to achieve what we wanted to achieve. Beyond that, Herbie was able to tie in the emotional aspects to the individual players and get them to perform at their highest levels. Herbie had a psychology degree from the University of Minnesota and believe me, he used it every day." — *Robb McClanahan, former Gopher & Olympic player*

"He was honest, smart and just did whatever it was that he believed in. When he went out to do something he didn't just do it on a whim. He analyzed it, studied it and went over it 1,001 different ways to figure it out. That was Herbie. Even for us, he took the best elements of the European game and combined that with the best elements of the North American game to come up with a style that was all his own. It was very calculated and he knew what he was doing at all times. The guy was just brilliant. He knew what he was doing and he knew where he was going." — *Buzz Schneider, former Gopher & Olympic player*

"His passion and his willingness to blend thoughts and ideas was what made Herbie so successful. He was also a great judge of character and a great judge of talent. He was also just able to bring out the most in people." — *Phil Verchota, former Gopher & Olympic player*

"He worked very hard at what he did. And, Herbie was a dreamer. He had a vision and he knew that if you worked hard that you could achieve your dreams. That is an amazing quality." — *Mike Polich, former Gopher player*

"As a coach the secret to his success was that he knew talent and he knew it took all kinds of different people with different skill qualities to make up a team. He got everyone to believe that they were important. Then, whatever they brought to the table, whether they were a shot-blocker, a penalty-killer, a play-maker or whatever, they were important to Herbie and they were important to the success of his team. I think that philosophy carried over into all aspects of his life too. He knew how to blend people together and to me, he brought out the best in everybody. He made you want to aspire to be the best person you could be, whether that was as a coach, parent, father, husband or what have you. He just made people feel important enough to where they wanted to aspire to be the best that they could be." — *Bill Butters, former Gopher player*

"He had a tremendous drive and persistence to excel. That was Herbie and he did that with everything in life." — *Roger Wigen, former St. Paul Johnson High School Hockey teammate*

"He put so much work into coaching. I mean when the game was done, he wasn't done. He worked so hard all the time and just never stopped trying to think up new ways to win. That was Herbie." — *Mark Pavelich, former player on 1980 U.S. Olympic Team & NY Rangers*

"Herbie was a very hard working guy. Contrary to what people might think, things didn't come easy for him. He did a lot of homework on whatever he was doing and he worked very hard. He studied everything and was well prepared for whatever he was doing. Herbie in the business world probably would have made a hell of a lot more money than he ever did in hockey. He was just that type of person. He was a very intelligent, hard working person, that was his secret." — *Steve Badalich, long-time friend*

"He was such a damn good people person. He understood people like nobody I ever knew. I would sit back and watch him talk to different people and was always just amazed at him. He just loved to talk to people about so many different things. And when he did take the time to talk to people, they felt like a million bucks. He had a gift that way. You know, if you knew Herbie a little bit, you knew him a lot. He was that open and that easy to talk to. Everybody wanted to say that they knew him, that was for sure." — *Butch Bloom, longtime friend*

"His passion for the game and his passion for life. He just really enjoyed being around people and then making them feel good or even better about themselves. He really encouraged people in whatever he did and sincerely wanted them to be successful. You know, with Herbie it was never a job, it was a real love that he had for the game and for people. I remember once when his wife, Patti, told him that he loved hockey more than her, and Herbie said, *'Yeah, but I love you more than hunting or fishing!'* That was Herbie. You know, he upset some people along the way too, but Herbie believed in what he thought was right and was not afraid to tell you that. You may not have always agreed with him, but he let you know exactly where you stood with him and what his beliefs were." — *Tommy Reid, former North Star & current Wild radio analyst*

"Herbie was a very organized person, which always impressed me a lot. I always felt like whenever I showed up for a practice that he had a plan for me that day. He was just always well prepared and he stuck to his plan. I believed in him so and I bought into the things he did. He just had that affect on me. Beyond that, he was so committed to what he believed in and he was very loyal to the Minnesota kids. I appreciated that about him a lot." — *Steve Christoff, former Gopher & Olympic player*

"It just came down to hard work with that guy. He worked us like I have never been worked when I played for him. I never worked harder for any other coach. But, he also put the right players out there together too, and he had a gift for seeing that. He just knew how to put a team together and then get them ready to play and win. He put together all the right pieces, from the goal scorers to the grinders, and then he got the right personalities that fit together too. It was a puzzle for Herbie and I think he loved that." — *Reed Larson, former Gopher player*

"Herbie was just very smart. And, he did things his way. Sure, he took advice from other people, but in the end it was his going to be his decision. There was no other way for Herbie. People had a lot of respect for him because of that." — *Greg Malone, Pittsburgh Penguins head of scouting*

"Herbie was probably one of the best judges of talent around. He could just tell if a kid was capable or not. Then, you add in his brutal honesty, and that is what made him unique. You know, my youngest brother, Dan, tried out at the University of Minnesota when Herbie was coaching there. Herb worked him out and then told him that he had better get another sideline, because he wasn't going to be a hockey player there. It was cold reality but it was the truth, and my brother accepted it and moved on. So, even though we were friends and what not, Herb just said it like it was." — *Bob Paradise, former teammate & father-in-law to his daughter*

"I think Herbie had a master plan for every team he coached. He was always very organized and he built a foundation from the ground up every time. He created a plan, then stuck to it and that was how he achieved success." — *Phil Housley, former 2002 Olympian under Brooks & former NHL All-Star*

"He was just a very smart hockey mind. He was also very honest. I mean he would always say, *'I can't be your friend, because then he I won't be able to coach to you.'* I totally respected that. He just kept us at a distance, yet we would all do anything for him. You just didn't want to disappoint him." — *Steve Ulseth, former Gopher player*

"He was so smart and so intelligent. He also had a great wit and was actually a very funny guy. Then, he was such a great motivator. He could really read people and his players knew that he cared about them. You know, when people know that someone cares about them, them will do extraordinary things to achieve a goal. He was just so passionate and cared so much for the people that he was trying to motivate. A lot of times that didn't come out right away with Herb, but there was a method to his madness in the end." — *Joe Micheletti, former Gopher player & current Fox Sports TV hockey analyst*

"The crispness and cleanliness of what he thought was right and that fact that he always kept that in focus and did not deviate from it." — *Noel Rahn, longtime friend*

"He was just a great coach. You know, even when I was playing with him way back when, he used to always coach me out on the ice, telling me what I was doing right and wrong. He just knew everything about the game and was so smart. So, I would say he was just very intelligent." — *Paul Johnson, former Olympic teammate and longtime friend*

"Herb knew what made guys tick. He studied their personalities and he could read them. He knew who he could push and who he had to back off of. He was also a good judge of character too." — *Mike Ramsey, former Gopher & Olympic player and current Wild assistant coach*

"Herbie wanted to win. Period. He knew how to push the buttons of his players to motivate them. He had a real knack at figuring out which buttons to push on each player, and once he did that he was able to get them to be winners. That was how he was so successful, he had a real gift." — *Paul Holmgren, former Gopher player & NHL player and coach*

"Herbie had the ability to elevate people to another level and was just a great motivator. He just had a gift. That was Herbie." — *Larry Pleau, former teammate on 1968 Olympic team & current St. Louis Blues GM*

"Herb was a good detail man. He was a fierce competitor. He was a very good judge of talent and character. And, obviously he had good players, because no coach wins without talented players. But, he knew how to put it all together and could motivate his players like no one I had ever seen. He was just a tremendous leader too. He took charge and got things done. There was no secret. He just worked hard and was real intelligent. In fact, that might have been the thing that was the most impressive about him, his intelligence. Then, I was also really impressed by the thoroughness that he exhibited with regards to scouting players. I mean he hated to cut people, so he would fly back and forth across the country, three or four times, to see guys play as much as he could. He just didn't want to make a mistake and pick anybody for his teams that wasn't deserving. Then, we would have discussions about players for hours on end, debating every little detail about them and what they could bring to the table. He was very good too about listening to everybody's input and valuing their opinions. You know, there were some really good players that he wasn't able to select for that 2002 team and that tore him up inside. He knew that those players would take it personally, and that hurt him. But, he was the boss and he knew that he had to make some tough decisions. Herb was a gamer, and I totally respected that about him." — *Lou Vairo, head coach of 1984 U.S. Olympic team & assistant under Brooks on the 2002 U.S. squad*

"He was an innovator. He was also very progressive in how he coached. He just really knew how to push the right buttons on people to get the best out of them. I would also say that his teams were very well prepared and in just great physical condition too." — *Don Lucia, Gopher Hockey head coach*

"He was a great motivator. He knew what buttons to push on what people and could just get the most out of his players. I will never forget back to just before the Olympics in 1980 when he called me into his office and just flat out said he was going to cut me. Actually, he said he would say that I hurt my back or something so I could still travel with the team and come to Lake Placid. He was always playing with your mind a little bit, and I wasn't sure what he was up to at that moment. He was trying to see how close the team was and it might have been the last hurdle that he placed in front of me. I mean the guys were pissed off that he would consider cutting one of us and bringing in somebody from the outside. We rallied together though and that united us. His thought was to get everybody against him so that we would all be on the same page. He was just a very demanding coach and could be difficult to play for, but you couldn't argue with the results. He was like your dad. I mean sometimes you loved your dad and sometimes you hated him because he made you do things you didn't want to do. That was Herb." — *Mike Eruzione, former 1980 Olympian*

"He was certainly a hard worker. He also had goals that he set and then had certain ways that his players had to play in order to achieve those goals. If they didn't, then they didn't play for him. He was very opinionated on how the game was supposed to be played, and he tried to change you. So, if you didn't change for him, then you didn't play very much. He was a very strict coach and really got his guys into shape. His practices were legendary. So, all of those things went into it I think." — *Willard Ikola, former Olympian and longtime Edina High School Hockey Coach*

"Obviously, you win with talent, and don't get me wrong, he could recruit and was a good judge of talent, but Herbie was also a great motivator. He was a great tactician of the game too. He just had all the attributes of being a successful coach from top to bottom. He had it all." — *Eric Strobel, former Gopher & Olympic player*

"Herbie had a lot of good qualities. He was very organized, very intense and very smart. He was just the total package. If you ever heard him speak, then you know what I mean, he was just captivating to listen to. He had a gift. He could get his players to buy into his systems and then motivate the heck out of them to win. He also developed skills and fundamentals in his players and that was important to remember too. He was a really special person." — *Dean Blais, former Gopher player & current head coach at the University of North Dakota*

"Herbie knew how far he could motivate people before they would quit. He could push that button with everybody to push them just far enough to get them to do things that they never thought they were capable of doing. He just made sure that everyone on his team was giving their maximum effort towards the team's common goal." — *John Harrington, former Gopher & Olympic player*

"Herbie was a great communicator. He just said the right things at the right times and the kids performed accordingly. He was able to speak their language and that is how he could communicate so well with them. You know, Herbie never ran a personality contest, but you could never argue with his win-loss record. He just demanded respect and he got it. He earned it. You see, success doesn't come in cans, you have to earn it, and nobody worked harder than Herb Brooks. He just made people believe in themselves and from there anything could happen." — *Lou Cotroneo, former St. Paul Johnson High School hockey coach & longtime friend*

"Conviction, belief, passion and hard work. He really believed in people and tried to put them into situations where they could do their jobs and then succeed. The guy was brilliant. He had a passion for the game unlike anything I have ever seen. I remember when I coached with him in New Jersey and one time he called my room at like 2:30 in the morning. I said, 'what the heck are you doing I am sound asleep?' and he said, 'take out a pencil and a piece of paper and write these lines down — then tell me what you think of them tomorrow in practice.' I mean he would think about hockey all the time, it consumed him." — *Warren Strelow, former goalie coach under Brooks and longtime friend*

"Herbie was just able to motivate players who maybe weren't quite as talented as other people, but he knew how to get the most out of them. He knew that he could count on them down the stretch and that was big to Herbie. He recruited people like that and understood that teams needed all types of players. He was just so innovative and creative with what he had to work with. He was just a great coach in so many aspects. Then, he got us in such good condition. I mean our teams were the best conditioned teams in the country, without question. I mean nobody beat us in the third period and nobody ever out-skated us, that was for sure. You know, I will never forget his practices. It was hell, I can remember falling down those stairs to the locker room afterwards because my legs could no longer stand. Our big joke was that we would get out of shape on the weekends, because we had games instead of practices!" — *Bill Baker, former Gopher & Olympic player*

"He loved his players. It was more of a father/son relationship, but he loved them." — *Neal Broten, former Gopher, Olympian and North Star*

"Before you can become a great coach, you have to be a great person. And that was Herbie. There were no hidden agendas with him. He was so passionate too, and just stuck to his guns on things he believed in. I respected that about him so much. Now, some guys were threatened by him, but that didn't bother him. He was just very outspoken and very altruistic. He did very little for financial gain, yet did so much out of love and compassion. He just loved hockey and always wanted to improve the game for the next generation of kids. That was what Herbie was all about. He just wanted to make better people out of everybody. You didn't have to like him when you were playing for him, but when you were done, that was when you realized what he was trying to accomplish. He was hard on his kids, and even tougher on his superstars, because he knew that they had more to give. He just always wanted to raise the bar for everybody, and that was why the guy was so successful." — *Gary Gambucci, former Gopher and teammate on two U.S. National teams*

"His passion, no question, you could feel it. He just had a passion for success in whatever he did and that was amazing. That was what separated him from the others, the fact that he could instill that passion into his players and then motivate them to do things that they never thought they could do." — *Craig Sarner, former Gopher and player under Brooks on 1979 U.S. National Team and in Europe & longtime coach at various levels*

"He was so dedicated and so willing to learn. Then, he would take what he learned and put it into practice. He just had an innate ability to get people to accept what he was preaching. The result was usually success." — *John Mayasich, former teammate on U.S. National Teams & longtime friend*

"Herbie was a great judge of talent, but was also brutally honest. So, if he saw someone with talent, he would encourage them to work hard at their abilities. But, I know dads who he had told them that their kids weren't any good. He would tell them instead to have them get a good job or find a good woman and get married and have a great life. He would tell them that they weren't going to be a hockey player. They would be something else, but not a hockey player. So, he was very honest and I respected that." — *Bob Rink, next-door neighbor and longtime friend*

"He was a great people person. He was very honest, earned the respect of his players and worked very hard. Then, he had a great, great knowledge of the sport." — *Frank Messin, former hockey referee and longtime friend*

"It was his intensity, his competitiveness, the fact that he was not afraid to take chances, his motivational skills, his ability to read players, and his work ethic. It was all of those things and more." — *Jeff Sauer, former University of Wisconsin & Colorado College Head Coach*

"Herbie knew how to put a team together. He knew that you needed different personalities and you needed different types of players to be successful. You know, I always felt that (Doug) Woog always went for the all-state superstars, but Herbie knew that you needed a blend of players. He understood that you needed a few guys who worked their way up through the junior ranks, and that you needed a few muckers and grinders to balance everything out. He knew that you couldn't win with just all superstars, and that was why he had guys like Billy Butters and Jim Boo on his teams. So, Herbie knew that and then was able to get the most out of them. That was his gift, to put a team together and then to get them to play together. No one was better at that than Herbie." — *Gregg Wong, former Pioneer Press columnist*

"Herbie was very prepared. He knew what to expect from his opponents and he was able to communicate that to the players. He had a way of building up his players and then occasionally tearing them down at certain times. He was an outstanding motivator and just really knew how to get the most out of his players. Then, I would say that he was a tremendous student of the game. He learned so many different systems from around the world and wasn't afraid to try them with his own players." — *Walter Bush, Chairman of the Board, USA Hockey*

"Herbie never sold himself to anybody. He did what he thought he needed to do and he did it on his own terms. Herbie was his own man, and good or bad, that was how it was going to be with him. I respected that a great deal about him." — *Doug Woog, former Gopher Hockey Coach & teammate on a U.S. National team*

"It would have to be his ability to motivate because he wasn't necessarily going to always get people to be in his camp. You know, with Herbie it was *'my way or the highway'* with a lot of the things that he did. So, in order to motivate people within those parameters, that was a pretty difficult thing to do. But, he did it and that was why he was so successful. He was just a brilliant motivator." — *Frank Mazzocco, Gopher Hockey TV Analyst*

"His passion. He couldn't hide his passion. He loved hockey so much and would do anything for it. I mean if he had an issue with something, watch out! He was so determined and so focused that nothing could stop him. He was so salty and cantankerous too. He didn't care if he pissed a few people off along the way, he was just going to do things his way no matter what. I used to love too when he would give guys that he didn't really like back-handed compliments without them even knowing that he was slamming them. He was just a classic." — *Joe Schmit, KSTP-TV sports anchor*

"His passion. Herb just loved to coach. I mean I remember seeing him at the Olympics in Nagano, when he was coaching the French National Team, and asking him what the heck he was doing over here! Sure, winning the gold medal was great, but he just loved to coach — that was Herbie. He was truly born to be a coach. I think he felt the most at ease and the most comfortable in this world when he was behind the bench or at practice teaching kids." — *Mark Rosen, WCCO-TV sports anchor*

"Herb was very intense. I remember during the 1980 Olympics when we were playing the Soviets, it was late in the third period and we got screwed up on a line change while we were killing a penalty and I counted six guys out on the ice. So, I grabbed Neal Broten by the jersey as he was heading over the boards and pulled him back. Just then, Herbie came all the way down the bench and said, *'Smitty, way to stay in the game!'*. That was Herbie. You know, Herbie loved his players but he would never let them know that. I remember he would tell me from time to time that he would love to be able to go out and have a beer or two with certain guys, but he never let himself. He always kept himself distant. Herb was kind of a loner and I think he liked the mystique of that.

"You know, there was always somebody to kind of calm things down after he ripped em' a new one, and one of those guys was Robbie McClanahan. Herbie picked him for that role because he knew that he could handle it. I remember playing against Sweden during the 1980 Olympics. It was the first period and Robbie bruised his thigh pretty badly, so I took him back to ice it in the locker room. So, Herbie came in after the period and went after him like there was no tomorrow. He called him the biggest pussy that ever walked the earth and that he wasn't tough enough to play in the National Hockey League. Robbie, meanwhile, has a huge wrap around his leg, and he jumps up and goes after Herbie. The ice bag flies off and the two of them are screaming at each other out in the hall. The Swedes are right next door in the next locker room and are wondering what the hell is going on. So, Herbie brings him back into our locker room and is reading him the riot act. I am standing there thinking *'Oh my God, we are at the Olympics and Herb has lost it!'*. And as I thought that, I looked around the room. I could see that every one of his teammates was getting more and more pissed off at Herb over the way he was treating their teammate. So, they rallied together and went out and beat the Swedes, just to spite Herbie. Herbie, however, was a psychology major, and knew that all along. He sold his theory to his players, and they bought it. He just knew how to deal with people in his own way, and that was the secret to his success.

"Another thing with Herb was his ability to polarize his teams in an 'us versus them' situation. I mean, I will never forget back to when we played Boston

University back in the semi's in 1976 and we got into a big fight with them. Herb loved that because it became us versus them. It was Minnesota versus the East Coast preppies and Minnesota versus the Canucks. He always drew those lines and that got his players to rally together. Well, we won that battle and won the national championship that year. That was Herb. I remember walking into Blue Line Club luncheons at North Dakota or Madison, boy, it was tough. I mean there were four or five of us against an entire room full of people who hated us. Herbie loved that. He thrived on it and it motivated him. But he was not petty about things or held grudges either. An example of that was when I found out that Mark Johnson was named to the 1980 Olympic team. I was shocked because I knew that Herbie and Badger Bob, Mark's father, were bitter rivals. But, Herbie knew that Mark was a great hockey player and thought he was a great kid. He didn't hold that against him and I respected that a lot about him." — *Gary Smith, trainer under Brooks at the University of Minnesota and on the 1980 Olympic Team*

"Herbie had a very rare combination of instinct, understanding people, knowledge of hockey, hard work and an ability to motivate. He understood the Xs and the Os of hockey better than just about anybody plus he had an ability to really know how to push people's buttons. He treated all of his players differently and just knew what it would take to motivate each one of them individually. He was very interested in overachievement. High achievers weren't good enough for him, they had to raise their own bars to achieve beyond what they thought they were capable of. He was just never satisfied and a real perfectionist. The guy was brilliant." — *Wayne Ferris, lawyer and business manager*

"His intelligence. His genius was being able to take a group of people who were all going after a common goal, dissect what their roles were, and then convincing each of the individuals that the success of the team would come down to how well each of them did their jobs — because each job or role was just as important as the next. And no matter how big or small their role was, he made them feel that it was not only meaningful, but critical to the group's success. So, in hockey he knew that you needed grinders and checkers to compliment the goal scorers. And in the end, if everyone did their job, the team would be successful." — *Dave Knoblauch, longtime friend*

"His determination to succeed and to excel was unbelievable. He worked so hard at whatever he was doing and just had an incredible work ethic. He burned the candle at both ends for a lot of years and spent a lot of time on the road. He just had a passion for hockey and a passion for life. And, if people asked him to come to their functions or award ceremonies or what have you, he was there for them. He was so generous with his time and that meant so much to people." — *Don Saatzer, former Hastings High School hockey coach and longtime scout with the Boston Bruins*

"His work ethic. He put so much effort into whatever it was that he was working on and that was why he was so successful. He wasn't there to make friends, he was there to get a job done. Another thing with Herb as a coach was that he always got his teams in great shape, no matter what. He insisted on that and that was very important to him. From there, he just believed and then he got his players to believe — that was his secret." — *Paul Coppo, former teammate on several U.S. National Teams and longtime friend*

"Herb Brooks was a great listener. As dynamic a person as he was, he would always listen to the advice of others. Then, he worked very hard at whatever he was doing.

He could motivate his players to do just about anything too, and that was how he was able to win so much throughout his career. He was just a fabulous coach all the way around." — *Bob Utecht, founder of Let's Play Hockey newspaper*

"He knew how to get players to buy into his philosophy. Then, he knew how to be creative. He just had the ability to get guys to believe, and I was one of those guys. I would have followed him anywhere. You had to work hard for Herb, but it usually paid off in the end. He was also an information guy, and really understood the value of good information. He didn't trust a lot of people either, so if you were in his circle, it was a real honor. He surrounded himself with the people he trusted the most and that was important to him. The guy was so determined, in whatever he did, and he was very honest. That was the secret to his success." — *Nick Fotiu, former New York Ranger under Brooks*

"For me it was one word, passion. This guy was passionate about everything he did. I mean I didn't always agree with him. In fact, we had a lot of disagreements over a lot of different things, but I never ever questioned his passion. It was just larger than life. I really respected the guy." — *Brian Lawton, hockey agent and former North Star under Brooks*

"Herbie was very driven and very passionate about everything he did. He used to say that what you can't give a player is a heart transplant. For Herbie you either believed it and were passionate about it, or you weren't. I mean I certainly didn't have the talent that the other guys did, but Herb got the most out of me. He enabled me to believe in myself and I worked very hard for him. He just had that ability to do that with everybody, and that was the secret to his success." — *Jim Boo, former Gopher player*

"Herbie was a very thoughtful person and he would analyze everything from practices to the evaluation of players. He was very effective at that. And, of course, he was a great communicator and motivator with his players. You know, players don't always like to hear the truth and it takes a special person to do that, whether you have to raise your voice or not. That is the difficult part of coaching, but Herbie stuck with his convictions on things that he believed in. Let me tell you, chewing butt is not easy work, for any of us. You have to be determined. I didn't relish raising cane with people, but it was a job that had to be done because the team has to come first. I think Herb was able to be tough, but still was able to command the respect he deserved from his players. That was unique. As a colleague, I certainly respected his hard work and the determination that he had." — *Bob Peters, longtime Bemidji State University head coach*

"He was very, very bright. He was a thinker and was not afraid to try things. Then, the things that he did try, he really thought them through and researched them. He prepared for everything and never left anything to chance. He was also a man of his convictions too. I mean once he got something into his head, he was going to do it, no matter what. So, all of that, plus a lot of hard work, that was Herbie's secret." — *J.P. Parise, former North Star player and assistant coach with the North Stars under Brooks*

"You know, when you talk about money, sure, Herbie did pretty well for himself, but it wasn't because he was thinking about money. It was because he was thinking about motivating people and helping people and trying to impact their lives. So, it is like anything else, if you become good at something and are passionate about what you do, then you don't really even think about the results. You think more along the lines of loving what you are doing, having fun and being committed. From there the results fall in the wake of doing the right thing. That is what Herbie will be known for. Sure, he was cantankerous, sure, he was somewhat misunderstood by a lot of people and sure, he had the ability to create enemies. But he did things his own way and that enemy he had one year might be his best friend the next. That was Herbie." — *Paul Ostby, former Gopher player and business associate*

"Herb was a thinker. He was just very smart when it came to studying the game and understanding strategy and all of that. He just took his hockey very seriously and I respected that. We had some good battles with each other over the years, but I liked him. He was a good hockey man. You know, I used to always kid him that I was the real reason that he got the 1980 Olympic job. You see, we were playing him in Lansing, when I was coaching Michigan State, and he beat us in triple overtime to advance onto the final four. They won the title that year and I am sure that helped his cause. So, I used to tease him about getting him his big break, and he got a kick out of that." — *Amo Bessone, former Michigan State and Michigan Tech Head Coach*

> # LIKE HERBIE CARRIED JOHN MARIUCCI'S TORCH, HOW ARE YOU NOW GOING TO DO YOUR PART TO CARRY HERBIE'S TORCH?

"John Mariucci was a fantastic character and an icon, and Herb played for him at Minnesota. Maroosh was inspirational, and he broke down barriers to promote U.S. players and Minnesotans in particular in a Canadian-dominated hockey world. But he wasn't a tactician; he was the opposite of what Herb was to become. Maroosh was the Godfather of Minnesota (and U.S.) hockey, and Herbie was the Crown Prince who became King. So Herbie didn't carry John Mariucci's torch. Maroosh broke down the door, and Herbie raced through it as the best and the brightest. But he never carried anybody's torch except his own. Nobody can carry on what Herb meant to the game, although setting lofty goals and being determined and unafraid to pursue them would be a proper tribute to him. When it comes to hockey, coaches have a responsibility to carry on Herbie's ideals by studying and trying new and creative ideas, instead of settling for the traditional easy way out. The hockey world needs innovators, more than ever, since August 11, 2003." — *John Gilbert, former Star-Tribune hockey reporter and longtime friend*

"You know, he was always battling USA Hockey. Always. It was a love-hate relationship, either he was coaching an Olympic team or he was arguing with them about something at the youth levels. So, I remember one of my last conversations with him about a month before he died. I had told him that I was working with USA Hockey to develop a bunch of his ideas under their flag. Well, Herbie was pissed about that. I told him that we were even getting rid of traveling squirts this year, and instead focusing just on European skill development. Herbie was big on that, he wanted to have the younger kids focus more on skills and less on traveling and that kind of thing. So, Herbie is pissed at me and giving me sh-- about it. He would razz me by saying *'Larry, Larry, I can see it now, you used to be a warrior, but now you're just a sell-out to USA Hockey. So, go ahead, cash your checks, and get out of here. In fact, why don't you just go live in the woods. That's right. Get out there, take your damn dogs, and live off the land. Go to your cabin up north and live in seclusion. Go where it is safe, where no one will bother you out there. Don't take on USA Hockey, just hide and go where it is safe!'* Well, Herbie was like that. He was always challenging you. So, I want to do in my own way what he thought was going to make kids better hockey players. That is my goal. That is why I have been on the ice for eight straight days and will be on for four more, then after a day off, I will be on for 10 straight more after that. I am on a mission doing all of these skill clinics, and I know that by doing my part we will make hockey better. That will keep Herbie's legacy going. You see, Herbie was big on conditioning and big on letting young kids just play the game and having fun. He was also against young kids playing so many games and not getting the skill base. He was even against kids having to represent their community when they were seven years old, so if they lost they had to feel bad for three days — like they let the entire community down. Herbie knew that when a seven year-old's game was over, he didn't care about who won or lost, they probably wanted to go sliding at the park, or better yet, go back to the outdoor rink and play again. That was Herbie. So, my personal challenge is to train coaches on how to train players. That is my theme, whether it is dry-land training or on the ice. You know, one person can't fight his battles now that he is gone. Herbie was bigger than any one of us guys. But as a group, we can make a difference." — *Larry Hendrickson, former area high school hockey coach and longtime friend*

"As ambitious as I would like to be, I could never hope to carry a torch like Herbie carried John Mariucci's. I don't think anybody can. His impact on me, however, is that I will do what I can to try to remain as true to my values as Herbie was to his." — *Jack Blatherwick, Brooks' former strength & conditioning coach and longtime friend*

"That is a pretty heavy torch! I don't have the answer to that. I think we got along so well because he believed in what I was doing. He believed in my philosophy and my approach in dealing with clients, and respected that. So, I will try to continue to represent my clients the best way that I can and do my part to carry his legacy on." — *Neil Sheehy, hockey agent and close friend*

"I don't know if anybody can carry Herbie's torch. It really takes a special kind of person to wear those kinds of shoes. I mean John (Mariucci) had a vision of wanting to help Minnesota hockey become better and he stuck to his theory of recruiting Minnesota kids. He wanted to get them more opportunities, knowing that it wouldn't really pay off immediately, but it would down the road. Herbie, on the other hand, took that vision several steps further and it was truly incredible what he was able to do. You know, when I think of Herbie I have joy because of the legacy he left and the lessons and examples that he set for me and others who knew and loved him. So, what I am going to try to do is to remember that and do my part. I will constantly remind myself too, that it might not be about what is happening today, but it's what is going to happen down the road. I think that if you stay true to the values of work ethic, intelligent work and caring about people, ultimately that will leave a pretty good legacy because those are great values." — *Craig Dahl, St. Cloud State Head Coach and former Brooks assistant*

"I am not going to settle for mediocrity just because that was the way it was done. I will try to experiment with new things and go outside the box. Those are things Herbie influenced me on, and I will carry them forward in my own life." — *Tom Vanelli, former Gopher player*

"I think I will try to keep the respect going that Herbie instilled in us. He passed that on to me and I will do my best to pass that on to others as well. You know, he always said you don't want to be a sh-- bum hockey player. And what he meant by that, was don't turn into some kind of a load. Don't be a screwball. Respect yourself and respect the game, now, and for the rest of your life. That was Herbie." — *Pat Phippen, former Gopher player*

"I am not that involved in hockey any more, so I won't be able to carry the torch as Herbie did. But I have often said that he was the best coach that I have ever played for. Period. And I played for Scotty Bowman. So, for Robb McClanahan, Herb Brooks was the best coach I ever had. I will tell that to anybody and everybody." — *Robb McClanahan, former Gopher & Olympic player*

"What I can do is to challenge some of the status quos and just stand up for things that I think are right. If we all do our own small part, then Herbie's legacy will live on." — *Phil Verchota, former Gopher & Olympic player*

"I still ask myself why the good Lord would take a guy who could still have such a huge impact on a lot of people. Well, you try to figure that out whatever way you can. I think there was a reason. I think that he fulfilled his mission here on earth. He touched a lot of people in a lot of positive ways and now those people that he touched, they have to go on and carry out for him some of the things that he instilled in them. He carried so much of John Mariucci's vision forward and it is just up to us now to do the same for him. He believed so strongly in the abilities of Minnesota hockey players and really made us proud. I mean he won three national championships with all Minnesota born players, and that says a lot. So, how can I carry Herbie's torch? I am not coaching but I still feel like I want to do my part. So, I guess if somebody comes to me and asks me about hockey, or whatever, then I could try to answer their questions by reflecting back to ask what Herbie would have done. That will continue his legacy and hopefully I will also be able to just lead by his example in my own life with honesty, integrity and hard work. Then, when I have success, I will be humble, just like Herbie." — *Mike Polich, former Gopher player*

"I don't really have the platform that Herbie had, nor do I have the respect that he had. Those guys (Herb and John) were almost idols or heroes of so many people for their accomplishments, so I don't know if anyone can pick up their torch. I think it is probably going to be more of a conglomerate of people who are going to have to aspire to carry Herbie's torch. But what I would like to do is emulate some of the qualities that he had and be passionate and committed. Then, I am going to go out of my way to make the people that I know feel important." — *Bill Butters, former Gopher player*

"I don't know if there is any one person who could carry Herbie's torch. He stood alone. I certainly don't see anyone stepping forward to fill that role, but hopefully there will be someone who can down the road. The best thing that I can do is to promote the game as best as I can, and with that, Herbie would be proud." — *Tommy Reid, former North Star & current Wild radio analyst*

"I couldn't carry his torch, but I can pass down what I learned from him to others. That is what I will do." — *Reed Larson, former Gopher player*

"I am going to try to get into coaching. That is what I want to do. I want to make a difference the way he did, and that is what I am going to do when I am done playing. I could only hope to be as successful as Herbie, but I want to follow in the same sort of footsteps that he did. I have a passion for the game and found that I get those same emotions from coaching that I do from playing, so that is what I want to do." — *Phil Housley, former 2002 Olympian under Brooks & former NHL All-Star*

"I am in the hockey business, so I will do my part to promote the game and to make it better. Beyond that, I will try to wake up every day and be honest and say what I think. That would be my way of honoring Herb Brooks and to keep his legacy alive." — *Steve Ulseth, former Gopher player*

"Being an American hockey player from Minnesota, I will just do what I can to help grow the game and to make sure that his vision of getting more kids involved comes true. You know, one thing that I recently did that I am very proud of is I created a scholarship at St. Cloud State. So, I am trying to give back to say thanks, the same way that Herb did for me. Hopefully I can start a legacy at St. Cloud." — *Bret Hedican, current NHL All-Star*

"We just need to keep his vision going forward, and that will take a lot of people. You know, Herb had more people who were fighting against him than were with him. He was out there on his own a lot with his ideas and convictions, and it will be tough to keep a lot of them going. Herb was never intimidated by anything or anybody, he was so just principled and determined." — *Joe Micheletti, former Gopher player & current Fox Sports TV hockey analyst*

"Herbie is a constant reminder to me that you have to stand for the values that made this country great. So, whenever I get into a situation where those values are tested, I remember Herbie and stay true to what I believe in." — *Noel Rahn, longtime friend*

"That is an awfully big torch. You know, I am in the hockey business and I certainly love the game. I don't know if anyone can love the game as much as Herbie did, but I am going to try. So, that is what I am going to do." — *Paul Holmgren, former Gopher player & NHL player and coach*

"I am certainly going to do my part with the Gophers. Then, I will try to get involved at the state level to do what I can there too. I mean when you lose someone like a Herb Brooks, other people have to try to step forward and fill that void. So, with the position that I am in with the Gophers, people will look to me to do that and I will do what I can. Nobody can fill Herbie's shoes, but we need people to try to take us down the path of where hockey needs to go in the upcoming years." — *Don Lucia, Gopher Hockey head coach*

"I just think to live my life the way Herb would have appreciated, which is working hard and being up front and honest with people. Then, I try to represent the 1980 U.S.

Olympic team the best as I can, and as the captain I feel that it is my responsibility to do so. Whether that is making an appearance or just keeping everybody informed regarding decisions that might affect us, I have taken on that role and just want to do the right thing. Hopefully Herb would be proud of that. In addition, I always wear my seat belt now, which was more of a side affect of what happened, but every time I buckle up I think of Herb." — *Mike Eruzione, former 1980 Olympian*

"You know, I have two daughters in high school now and I help coach youth hockey in the Eastview school district. So, many of the things that I learned from Herbie, not only in hockey, I try to pass down to these kids." — *Eric Strobel, former Gopher & Olympic player*

"I will just do what I can to continue Herb's vision. Certainly, I am in a position where I can influence young people, and hopefully I can teach them as well as Herb taught me. Whether that means putting on clinics or speaking at different youth hockey functions around the state, I will just do my part." — *Dean Blais, former Gopher player & current head coach at the University of North Dakota*

"I know that Herb was very outspoken about improving the game from the ground up, rather than the top down. So, Herb did not want to just work with the best players, he wanted to build the base of the pyramid wider so that more people would be involved with the game at the lower levels and could then move up as they got better. So, I will do my part as a coach to keep his vision alive." — *John Harrington, former Gopher & Olympic player*

"I could never carry Herbie's torch. Ever. But, I can help kids as much as I can and I can help people to achieve their goals through my coaching and through my goalie schools." — *Warren Strelow, former goalie coach under Brooks and longtime friend*

"I don't think that is what Herbie would want. It wasn't about carrying on what he believed in, it was more about you standing up for what you believe in and then carrying that on. So, that is what I will try to do." — *Bill Baker, former Gopher & Olympic player*

"I couldn't even come close to being able to carry Herbie's torch. I guess I will just do my part and be a good ambassador for the game." — *Neal Broten, former Gopher, Olympian and North Star*

"I work at the youth level and just try to do what I can. If everyone works hard at whatever their sphere of reference is, then we will continue to grow the game. I am involved with youth hockey and I also run summer hockey schools. We do a lot of different things there, and much of that goes back to the things that I learned from Herb. So, I will do my part and hopefully everyone else will do theirs so that we can keep his vision alive. And, so that we can just keep hockey growing at all levels." — *Craig Sarner, former Gopher and player under Brooks on 1979 U.S. National Team and in Europe & longtime coach at various levels*

"Herbie wanted to see every young kid have the opportunity to play the game. Then, he wanted to make sure that the dollars that were raised for them were well spent and benefited the masses, versus just the top level kids. He also wanted to make the sport less structured and more available to more people. I certainly agree with that and will do my part to keep Herbie's vision alive." — *John Mayasich, former teammate on*

"You know my last conversation with Herbie was at the Hall of Fame golf tournament the night before he died. He said, 'You know Jim, this is definitely on the upswing. This whole thing (the Hall) is going gangbusters and you have got to keep it going. You just have to keep it going because we need to get America going the right way.' That was the last thing he said to me. So, what I would say to Herb is that I will do my best to keep it going." — *Jim Findley, President of the U.S. Hockey Hall of Fame*

"You know, hockey is such a small fraternity. We all know each other and we all respect each other for our abilities, but it is much more than that. It is very important for the young coaches to know about the contributions and sacrifices that the Herb Brooks', John Mariuccis, Bob Johnsons and Dave Petersons of the world made before them. So, I will do my part to keep their legacies alive and make sure that we are doing what we can to continue to grow the game. That is what they would've wanted." — *Jeff Sauer, former University of Wisconsin & Colorado College Head Coach*

"You know, John Mariucci made it possible for Minnesota kids to have the opportunity to play college hockey, but Herbie was the guy that took those kids and made them winners. He took them farther than John ever did. I mean, Mariucci may have planted the seeds, but it was Herb who took it to the next level. I think that was significant. Mariucci got the ball rolling, but Herb produced champions. So, in my opinion, if John Mariucci was the Godfather of Minnesota hockey, then Herbie would be the next level above that." — *Gregg Wong, former Pioneer Press columnist*

"From a personal standpoint, that torch is too heavy for me to carry. I am not a champion of causes, that is just not in my make-up. You know, what I can do as a journalist and television analyst is to promote the game of hockey, to sell it and to convey its excitement." — *Frank Mazzocco, Gopher Hockey TV Analyst*

"I will just say that as long as I am on this earth, he will always be in my thoughts and will always be a part of whatever I do. We will just keep raising the flag at Iwo Jima together and hope that other people can do the same." — *Bob Utecht, founder of Let's Play Hockey newspaper*

"The reality for us, at Octagon, is that nobody represents more American born hockey players than our firm does. That is a fact. So, we hope to continue to do that and to expand even more. We strongly believe in keeping kids in school and having them build a solid base before they become professionals. The one thing that we do well as it relates to Herbie is that we try to bring everybody into the fold and get them on board as members of our team, our family. Herbie was always big about hey, we may disagree, you may be from the east and I may be from the west, but in the end, we are all on the same team. So, that is the way we approach things with our clients." — *Brian Lawton, hockey agent and former North Star under Brooks*

"I will just do my best to communicate how much of a friend, mentor and leader he was to me. Herb was a great, great man and hopefully I can do my part to keep his memory alive." — *Jim Boo, former Gopher player*

"For me, I am not going to carry his torch. But in some small way, what I have been doing over the past 20 years and am continuing to do, will help in that end. I have always believed that the grass roots level of hockey with young kids is the best level of all hockey and I know that Herbie felt the same way. Herbie was always thinking about how he could help more kids to get better. So, I will continue to do my part and hopefully I can make a difference. You know, what is funny about this is that as much as we all think we are doing, Herbie would expect each of us to do more. He was always asking for more out of people, no matter what it was. I mean, for Herbie it was all about surpassing your expectations and getting over the wall. And Herbie wasn't just a teacher who said to do it either, he was a guy who had already done it himself. So, that will be all of our challenges now that he is gone." — *Paul Ostby, former Gopher player and business associate*

OK, LET'S HAVE IT, YOUR BEST HERBIE STORY!

"There are too many to have a favorite, over 40 years. So I'll go with my last conversation with him, two days before he went up to the fateful last golf tournament. We talked for over an hour, discussing his life, my life, our families, and our futures. We also talked about the Mike Randolph situation. Randolph, perhaps the best coach in the state at Duluth East, who had been something of a protégé of Herbie's while winning over 300 games in 15 years, was fired by a principal who had never spoken to him, but whose son he once cut as a sophomore. Herb asked me for some details, and got pretty animated about how Randolph should fight the situation. The phone conversation ended at about 10 p.m., and an hour later Herbie called me back. 'I just got off the phone with Mike Randolph,' he said, and proceeded to tell me the advice he had given to Randolph. The next day, I called Randolph, who told me that he had already gone to bed when Herbie called the night before. He was amazed that Brooks would take time to call him, and also said he couldn't get back to sleep because he was so fired-up by what Herbie had said. Right to the end, Herbie's inspiration was unlimited." — *John Gilbert, former Star-Tribune hockey reporter and longtime friend*

"I remember once when we were playing together on a U.S. National team in Geneva back in the late 1960s. We got into town and had a few days off, so he and Doc Rose decided to sneak out of that night and see the town. So, I made up his bed with a bunch of pillows shaped like his body. Sure enough, our coach came in to do a bed check later that night, and I told him to be quiet because Herbie was sound asleep and I didn't want to wake him. He bought it, and Herbie got a free night out on the town!

"Another time, during the Olympics, we had a day off and we wanted to get out and see the town. We had a curfew, but Herbie wanted to go. He said that he had found a good way out over a fence, so we snuck out. I didn't really want to go, but went along anyway. So, I climbed up and over the fence first and when I got down I fell right into a big pile of mud. Herbie asked if it was OK to follow, and it was dark out so I said 'sure, come on over, it's all clear.' So, Herbie came flying over and went right into that same pile of mud and got stuck right up to his knees. I helped him out and we laughed about it over some wine and a nice Italian meal. Those were the days!" — *Lou Nanne, former Gopher and North Stars player & GM*

"You know the funny things with Herbie kind of happened by accident. He didn't sit down and tell jokes, that was not him. He was a very serious, intense guy, so things just sort of became funny with him. I don't have any great Herbie stories, but yet I remember laughing with him so much. It is an odd thing. From building decks to gardening, Herbie was a funny story waiting to happen, you just had to be in the right place at the right time. You know, he loved building decks, yet he never had the time to actually sit down, relax and enjoy the decks. He just loved projects, the start and finish of a project, and the perfection of seeing it completed — whatever it was.

"One of Herbies best friends, LeRoy Houle, is a classic example of his wide range of friends. LeRoy was a tree trimmer who he hired to cut down some trees at his house on Turtle Lake. Well, when LeRoy got there, Herbie had a chain saw with him and told him that he was going to cut down some trees too, to save some time and money. LeRoy asked him if he had ever cut before, and Herbie said 'sure, sure, hundreds of trees…' Well, Herbie didn't know what the heck he was doing. So, they are cutting and eventually LeRoy says 'Mr. Brooks, no offense, but you are not going to do any more cutting today. Please just go stand over there and tell me what you want done and I will do it. I do not want you to get hurt.' Well, Herbie was pissed, and wanted to cut down some trees. So, he says 'f--- you!' LeRoy then turns around and says 'f--- you too!' So Herbie says, 'Well then, SUPER F--- YOU! Don't tell me what I can or can't do on my own damn property!' LeRoy says 'SUPER F--- YOU!' right back, 'I am not going to let you get killed by a falling tree out here!' So, they both start laughing hysterically right there, and afterwards they went out for some beers. From that moment they became best friends. That was Herbie. The two of those guys together were a riot. LeRoy would pick up Herbie on his Harley Davidson and drive around together, and they just had a ball together. Herbie had friends from all walks of life, and that is what made him so unique.

"From spending time at my cabin, to camping to going grouse hunting with him, we did so much. He was an expert on everything, right? Or at least he thought he was! He was always coaching you, whether it is in hockey, golf or grouse hunting, he knew it all. I mean I remember when we went hunting together for the first time, I spent half the day down on one knee because he would spin around talking to everyone with his gun barrel pointed right at my head all the time!" — *Larry Hendrickson, former area high school hockey coach and longtime friend*

"My brother and Herb were actually roommates together on a U. S. National team back in the late 1960s, but I never really knew him. I remember the first time I ever met him. I was a freshman playing at Harvard and my very first game there was against the U.S. Olympic team which Herbie was coaching. I had a pretty good game and was hitting some guys around out there. Well, after the game the media asked Herbie about me and what he thought. Now, there are some coaches who would always say 'that guy could never play at my school,' and defend their own turf or whatever, but not Herbie. He was always trying to push and help the Minnesota kids. So, Herbie just simply responded, 'Well, let's just say that if I were still at the University of Minnesota Neil Sheehy wouldn't be at Harvard.' Which was completely not true, but it was a way for him to plug another Minnesota guy and I totally respected that. That was what Herbie was all about. He was always praising the local kids. If he couldn't get somebody, then he would call another coach and tell him that this guy was a player and that he should take him. So, when I finished playing hockey we got together and I told him that I was going to become a lawyer and an agent. Herbie always had a thing for Harvard and we just hit it off. Later, when he scouted, we would drive all over the place together to scout talent together. We talked all the time and really got to know each other. It was great.

"Early on Herbie used to always rip into USA Hockey, complaining about everything that they were doing. Well, I later got involved with them and it drove Herbie nuts. He would tell me 'Yep, all those kids from International Falls sending in their $32 bucks a year (annual dues) to send you guys high on the hog to Florida (for their annual meeting).' Well, one year I called him from Florida to tell him that I had been elected to the Board of USA Hockey. It drove him nuts. He said 'Oh Sheehy, you sold your soul! All those kids from International Falls are spending their hard earned money now to send you high on the hog down to Florida in the Winter to do nothing...' Well, Herbie later told me about all the money that USA Hockey was paying for insurance, and what a problem it was. So, I later became the chairman of the insurance committee and helped to redo the entire plan which ultimately saved them over $1 million a year. So, I called Herbie to tell him this and he says 'You see, I told you so, I told you so...' and I said 'no Herb, what you told me is that I couldn't change anything if I got involved. So, just remember Herb, it was the best $32 investment those kids from International Falls ever made by sending me down to Florida!' Our relationship just grew from there. I believe that you couldn't change the system unless you a part of the system, and he didn't agree with that. He would say, 'OK Sheehy, you go be a part of the system and I'll be Ralph Nader over here throwing grenades from the outside!' We had that kind of relationship, where he respected me as a guy on the inside facilitating change, but that was definitely not his style. We worked well together though.

"Another story happened in 2000 when one night I couldn't sleep. So, I got up and called Herbie at the hotel he was staying at around four in the morning. I woke him up and told him that I had had an epiphany and that he needed to get back into coaching. I told him that he needed to coach the U.S. National Team and then the 2002 Olympic Team. Herbie pauses and then says 'Sheehy, you're fu---- up!' Then I said, 'I know Herb, but I haven't been drinking!' So, the next day I called him again and could tell he was intrigued by the idea. Well, we had a bunch of blow-ups over it over the next few weeks, but eventually he agreed. I can remember on several occasions him just melting down with USA Hockey, and him calling me to say 'Neil, if they don't want me, then that's it! I am out. I am done, that's it!' So, then I started writing him notes on why he should take the job. One of them read: 'Herb, if you are serious about coaching, seize this moment. If you prefer to sell long distance service or sporting goods, respectfully decline and continue selling. (Herb had offers he was mulling over to get into other business ventures.) If you are more interested in selling Christian Brothers Hockey Sticks than in being behind the bench, then forget about this short term coaching opportunity, because it is not worth it. If you want to watch a few games a year and spend three months a year in Florida golfing, forget that I thought this was a good opportunity, it's not worth it. If you don't get a thrill by directing 20 men into war and teaching them to believe in themselves for the benefit of each other by winning, forget that I called you at four in the morning, thinking that this was a good idea, it wasn't. I believe that if you really want something in life, you do everything in your power and give everything in your belly to get it. It may not happen, but the effort was worth it. If you don't care to coach again, forget about it, it is not worth it. You have a tremendous God-given ability to influence people to believe, the only tragedy I see is that I am not sure that you believe. I do not believe that there is a better coach on this planet than you, I want to make the journey with you. Seize the moment. But, if you do not believe, forget it. It is not worth it.' He called me right after that and told me that I was a no good son-of-a-bitch and was really ticked off. He thought he was the only one who knew how to play mind games. But hey, the next thing you know he got back into coaching, first with the Pittsburgh Penguins, and then with the 2002 Olympic Team. It was a great story.

"You know, a lot of people don't realize just how close he was to accepting the New York Rangers job here last year. He actually accepted it one night at dinner with Louie Nanne and I at the St. Paul Hotel, but then after sleeping on it that night, decided to turn it down. I think he didn't want the stress of it all and didn't want to be alone like he was in Pittsburgh. He used to always tell me and Paul Ostby, when we were traveling on scouting trips together at places like Des Moines, Dubuque, Waterloo and Grand Forks, that he only had so many Friday and Saturday nights left on this earth and that he didn't want to spend them with a couple of sh-- bums like us! I told him that Manhattan was a lot better than Des Moines, Dubuque, Waterloo and Grand Forks, but he decided against it. Who knows what could've been. I think he still had the coaching bug in him, but he just couldn't make up his mind. So, he wound up spending more time with a sh-- bum like me, which, in reality, was wonderful for me anyway. I tried to push him and pull him into doing it, but he had had enough." — *Neil Sheehy, hockey agent and close friend*

"I remember when he was playing on my St. Paul Steers club and he broke his arm. It was a good thing he did too, because when he went to the hospital he met a pretty nurse named Patti, who just happened to later become his wife." — *Murray Williamson, former Gopher teammate and 1972 U.S. Olympic coach*

"I remember when we were lobbying for our new arena. Herbie stayed up at my apartment one night after we were out working all day and I got a phone call at about 6:30 a.m. from the president of the university. He asked for Herb, so I give him the phone. Herb gets up right away and starts talking. A few minutes later he hangs up and says, 'I gotta get dressed right away because the legislature is having their final push this morning with the speaker of the house and head of appropriations.' So, he got up and took off. He came back later that day and said, 'we're going to get our arena.' He was right. Sure enough, he helped to push it through and we got our new arena. I can't imagine where our program would be today without it. That was Herbie, he had a lot of clout and could just get things done." — *Craig Dahl, St. Cloud State Head Coach and former Brooks assistant*

"Herbie always played a real tough guy role, that was just his persona. Well, one day in practice I got hit in the face with a stick and I went down on the ice like a ton of bricks. Herbie, meanwhile, didn't see what had happened. He turned around and came over and just assumed that I was sneaking a breather in from one of his exhausting practices. So, he comes over and says to me to get up and shake it off. Then, when I rolled over and stood up, I spit six teeth out in a bloody mess. Right then his jaw just dropped, it was hilarious! I just told him to f--- off and I headed to the locker room. He was tough, that was for sure!" — *Tom Vanelli, former Gopher player*

"I'll never forget during my junior year with the Gophers, 1979, we were in a slump and had lost like six straight games in a row. It was a really tough stretch and we were just down. So, I remember we were in Denver, and we had just lost. Herbie then brought everybody back to the hotel and said that nobody could go out that night and that everybody had to stay in. Then, he led us to a conference room at the hotel that he had gotten and in there was beer and beer and beer and beer. I can't even remember if there was pizza in there or not, but we stayed in there all night and drank like fish. We just had a great time and really blew off some steam. We talked, we let our hair down and we relaxed. That was hard for Herbie to do, but he knew when to do that kind of thing and when not to. Shortly thereafter we got it together and we went on to win the national championship that year. That was Herbie. When we were playing poorly he laid off of us a little bit, but when we were playing well — that is when he really kicked our asses. Games were like days off for us because we didn't skate half as hard as we would've in one of his boot camp practices." — *Robb McClanahan, former Gopher & Olympic player*

"I remember just this past Spring I was at my son's junior hockey game down in Iowa. Well, my cell phone rings and its Herbie. 'Michael,' he says, 'I just wanted to give you a call. I don't know if you heard, but Mrs. Micheletti passed away. I know you're from Hibbing and you know the family, so I just wanted to let you know.' I hadn't heard yet, so I told him I was very thankful for the call. Then, I asked where he was at. He says he's in Montreal. And I am thinking here he is, off in Canada working, and he still has time to call me over something like that. That was the kind of caring person Herb Brooks was." — *Mike Polich, former Gopher player*

"I remember at the start of my senior year Herbie called me in and said, 'Bill, what do you think you are on this team for?' I said that I was the captain. 'Well, you're not here to score goals,' he says, 'you're here to run people over and get in the occasional skirmish and what not.' Now, at the time, we hadn't even played any games yet, we were still just practicing. So, I said 'do you want me to fight guys on my own team?' and he said 'You bet I do! This team won only seven games last year and we've got to get this team tough, and I need your help.' That was my first one-on-one meeting I ever had with Herb Brooks. So, that set an early tone for me I guess. Later that year, I did probably the most famous thing that I am remembered for — diving into the Colorado College bench at their own arena to take them all on. So, afterwards, Herbie and I had to go meet with the athletic director, Paul Giel. Before we went in Herbie told me, 'Bill, remember, don't say anything, let me do all the talking.' So, we are in there and Paul looks at me and says, 'You know, people tell me that you are a pretty good guy, so what do you think we should do about this?' Well, Herbie butts in and says 'You know, we have kept Bill under wraps all year and he has done a pretty good job. He just snapped, that's all. So, let him go and I will guarantee you that I will keep him under control for the rest of the year.' Giel agreed, and it was back to business as usual for me! Herbie really pumped me up to do that stuff and that was fun. To me that wasn't degrading or anything, because that was my role on the team, that is what I did. I even took that style with me to when I was coaching as an assistant with the Gophers too. I mean I had guys like McAlpine, Skarda, Pitlick and guys like that who I could lean on every now and then. All I had to do was tap them on the shoulder and say, 'smoke!' I didn't have to say much, they knew. Herbie loved toughness and guys would go to battle for him." — *Bill Butters, former Gopher player*

"You know, Herbie was very inquisitive and always wanted to understand how things operated. I remember when he was coaching the Rangers and I went out to see a game with his family one time. So, we went out for dinner and then saw the play 'Annie.' Afterwards, Herbie asked me what I was doing going to see that sissy kind of stuff. I told him it was great and that he should see it. Well, he wound up going to see it and he loved it. In fact, he saw it at least five more times after that. That was Herbie.

"I remember another time when I was out in New York to see him and we were talking about Mark Pavelich, from Eveleth, who was playing for him on the Rangers. They said he was too small to play in the NHL, but under Herbie he scored 40 goals one year. So, I asked him how he was doing out there, you know, a small town kid from the Iron Range living in New York. Well, Herb said it worked out great because he had him rooming with this guy from Denmark. I asked him how he ever came up with that combination and he said, 'It was perfect, Pavelich doesn't talk and the other guy can't speak English!' " — *Roger Wigen, former St. Paul Johnson High School Hockey teammate*

"One of my friends who is a trainer now, but at that time (during his playing days with the New York Rangers), was an employee at Madison Square Garden, told me a funny story about Herbie. He said that after games, particularly when we lost, that Herbie used to mill around the locker room for a while. So, the janitors would eventually come in to clean the locker room. Well, Herbie would have to vent his frustration at someone, so he would drag these guys in. Now, these guys knew absolutely nothing about hockey, in fact I don't even know if they spoke English, but they would come in and Herbie would sit them down and then break down plays on the chalk board for them to analyze at like midnight. They would pretend like they were interested, but they just wanted him to shut up so they could finish their jobs and get home. So, after that, these guys would totally avoid him and hide until they saw him leave. When I heard that I just had to laugh, because that was so Herbie." — *Mark Pavelich, former player on 1980 U.S. Olympic Team & NY Rangers*

"I remember my sophomore year, 1976, when we were up at Michigan State. We lost the series and afterwards Herbie told everybody to get back to their rooms. Well, we all thought we were in trouble, but instead he showed up with pizza and beer. Nowadays you couldn't do that, but back then you could. The drinking age was 18 and it was just a different time. I remember we were all sitting around and talking. We were depressed because none of us liked to lose, but I still remember that time vividly. Herbie knew when to ease up on us and when to work us.

"Then, another fun story I remember came after we got swept at Michigan Tech. Herb was so upset that instead of flying home he made us take an all-night bus trip back to Minneapolis. I can still remember stopping in the middle of Wisconsin to take a leak on the side of the road because the beer was about three inches deep on the floor of the bus. Then, we were out in the snow banks having a snowball fight on the side of the road and shoving each other into the deep snow in the ditch. That was just a hilarious time and something I will never forget. Herbie would punish us by making us bus home, but then reward us with beer — knowing that what we probably needed was to just hang out and let our hair down a little bit. Well, we went on to win the national championship that year. Not bad!" — *Reed Larson, former Gopher player*

"I remember one time when I was a freshman I was trying to break into the lineup. Well, we had just lost a game and we were sitting there afterwards and Herbie is chewing us out pretty good. Then, out of the blue, he says, 'Ulseth, what did you think?' It totally caught me off guard and I made the ultimate mistake of saying to Herb Brooks, 'I don't know...'. Well, Herbie just looked at me and sort of smiled and said, 'You don't know! Young man, you better get a f------ opinion in life or you are going to go nowhere!' I just shrank and thought to myself, ' that went well...' So, the next day I am walking on campus, and this is right during the time when people were out protesting the U.S. to get out of South Africa. Well, some of the protesters were selling tee shirts which said that, so I bought one. That afternoon at practice I saw him and said, 'hey coach,' and I opened my coat to show him my new shirt, 'look, I got a f------ opinion!' He just laughed, and said 'atta-boy!' " — *Steve Ulseth, former Gopher player*

"I remember once when Herbie was coaching in Pittsburgh, I came down to the locker room to talk to him before the game. Now, it was a pretty big playoff game, and I was trying to get ready to go on the air and I figured Herb would be nervous and getting ready to go too. Well, I go down there and instead of talking hockey, he starts talking about the stock market. He knew that I used to be in that business, so he liked to talk about new stocks and what not with me. So, he brings over the chalk board and proceeds to break down three different high tech companies, one by one, telling me the pros and cons of each one and what their long term forecast was in his opinion. He goes into this 20 minute dissertation about these companies and I was just blown away. Then, when he was all done, he erased the board and started talking hockey, diagramming plays like nothing had just happened. I mean the guy was just brilliant, and was intensely passionate about everything he did in life, no matter what it was. That was just classic Herbie, and I think he won the game that night too." — *Joe Micheletti, former Gopher player & current Fox Sports TV hockey analyst*

"I remember when we were playing together on the 1961 U.S. National Team and we had a game in Geneva. We had one game to go and if we didn't get any penalties in that particular game, we were all going to win a $5,000 Rolex watch. So, everybody said before the game that they were going to try like heck to play it clean so we could get our watches. Well, I wound up yelling at the ref in the third period and got thrown out of the game. Herb never forgave me! Whenever he came down to my bar in Waterloo, Iowa, he always charged his drinks to me and said that it was for payment of his watch." — *Paul Johnson, former Olympic teammate and longtime friend*

"You know, I can still remember when Herbie was recruiting me and he came to my house. He was trying to coax me into coming to the U of M on a partial scholarship and I was just drooling to go there. I mean I was 17 years old and ready to just walk-on, it didn't matter, I just wanted to be a Gopher so bad. So, my dad says 'no, he needs a full-ride.' Herb then says he has to think about it and he leaves. Now, I am just furious at my dad because I thought for sure he blew my chance to play there. Well, the next day he called and gave me the full-ride. From there on out Herb called me the 17-year-old prima-donna. That was how he got me back I think. Then, when I made the Olympic team, I was the 18-year-old prima-donna. So, I had to deal with that, but it was great. I will just never forget being in such great shape back then from doing all of those damn Herbies!" *(A Herbie was a skating drill: skate to the blue-line, back to the goal-line, red-line, goal-line, far blue-line, goal-line, far goal-line, goal-line, and then again...)* — *Mike Ramsey, former Gopher & Olympic player and current Wild assistant coach*

"I remember when I was playing for him back with the Gophers. We were in the middle of a game and I was out there on a shift when the goalie made a save and the ref blew the whistle to have a face off. Well, I wanted to stay out there, so, when the two new defensemen came out I waved them back, to signal to them that I was OK and I wanted to stay out there. Needless to say, those guys came out and when I got to the bench Herbie said 'Grab a fu----- seat back there!' And that was where I sat for the rest of the game! He was pissed, and after the game he grabbed me and took me aside and said 'Don't you ever try to fu----- try to show me up again!' You know, it was over after that and he didn't hold any grudges, but he wanted to make his point. Herbie just had a certain way of making points, and that was Herbie." — *Paul Holmgren, former Gopher player & NHL player and coach*

"I was an assistant under Herbie at the 2002 Olympics in Salt Lake City. So, we are staying together in a room along with John Cunniff and Herb wakes up at like five in the morning. I said, 'what the hell are you doing up, it's five in the morning?' And Herb says, 'I can't sleep because of you f---ers.' I said, 'What, did we wake you up somehow?' 'No,' he said, 'I should've gone with eight defensemen and 12 forwards instead of seven and 13, which was what you bastards convinced me to do. I had a dream last night that we were playing Finland and Teemu Selanne came down the outside, broke to the inside, beat our defensemen and tucks it in the side of net to beat us 3-2.' So, I said, 'That's funny, because I had a dream last night too.' Herb says, 'Yeah, what did you dream?' I said, 'The same thing. Only in my dream Selanne came down the outside and broke to the inside, but, instead of beating our defensemen, our guys poke-check it up and we get a two on one breakaway. We then pass back and forth, deke the goalie and bury it to win, 3-0. Now go back to f---in bed!' And do you know what? We actually won that game 6-0!" — *Lou Vairo, head coach of 1984 U.S. Olympic team & assistant under Brooks on the 2002 U.S. squad*

"You know, I played for UM-Duluth, and Herb used to give me so much crap about that. I mean when I was at UMD we had not beaten the Gophers in like 23 games. So, Herb used to always bring that up to me to rub it in. Well, one time when I was playing for him in 1980 he came up to me as I was walking through the locker room and said, 'Harrington, I can't believe UMD, I mean that is amazing. I wouldn't let my son go there if that was the last college on earth...' So, I look over at Mike Ramsey and Eric Strobel, who both played for him at Minnesota, and they said, 'You're lucky, you only have a year of him, we had to put up with him for five!'

"Herb just used to razz me. I remember another time I came to the rink a little early before practice and as I was tying my skates Herb comes up to me and says, 'Harrington, you are the worst defensive player I have ever seen.' So, I look up and I see that there is no one else in the room but me and him. And, he is not joking. So, he goes on and on with this, saying, 'Harrington, do you really think Winnipeg is going to sign you? Come on, they will run you out of town on a rail. You couldn't even check your hat...' Then, that was it. He left. He just shrugged his shoulders, and I shrugged my shoulders and I went on the ice. So, needless to say, I gathered from our conversation that he wanted me to work on my defensive skills! I mean, that was his way of saying I needed to work on my defense. I got the message Herb. Sometimes he had a very unique way of showing you he cared about you, that was for sure!

"You know, it was funny, because several years later, when I was an assistant at the University of Denver, Herb's son, Danny, came to play for us. Boy, was Herb different to me then! It is funny how things changed. But really, we became good friends after that and that was a lot of fun." — *John Harrington, former Gopher & Olympic player*

"You know, Herbie and I lived by each other as kids and would play hockey together every night until they shut the lights out on us. Then, we would sneak back in and turn the lights back on and play for a few more hours. Sometimes the park cops would come down but they would let us play, they were great. Then, years later, every Sunday night we would go over to the outdoor rink to play. I had the key to the warming house and we would all go over there and play a game. Some of the old guys who played on the Olympic teams would join us and we would scrimmage against the high school kids. He just loved that more than anything. Those were some great, great memories. The kids even talk about that to this day. It meant so much to them. I mean every Sunday he was out there with us, and that was so special.

"Later, we had a ritual after every Gopher game. We lived by each other so I would ride to the games with him. Well, after every game, we would stop at the

Happy Chef restaurant. There, he would draw Xs and Os on the napkins. I mean after every game that is what he would do. It was great, that was Herbie." — *Warren Strelow, former goalie coach under Brooks and longtime friend*

"I remember when I was playing for him back during the 1980 Olympics. We were over in Norway, playing some games over there in preparation for Lake Placid, and we wound up tying this club team. Well, Herbie was really upset over how poorly we played. So, after we shook hands with the other team, Herbie says, 'Stay on the ice gentlemen...' Well, he proceeds to start skating us right then and there. We are skating laps and sprints and he is just working us. I remember the East coast guys couldn't believe what was happening. They were absolutely dumfounded that their coach would actually make them skate after a game. Well, for the Minnesota guys, it was like no big deal. I mean, after all, this was Herbie, and we had done this plenty of times before. I remember, Buzzy Schneider, who had gotten kicked out of the game earlier, was up in the stands and he had to get dressed again and join us too. So, what was so funny was as we were skating around, the Norwegian fans stuck around because they thought we were putting on some sort of an American skating clinic. They are now clapping up in the stands and this is just making Herbie madder by the minute. We all had to fight back the smiles over that one, but that was Herbie." — *Bill Baker, former Gopher & Olympic player*

"I remember one time when I was playing for him in Davos, Switzerland, and I was in bed one morning with my wife. Well, my wife hears something downstairs, and I sit up and sure enough, the door cracks open and in peers Herb. Now, most people would say 'excuse me or sorry to bother,' but not Herb. He just says, 'I'll put the coffee on...' When Herb wanted to talk hockey, you were going to talk hockey — no matter where you where or what time it was!" — *Craig Sarner, former Gopher and player under Brooks on 1979 U.S. National Team and in Europe & longtime coach at various levels*

"I remember sitting at a Wild game with Herb last year and I told him that my five year old son was getting into hockey. I told him that I had built a hockey rink out in the front yard and he just got all pumped up about that. 'That is the way hockey should be played; that is the way to teach him; he will be out there all the time,' he said. Well, three days later I got a numbered print of the 1980 U.S. Olympic Team beating the Soviets in the mail and it was signed 'Matthew, go for the gold, you can do it! Herb Brooks, 1980 Olympic coach.' I got it framed that week and it has been hanging on the wall above his bed ever since. That was Herbie. What a guy." — *Joe Schmit, KSTP-TV sports anchor*

"I remember one time when I was playing for him with the North Stars and I was walking down the corridor at the Met Center past the locker room and towards the ice for the start of a game. Well, as I got there I saw Herbie waiting for me. 'Lawton,' he says, 'get over here!' So he grabbed me and pulled me aside pretty firmly by the arm and said, 'if you don't score tonight I am going to have to trade you.' That was it. That was all he said. And he was dead serious too. Well, luckily for me, because I hadn't been playing very well at the time, I scored on like my third shift of the game when a slapshot deflected, literally, off of my ass and into the side of the net. It was not a pretty goal by any stretch, but I was elated. I remember skating over the ref and making sure to tell him that the puck definitely hit me and to make sure I got credit for the goal. So, I headed back to the bench and told Herb that I tallied that one just for him. Herb just looked at me and said, 'You're pretty damn lucky Lawton...'. You know, we used to laugh about that whenever I saw him. He had some strange ways of motivating guys, but that one took the cake for me." — *Brian Lawton, hockey agent and former North Star under Brooks*

"I remember the very first day of practice, I walked in wearing a rabbit fur coat and had on diamond earrings. I can't remember exactly what Herbie said to me, but it wasn't the kindest words I have ever had spoken to me.

"You know, I was never known for being a goal-scorer, but I remember one of my first goals. It came up at North Dakota when I miscalculated a clearing pass and scored on our own goalie. I felt terrible, and out of frustration I hacked the guy out front who was poke-checking me. The ref gave me a quick penalty, and to add insult to injury, I got hit in the head with a dead fish on the way to the penalty box. Well, after I got out of the box — which was the safest place to be at the time, as far away from Herbie as possible, Herb says, 'Well Boo, you finally got one!'.

"Then, I remember one night we were playing in Denver and my father made the trip to see me. Well, we lost, and afterward I snuck out of the hotel to see my dad for a few beers. Well, wouldn't you know it, but as I am sitting there with my dad having a cold one, the waitress comes over and says the man across the bar bought me a beer. So I look over and who do I see, Herbie. I knew right then and there that I was in big trouble. So, he comes over and says 'Jimmy, you might as well enjoy this one because you are going to pay for it tomorrow...'. Well, when we got home that next day we went right to the rink and put on our wet equipment and skated and skated. So, I am just dying out there doing laps and he skates up to me and says, 'How's that beer tasting now Jimmy?'. — *Jim Boo, former Gopher player*

"I never used to wear a mouth guard. So, one time at a game in Wisconsin, Mark Johnson, the centerman against me on the face-off, told on me to the ref. So, the ref gave me a 10-minute penalty, and there were only 10 minutes left in the game. Well, when we got back to Minneapolis, Herbie made me skate laps after practice with a huge mouth guard. I skated for a half hour with Herbie lecturing me on wearing mouth guards the entire time. The next game I had gotten a Pro-Form (custom fit) mouth guard and was all set to play. So, I checked a guy in the boards, and he hit me in the mouth knocking out all my front teeth. I went to the bench, and pulled out my bloody mouth guard with all my top teeth still in it. I said to Herb 'Look at your damn mouth guard you made me wear!' The first time I ever wear a mouth guard, I lose all of them. So, after the second period, I had stitches, and I went back out to play. I couldn't wear a mouth guard after that, so I skated with my mouth closed. Well, I was in front of the net and a guy came by and butt-ended me in the mouth, knocking out all my bottom teeth. I just said the hell with it and gave up after that." — *Steve Christoff, former Gopher and Olympian*

"One time when we were on our way up to Michigan Tech to play a weekend series. We used to take an old North Central puddle jumper up there and it made a bunch of stops along the way. So, we are stopped in Green Bay, and somebody egged on Jeff Tscherne, our goalie, to make a joke about having a letter bomb in his suitcase. Well, he did, and of course, the cops jumped him and arrested him. I mean they don't mess around with that stuff, so they cuffed him and took him to jail. Well, Herbie wasn't about to delay our whole team from getting up there, so he just said to leave him in the clink and we would pick him up on the way back. No one thought he was serious but that is exactly what we did!" — *Pat Phippen, former Gopher player*

"Herbie had just finished coaching the North Stars at the time, and they had just a dismal season. So, afterward Herbie came out to ski with me in Colorado to relax. Well, one day after skiing, we went to a local watering hole. The proprietor of the place had prided himself on being a big sports fan and claimed to know a lot about sports. He sees Herb and is real impressed. So, the free beer and pizza started rolling out and we were all having a great time. Then, all of a sudden, a real big guy wearing bib overalls and a Green Bay Packers hat, comes over to Herbie, sticks out his hand, and says 'Bob Johnson, I have always wanted to meet you!' Apparently the bar owner had talked to this guy just before he came over and gotten the two mixed up. Well, Herbie's head went down and I will never forget what he said, 'A perfect ending to a bleep-bleep year!' " — *Bruce Telander, former Gopher Blue Line Club president and longtime friend*

IS THERE ANYTHING YOU WOULD WANT TO ADD, TO SAY GOOD BYE TO YOUR OLD FRIEND?

"I think Bob Dylan said it best, 'Farewell my friend, until we meet again… not good-bye.' He was a great man and I will miss him. I think we will all miss him." — *Mike Sertich, former UM-Duluth Head Coach*

"So much has been said about him since he died. The week after he died it was so obvious to people who knew him that in reading the paper why he was such an incredible person. I mean every article you would read was a reflection of his life. On one half of the page it would be all these stories about his mini-miracles on ice, not just the big one in 1980, and on the other half of the page there would be some article about a cook in a small tavern over on Payne Avenue. Then, the next day there would be a big article about his accomplishments and on the other side there would be a story about some coach who asked Herbie if he could spend a minute or two with him and Herbie spent several hours. That was Herbie, and that came to life after his funeral. Those of us who knew him, however, knew that every day was really like that for him. It was a real dramatic dichotomy with Herbie, and that was his life. Maybe it was because his dad was such a plain old East Side kind of guy who spent his whole life working on behalf of kids, that Herbie would migrate towards those kinds of people as well. He was just a great person and a great friend. I am going to really miss him, I already do." — *Jack Blatherwick, Brooks' former strength & conditioning coach and longtime friend*

"You know Herbie was just starting to wind down his career and was going to spend more time just relaxing. So, I am sad that I wasn't able to get together with him more recently to have lunch and rekindle our friendship. We used to have a pretty close, personal relationship together, and it would have been nice to see him more often. I am really going to miss him." — *Murray Williamson, former Gopher teammate and 1972 U.S. Olympic coach*

"Herbie, we all loved you, and we will all miss you. Our years with you were some of the best of our lives, so thanks." — *Pat Phippen, former Gopher player*

"I just loved the guy and would just want to thank him for the opportunity to have played for him. He was like a father-figure to me and aside from being a wonderful coach, he truly made a difference in my life." — *Buzz Schneider, former Gopher & Olympic player*

"I am just really going to miss him. He was such a great guy. There are still days where I get up and really can't believe he is gone. I don't know when that will go away, or if it will ever go away. I just miss him, he was a good friend." — *Mike Polich, former Gopher player*

"Like I said in his eulogy, Herbie took characters like me and made us men of character. I will miss him. As a 53-year-old man I can honestly say that I loved Herbie Brooks as a friend. I looked up to him as a dad and I respected him probably more than any man that I have ever met. And it was not because he was a great coach, it was because he said what he thought and he lived out what he said. He was just a man of his word. To be a guy like that is so honorable. I really admired him. He was a great, great man." — *Bill Butters, former Gopher player*

"I am sure he is running the show up there where he belongs and I am sure he has got an opinion up there too. He was the best. I really miss him." — *Steve Badalich, long-time friend*

"We will miss him. I even have a little tribute up at my restaurant where people have been signing a book with their thoughts and feelings about him, so that has been nice to see too. It is amazing to see how he touched so many people, even though he didn't even ever meet them. That was Herbie." — *Tommy Reid, former North Star & current Wild radio analyst*

"You know, when I heard Herbie died it was like when John Lennon died. It was the end of an era. There will never be the Beatles and Minnesota hockey will never be the same." — *Steve Ulseth, former Gopher player*

"Probably just thank you. You know, you go through life and you can pinpoint a small number of people who really helped you and made a difference in your life, and he was certainly one of them. Herbie loved a lot of people, and a lot of people loved him. I loved him, and I know he felt the same way." — *Joe Micheletti, former Gopher player & current Fox Sports TV hockey analyst*

"Thanks for the memories and thanks for influencing my life. I will miss you old friend." — *Noel Rahn, longtime friend*

"I miss Herbie and I feel for his family every day. I just have some very fond memories of him and that is how I will remember him." — *Paul Holmgren, former Gopher player & NHL player and coach*

"All of us in the hockey world are saddened by his passing and we are just going to miss him. He gave so much of himself to hockey and really made a difference. He was such an innovator and passed on that legacy for future generations as well." — *Larry Pleau, former teammate on 1968 Olympic team & current St. Louis Blues GM*

"He was just such a unique person and did so much for the hockey community. Sure, he had his battles along the way, but he did what he believed was right. We are really going to miss him." — *Willard Ikola, former Olympian and longtime Edina High School Hockey Coach*

"You know, when the 1980 Olympic team was inducted into the U.S. Hockey Hall of Fame this Fall, if I could tell him something, I would say this: 'Herbie, you are up there watching over us. But without you, this would have never been possible. So, thanks for everything.' " — *Warren Strelow, former goalie coach under Brooks and longtime friend*

"I loved and respected him as much as any person in my life, even as much as my father and my uncles, who I adore. And I know that Herbie loved the Gambucci family too. So, good bye old friend, we will miss you." — *Gary Gambucci, former Gopher and teammate on two U.S. National teams*

"He will be sorely missed. I feel like he is still around because it is so hard to believe that he has left us. It wasn't just hockey with Herb, it was a sincere friendship and a lot of fun. I will miss him." — *John Mayasich, former teammate on U.S. National Teams & longtime friend*

"I would say thank you for being my friend and for respecting me. I would also say thank you for giving us the most significant event to ever increase the population of kids getting involved in hockey. The U.S. hockey scene changed dramatically after the 1980 Olympics and Herb was a big part of that. His whole life was about hockey and he will be dearly missed." — *Walter Bush, Chairman of the Board, USA Hockey*

"The time we had together was wonderful, the fun we had was fantastic and I will never forget you. You know, I was lucky, I got to spend the last two and a half days of his life on this earth with him. We were just great friends. We tipped a few cold ones together in our day and just had so much fun. He was such an unselfish person and would do anything for me. I am going to really miss him." — *Paul Coppo, former teammate on several U.S. National Teams and longtime friend*

"I won't say good bye to Herb because he is with me all the time. I have his picture with me wherever I go and he will just be with me forever. When I go on the road he will be in my pocket and there is also a picture of him in my office and at my house too. So, there are no good bye's from me. He is just always going to be in my thoughts and in my teachings." — *Nick Fotiu, former New York Ranger under Brooks*

"For me, Herbie's death made me re-prioritize my own life. His accident just reinforces with me that the time we do have on the is earth is so precious. So, I am focusing on spending more time with my friends and family and am just reevaluating my own life. I was truly blessed to have known Herbie and I am just going to really miss him. He had a tremendous impact on my life and I will never forget him." — *Jim Boo, former Gopher player*

"I think the entire hockey community is going to miss his enthusiasm and determination to keep the U.S. hockey product marching forward. We will all miss him. I still find myself in denial. You kind of expect to see him walk into the rink, yet he won't be and that is tough. It will take a while, and it will certainly be a rough Winter this year without him." — *Bob Peters, longtime Bemidji State University head coach*

"I appreciate everything that he did for me. You know the greatest teachers in my mind are not the ones who are out front and center, calling attention to themselves about what they have done, instead they touch you kind of without you knowing it. That was Herbie and that was a part of his magic. He was just a warm, compassionate, incredible person and I will miss him." — *Paul Ostby, former Gopher player and business associate*

"I just that hope he and Badger Bob are getting along and aren't fighting up there!" — *Reed Larson, former Gopher player*

"You know, knowing Herbie as well as I did through the years I think the thing he would regret most about dying so suddenly was the fact that he didn't have the opportunity to tell at least 100 more people to go fu-- themselves!" — *Gregg Wong, former Pioneer Press columnist*

AFTERWORD
BY CHUCK GRILLO

Chuck Grillo was one of Herbie's oldest and dearest friends. Grillo, who works as a scout for the Pittsburgh Penguins, is a former teacher and coach from Bemidji, and the current president/owner of Minnesota Hockey Camps — which was founded by Herb Brooks. When I called Chuck and asked him to be a part of this book he told me that he had been writing about his friend nearly every day in the form

of a journal. After reading it, I thought it was so poignant and so heart felt. Really, I thought it would just make the perfect Afterword for the book. So, thanks Chuck, for sharing your intimate memories of your old friend and for giving us some more insight into just what kind of person Herb Brooks really was, both on and off the ice.

A few years back, I sent Herb a copy of some material that I used when someone close to me passed on. He was quick to call me and tell me how much he liked the material. He asked me, "If the opportunity is there, would you mind if I used this?" I replied, "Feel free, Herb, I probably got most of it from you at one time or another anyway." Little did I know that I would be using that same material in remembering Herb. It fits him better than anyone I know.

We have an obligation to our colleagues and athletes to take every experience and grow as much as possible from them. Herb Brooks' untimely death gives us an opportunity to think not only about him, but the important things in life as well. It gives us the opportunity to critique ourselves. His funeral was a special moment. This is something the Brooks family members can treasure forever. This final farewell has so many "tie-ins" to real life and so many lifetime lessons to learn.

I've known Herb Brooks close and up front for 27 years. Only my wife, Clairene, knows how many hours I've spent talking about life and hockey both on the phone and in person with Herb. He had a set of rules when communicating. He liked to agree to disagree. He believed in debate and was not offended if you disagreed. He also believed in free speech, so this gave him every right to express his beliefs.

If I had known Herb would be gone, there is no way that I would have recently passed on a golf game with him down in Florida. I was witness to the entire Pittsburgh staff wanting to golf with him so I felt I should back off because I could golf with him anytime. Herb is one of those lifetime relationships that are cultivated through the sporting world. This is the beauty about the world of sports. The hockey world is full of short-term relationships that last a lifetime.

I went to work for him at his hockey camp in Shattuck in 1976 and I've been trying to live up to his expectations since that day. The early years were tough and full of long hours. With everyone tugging on him for his time, I was one person who would work around the clock for him and enjoyed doing it. The lesson here is employers are quick to recognize those who "live their company." I am still "living the company" and I'm working for myself.

Herb was quick to recognize this and kept giving me a percent of the business because the profit margins were not good enough to pay me. It wasn't too long and I was part owner with 33% of the ownership in his business. This was all done with a handshake. When I couldn't afford tickets to Gopher games, he made me a goal judge. This is just one example of Herb's honor system. It was a way for my son, Dino, to have a unique seat for the games.

Herb's son, Dan, sent me a carved life size wooden duck that I had given to Herb back in 1980. I made it in the shop class at Rosemount High School for Christmas. He said, "Herb had it on his desk ever since he received it. He moved his desk several times and the duck was always placed a few feet away from his chair." Dan thought I would want it in memory of his dad. The duck is going to sit a few feet from my chair.

Herb taught me that the world is bigger than the small world I was part of. He gave me an opportunity to reach out to kids and my peers all over the world. He, Craig Patrick and George Gund III gave me an opportunity to work with some of the top hockey personalities in the game. Most importantly, he found out he had a talent that no one could take away from him. He found out that this talent had more meaning than anything during his playing days. His mentoring skills will stand the test of time.

What can be learned from Herb's lifetime experiences? Ten percent of life is what happens to us and 90 percent is how we react to it. I spoke with Dan within 24 hours of Herb's passing. Dan is a living example of someone who fits the role of life being 10% what happens to us and 90% what you do about it. Patti is responding likewise, and I'm assuming Kelly has the same strengths. They are prepared and are handling the situation as professionally as possible. I know Herb prepared Dan even though there may have been a time when Herb was telling him a lot of things he didn't want to hear.

Herb was both resilient and understanding. There were times when I wondered about those who claimed they had a respect for Herb's genius, yet many of those same people didn't get behind him when he wanted to be a coach/gm in the NHL. Their belief was that no one should take on the role of gm/coach. He was quick to tell me that this is the way life works and moved on to another project with the same passion he would have had for the job he was seeking. I just believed Herb was the exception that could be gm/coach.

I believe many of those same people would reconsider if they had another opportunity to support him because they did love the man. They would let their "hearts rule their heads." Herb wanted people to challenge him in the same manner he challenged his players. Herb needed them to do for him what he did for so many others. His competitors in life weren't bad choices, some made a name for themselves, but we are talking about competing for a job with a man who can walk into any boardroom in corporate America and feel right at home as well as make decisions. The lesson here is, "When someone is at the top of his game, he still may need the help of others to raise his game to yet another level."

Herb knew he didn't have the backing from some people he wanted to back him, and their reasons contradicted what they had to say about him; their assessment of his genius, passion and love for the game and life. Did he hold it against them? No! He just moved on and continued to maintain his friendship. He said, "I have my reasons for believing I can do the job; they have their reasons for believing I can't. Who's to say they aren't right? I was the last cut from the 1960 U.S. Olympic team. After they won the gold, my father told me they must have made the right decision." Thinking back, I let my emotions rule my head and have learned that decision makers have programmed themselves to make decisions based on their thought process; not their hearts.

Herb had a "take care of your own" theory. I believe the biggest single difference between Canadian and American hockey is the ability and willingness to promote our own. Take some time to look at the big picture. Canadians are represented at every level of hockey all over the world. This means people in management, support staff, coaches and players. We have to do a better job of "promoting our own"; no one else is going to do it. Herb and I shared the same respect for the Canadian people; they "take care of their own" and their aspirations are to be in the NHL. This is the underlying reason for the high percentages of Canadians playing pro hockey.

I do know that Craig Patrick (GM of the Pittsburgh Penguins) got behind Herb because he wanted him to have the same opportunities he had in the game. Craig was quick to recognize that when Herb Brooks was in charge of his own destiny, he responded. Herb is similar to Craig in that they spend their time focusing on their work and have the unique ability to "empower" their people. I believe "empowering people" is something Herb learned from Craig. He loved working for the man because he let him do his job.

Herb was capable of multitasking because he enjoyed the challenge and spent no time promoting himself. This is why he was qualified to be a coach/gm. He had people in place, had the time to manage, and had the ability to empower those people. There are some in the business who think they have to spend half their time doing their jobs and the other half promoting themselves. Herb was smart enough to realize that a job well done is all the promoting he needed. His 1980 experience solidified that.

No one is perfect, and it's unfair of us to expect him or her to be. In looking for flaws, we may be overlooking real talent. When I look in the mirror I see some things I wish I could change. I try to keep that in mind when I judge others.

Herb had that unique ability to get into your head, and believe me when I say he could get in to your head. But he did it out of his love and respect for you. There were times in our relationship that I had trouble understanding this but I always came back to his level of intelligence and how much good he did for me. I got something out of most every conversation we ever had. There was always something there if you cared to sort through what he was saying. As I look back, I regret questioning any of his motives.

As a scout in the NHL, I take time to document the assets and liabilities of prospects for our team. I made mistakes when I dwelled on the negatives. I look for a "glimpse of excellence" and then find ways to make it happen with regularity. Herb told me, "It's our responsibility as mentors to take your glimpse of excellence and make it happen over and over and over again; each time getting better."

I was one of those guys who learned how to "work a practice." Herb was adamant about working practices and working the bench. He said, "Anyone can run a practice; it takes a real mentor to work a practice."

Herb's talents went far beyond his playing skills and performance on the ice. His number one talent was his unconditional love for people and his passion for the game of hockey and for life. He had a unique ability to inspire people of all ages. Young people developed a passion for the game and for life by rubbing elbows, shaking hands or taking pictures with the man. He was bigger than life to many of them. He believed he was "giving back" when he spent time with young people.

Everyone has at least one unique skill; some more. Judge them on their execution and infectious level when they are in a position to use those talents; especially during "critical moments." Make sure they are aware of the importance of over achieving in their asset categories. This is the way a team and businesses are built! Each person feeds off the others' talents and each person improves in each skill category. Herb excelled during "crunch time" and he knew how to push the right buttons on each person he came in contact with.

First and foremost, Herb believed that good players had above average intelligence. His belief was that hockey, being the reaction type game at high speeds that it is, would make it impossible for anyone to perform if they were not intelligent. Creative players were in the upper ranges of being very good and having a high level of intelligence. This was the reasoning behind his "thinking" type system. He had a respect for the intelligence of his players. He believed that we should challenge their intellect. This is also why he believed that any great hockey player struggling in school was lazy, because he felt that you couldn't excel at the game without being intelligent.

On the ice, Herb was very observant. Once, he made a comment to me about how he likes his defensemen. He said, "Look at Mike Ramsey, watch how he keeps his feet moving in tandem, handles the puck at the same time, gains space for a good passing angle and delivers the puck while his feet are still moving. There are not many defensemen who can do that." I've always remembered this quote while studying the reasons why there are so few. The reason is simple. The human mind only likes to do one thing at a time. Mike programmed his mind to do multiple things. This is what the great athletes do. This is the very reason why a player's feet stop when he is thinking about catching a puck going down the wing. His mind only wants to do one thing at a time, so the feet stop while he catches the pass.

I'm sitting here with the original drill books that are hand written by Herb. There is a book for squirt, peewee and bantam/midget. There are three binders, all written in long hand. It must have taken him weeks to write them. This is another example of his passion for the game and willingness to help young players help themselves.

I remember one time at Madison Square Garden when the Rangers were playing Philadelphia. Philly had scouts in the press box diagramming the path of each player on each shift. One scout said to me, "I don't know why I'm doing this; they never go in the same pattern. They change every shift." This is just one example of how far advanced Herb was for the NHL. Herb wanted his players to play free, play proud, play smart and play on the edge with the consequences in mind. This means you know the score of the game, the time of the game, how your play affects your teammates and organization and what would happen if you made a wrong decision. He liked risk takers if they considered the consequences of their actions. Thinking back to the day Philly came in to scout in New York, Herb had another theory in the game. Preparation gets rid of any anxiety; let the other team worry about you.

Herb Brooks and our family's Greenhaven Rink in Hibbing, Minn., laid the foundation for our camp. The camp and the kids are the beneficiary. The real sadness about all this is that the whole world was just getting to know the "real Herbie." It wasn't his fault; it just took too many years for others to realize that he did things out of love and respect for others. He was no different than the rest of us. He had a basic psychological feeling to be liked or loved for who he was, what he stood for and his desire to fulfill the obligations of a true mentor.

Herb's funeral could easily have filled the Metrodome. You have witnessed the affect of a person with all the intangibles as a mentor. This is the ultimate test of our contributions to society. This is all about a relationship with a community, organization, family, extended family, peers and players. In Herb's case, he had a relationship with the world. Money, property, boats, cars, motors and toys do not enter into the equation.

Herb once told me, "When we die we get buried in a casket with our best suit, no money in our pockets and none of the material things we craved in life. All we have is our honor." Herb's honor came from his personal makeup and his personal achievements in life. Most are well documented. Others I know first hand from our relationship.

We have a number of thank you notes from parents and colleagues regarding Herb because they were unable to attend. They represent people from around the world, in and out of hockey. These are the highest honors a mentor can receive. Herb was exactly that. He was a hockey mentor, a true professional who looked forward to every opportunity he had to go on the ice and work with athletes. This is a special attribute, one that he took very seriously. Herb was one of those who would look for ways to be on the ice or in some arena anywhere in the world.

Development of people meant as much to Herb as Stanley Cups do to the winners. Herb was one of those unique individuals we've met in our lives. He was a very special and proud human being with an old fashioned upbringing. Those responsible can be proud.

The "real product" of his parents evolved over the years just like the "real products" of Herb and Patti Brooks are evolving now. I was fortunate to meet all of them. Herb believes anyone from his roots in St Paul is qualified to live on the Iron Range and anyone from the Iron Range would enjoy his roots in St Paul. Herb's fondness for Iron Range athletes was clearly evident and his long term relationship with many families is the true test. Herb was very gracious towards my parents and for this I am forever grateful.

He met his match when he met his wife, Patti. She had an equally vibrant personality, charisma, wit and charm. She could easily top his one-liners. She certainly didn't have any inhibitions; which I believe is a necessary ingredient in top athletes and leaders. She excelled at allowing Herb to "live his life" and he returned the favor. They had their own successful team and I believe it was because each empowered the other to become what they could be. Every girl dreams of the man they would like to marry. Something tells me that Patti married that man. Herb showed an unconditional love and respect for most every person he met. He impacted our lives more than anyone will ever know. Our children developed a relationship with him that only they can describe.

How do I come into his life 27 years ago and earn the right to be an honorary pallbearer? Easy. The hockey world is full of examples of dynamic short-term relationships that last a lifetime. The love generated when you work for a cause bigger than yourself is a love that lasts forever. Being an honorary pallbearer for Herb Brooks is the highest honor of my lifetime.

They have yet to replace the old fashioned value system. Remember the 3-R's that were so important to our parents? They were reading, (w) riting and (a) rithmatic. The Brooks family has one more; recreation. In Herb's case, recreation led to: Respect for self, Respect for others and Responsibility for your actions. Then it was Talent multiplied by "Relationships with mentors and people in general + Right expectations of assets + Reward system in place + Respect earned from the fans and media," which led to his productivity as an athlete and leader. Further into his life he had risks, run-ins with critics, resolve, resiliency, remembering and repentance, righting and now risen. Most importantly he was "real." The 3-R's opened some doors. The other R's developed the intangibles that stayed with him. This nurturing process ultimately determined his successes in life. This process gave him the ability to nurture players, which is a risky business. One mistake can cost a young person his/her career, and in some cases, his/her life.

The intangibles support and go beyond the 3-R's. Salt of the earth families have a deeper appreciation for the important things in life. The Brooks family believes in God, country, community, family, extended family, friends and kids. The kids and grand kids are the catalysts for their fun in life. Herb showed that at the rink throughout his entire life. I can feel that they believe Herb is in a better place.

The old-fashioned value system is all about kids, all about your extended family beyond your family and about family values instilled at an early age. We also believe that every child needs a minimum of six mentors beyond their immediate family. We would have trouble arriving at a final count of every child Herb impacted.

Kids are powerful. They bring out the best in people who care. More importantly, when kids realize you have a passion for the game and for their careers, they will respond regardless of your methods. It's a thing called "love." Herb had this and more. Kids are so powerful, they cause adults to build arenas before they have enough money to pay for them. This is why the Gold Medal Arena exists in Brainerd, and it exists for all the right reasons. The Gold Medal Arena exists for kids and those we care to memorialize. Herb is one that comes to mind. One phone call to this man and the Mighty Ducks (grant) money was on its way. This is the place to honor those who care about kids and their futures. This is the place to honor kids who choose to make something out of their lives. This is about a place to honor those who give back to the game.

Herb always gave back. Some labeled him as "distant." However, Herb was a master at telling others what they did not want to hear. He did not draw a line between players and his peer group. Herb labeled as "distant" is the furthest thing from the truth. I believe he became closer to every person; every time he chose to tell someone something that they did not want to hear. Anyone with any degree of intelligence would sense this because he did it out of love and caring. For some it takes years to figure this out. I could sense and feel it the day I met him.

Parents and players should count their blessings if they have a mentor who spends a season with them and has the courage and passion to tell them what they do not want to hear. The coach is really telling you he wants to play a significant role in your life through his teaching, guidance, friendship, uniqueness and unbiased thinking. The Olympic gold medal team of 1980 proved that after 20 years. He was merely fulfilling his commitment to spread his knowledge and insure people of maximizing their potential.

Herb was smart enough to realize that success breeds complacency. He guarded against complacency and the tragedy that followed successful people and teams. He worked hard to prevent tragedy happening to others.

Critics or no critics, we are all going to get a label in life. I've seen great people with great labels and not so great labels. I've seen not so great people having great labels and I've seen them labeled properly. There is not much in between when it comes to labels. The main thing about labels is they are tough to shake.

We've had the opportunity to work with so many people in the world of hockey at every level. Herb is one of those that we will remember for the rest of our lives for all the right reasons. His love for the game was so visible and can only be equaled; not beaten. He was at ease on the rink, in the classroom, in front of thousands of employees in corporate America and in corporate America boardrooms. He was one who turned heads when he entered the room. Things got a little better when he entered a room, joined a team or just struck up a relationship. He plain and simple raised the bar in every situation. If this is the reason for the distant label, then we need to take a long look at our value and awareness system in terms of what we are teaching our youth.

The old fashioned value system is all about respect and loyalty, earned the hard way. Herb did this through examples, conduct, attitude and work ethic. Our elders did things with their hands that we cannot afford to duplicate and they did it with a passion. They were always prompt out of respect for others. It is all about working and playing when you are sick or hurt, and achieving in spite of it. It is all about forging a mental toughness and resolve in spite of the critics you may experience. Critics are important to our society. They are put in place to weed out the weak and reward the mentally tough. Herb answered every critic's challenge.

Old fashioned values are all about having the resolve to "pay the price" to success. It is all about "giving back" to something or someone you loved or benefited from. And most important, it's all about believing that death is the beginning of a journey to a better place. Herb spent a lifetime "giving back."

He named his camp Minnesota Hockey Schools (It has since been changed to Camps). He didn't want it to be Herb Brooks Hockey Schools. He thought naming it after himself was too egotistical. This also shows you the vision of the man in terms of passing the camp on. His vision also made it simple to have an email address and web site easy to find on the Internet. If he were here, he would tell me he planned it that way.

The staff at the camp was devastated by the loss of Herb. The flags were lowered to half-mast the minute we heard, because we didn't need a proclamation. We all recognized his caring and professionalism. There are all types of professionals in life. Herb was what I would call a "real pro," when you judge his accomplishments. There are real pros who do everything they can and more. There are the regular pros who get the job done, and there are those who just get by. All of these are good people but the real pro stands out.

Herb walked into my office one day and commented on my cluttered desk. He then swept every piece of paper off my desk and on to the floor. Then he said, "That is what your desk looks like." When he came back he was surprised to see I hadn't picked it up. I told him that everything was easier to find spread out on the floor. He laughed and proceeded to help me pick everything up. I sensed at that moment that he liked the rebel in me. He knew that people capable of expressing themselves would come through in "critical moments." Herb also had a sense of humor that would equal any of his peers. This is why he could laugh at himself and with others. To this day I keep a messy desk; just in case he walks in. He would quickly organize it for me and we would have a good laugh.

The intangibles are as important as book learning, because intangibles are a necessary component in the success of an individual. Herb proved that there are people out there who can contribute to the total growth of your child beyond the classroom setting. He was both book smart and street smart. I don't know many people or players who could beat him on the street.

When Herb's father passed away, we were at the New York Rangers training camp in Rye, N.Y. He asked me to go for a walk. We sat and talked on a park bench for a long time. When it was time to go back he said, "Gringo, call your father and mother and tell them you love them."

Sometimes we think that the things that are happening to us don't happen to everyone else at some point. It's hard for us, and the people around us, to accept our "special circumstance" as the product of an unfair society or life. Hard times give us the opportunity to reflect on the good things and grow. As difficult and harsh as it appears, we need to honor the situation and turn our thoughts to the future with resolve. We need to remove the obstacles that prevent us from a daily critiquing of our lives. Then, we can move toward being a detailed person who cares about others, while in the process of building our lives and maximizing our potential. Herb was forever doing this. He did what he was doing, what he did and what he was going to do; and he did it all at the same time. His last phone call to me was prodding me to help him develop a cut proof referees glove.

They say, "Love has two winners or no winners." In this case, I believe there are thousands of winners; namely every kid, person and fellow coach the man came in contact with. I wouldn't want to guess how many people owe him to "Be as much as he believes you can be." This means you get up each morning to be what you can be and not who you are. He did it and would accept nothing less from his athletes or his peers. It is human nature to get up each morning and to be who we are. What's wrong with someone prodding us to get up each morning to be what we can be? Does this make him "distant" or someone who cares?

I attended a church on March 2, 2003, in Seattle, Wash., called the Church By The Side Of The Road. It was a rather unique and down to earth service. The sermon was interesting to say the least and I feel that it solidifies the philosophy of our camp and our involvement with Herb and others. The pastor said: "When we decide to bring someone into our lives we have to provide unconditional love for that person; we have to share in all their ups and downs."

My thoughts turned to teaching, coaching and Minnesota Hockey Camps. I also had thoughts on scouting, pinpointing talent, evaluating talent and ultimately drafting that talent. All of these jobs entail "bringing someone into our lives and nurturing them so they might maximize their potential." This could conceivably last a person's entire career or lifetime. He went on to mention our responsibility to the people who become more than just an acquaintance or companion, which includes our staff, colleagues, campers and players on our reserve list. The key word was nurture. We have to accept the fact that we share and carry other peoples' burdens and problems; when someone is hurt physically or mentally, we are all hurt. He stressed being patient, humble, gentle, kind and to show compassion while working with them. In a sense these people in our lives go way past the acquaintance and companion levels. They are closer to the "real friend" level where we can go see them unannounced, pour out our hearts to them and listen to them pour out theirs. We have the responsibility to "corner them" and tell them things that they may not want to hear, in addition to complimenting them. We have the responsibility to provide meaningful experiences so they can grow.

I found it interesting that this pastor solidified the very feelings and responsibilities we have always felt about those around us. He brought meaning to the conversation Greg Malone (scout with Pittsburgh) and I had at the Delta Hotel in Calgary, Alberta, on March 23, 2003. It was about the people we were working with and the players we were responsible for. He gave meaning to why I got so deeply involved with Herb Brooks, his life, his teams and his camp. He always considered me family and showed me unconditional love and respect. He gave meaning to why

Craig Patrick hired me when I felt a need to get back to work and why people commit themselves to our camp and to the players we come in contact with in our line of work during the Winter months. Craig Patrick's comment to me was, "Glad to have you back, Gringo; you're family." This tells me why Herb and Craig had a winning relationship.

It took me back to a relationship that was innocently developed at Bemidji Hockey Camp many years ago. Craig was quick to show me unconditional love and respect regardless of me just getting started in the game and being only a high school coach. I have never forgotten this. These experiences, as well as observing how my parents have always been "real givers" in life, has pretty much been the foundation for how I feel while working for Herb, the Pittsburgh Penguins and Minnesota Hockey Camps. It's all about people caring about people who mean something to each of us for whatever reason.

I had a good morning this morning because I know I'm in the right line of work for all the right reasons. I'm grateful for the relationships and all I have in life; especially Herb Brooks. I'm a lucky guy! Thank God that my family and our camp got to enjoy his talents over an extended period of time that will last forever. We will miss him, but we are all going to be better human beings because of him. We have a relationship that the late Vince Lombardi called "Love." The entire world should know how we felt about Herb Brooks. We can all learn a lesson from it. We will all hold ourselves to a higher standard because Herb raised the bar. He didn't spend a lot of time with people who failed to raise the bar after he had the opportunity to meet and spend time with them.

As I write about Herb I do so with the intention of being able to change the name when the situation calls for it. If every person took the challenge, and lived much of what I wrote about Herb, there would be a lot of churches full on judgment day. This would be more than enough to realize that our time spent on earth was as gratifying and fulfilling as possible. Because of him, I will raise the bar the rest of my life.

Peace of mind comes from knowing you overachieved in your asset categories and did something for someone who can never repay you. Herb Brooks, has peace of mind. — *"Ol' Gringo," an Iron Range hockey man who developed a relationship with a hockey man from Payne Avenue*

Thanks for the memories Herbie, we will never forget you!

ABOUT THE AUTHOR

Ross Bernstein first got into writing through some rather unique circumstances. You see, after a failed attempt to make it as a walk-on to the University of Minnesota's Golden Gopher hockey team, Ross opted to instead become the team's mascot, *"Goldy."* His humorous accounts as a mischievous rodent, back at old Mariucci Arena, then inspired the 1992 best-seller: *"Gopher Hockey by the Hockey Gopher."* And the rest, they say... is history!

Ross Bernstein

Bernstein is the author of several regionally best-selling coffee-table sports books, including: *"Legends & Legacies: Celebrating a Century of Minnesota Coaches," "Batter-Up! Celebrating a Century of Minnesota Baseball," "Hardwood Heroes: Celebrating a Century of Minnesota Basketball," "Pigskin Pride: Celebrating a Century of Minnesota Football," "Frozen Memories: Celebrating a Century of Minnesota Hockey"* and *"55 Years • 55 Heroes: A Celebration of Minnesota Sports."*

Bernstein also writes children's and young-reader sports biographies as well. Among these books include biographies about such superstars as: Minnesota Vikings All-Pro Wide Receiver *Randy Moss*, Vikings All-Pro Quarterback *Daunte Culpepper*, Timberwolves All-Star Forward *Kevin Garnett*, Seattle Supersonics All-Star Point Guard *Gary Payton*, San Francisco Giants All-Star *Barry Bonds*, Texas Rangers All-Star Alex Rodriguez, and Los Angeles Lakers stars *Kobe Bryant* and *Shaquille O'Neal*, among others.

In addition, Bernstein also writes an annual book for the U.S. Hockey Hall of Fame, entitled: **"The Hall: Celebrating the History and Heritage of the U.S. Hockey Hall of Fame."** All proceeds from the sale of the book, which chronicles and updates the history of the Eveleth, Minn., based museum and its more than 100 world-renowned enshrinees, go directly to the Hall of Fame.

Today the Fairmont native works as a full-time sports author for several Midwest and East Coast publishers. In addition, he is also a writer and contributing editor of *"Minnesota Hockey Journal."* A sister publication of USA Hockey's *"American Hockey Magazine,"* the Journal has a circulation of nearly 50,000 Minnesota hockey households.

Now working on his 30th book in 2004, Ross, his wife Sara, their one and a half year old daughter Campbell, and their sock-snarfing Jack Russell Terrier, "Herbie" *(named in honor of Herbie Brooks)*, presently reside in Eagan.

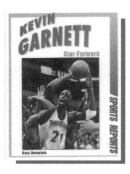

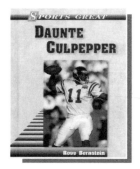